JUST WORDS

JUST WORDS

Law, Language, and Power

Second Edition

JOHN M. CONLEY AND WILLIAM M. O'BARR

THE UNIVERSITY OF CHICAGO PRESS

CHICAGO AND LONDON

The University of Chicago Press, Chicago 60637
The University of Chicago Press, Ltd., London
© 1998, 2005 by The University of Chicago
All rights reserved. 2005
Printed in the United States of America
09 08 07 06 05   1 2 3 4 5
ISBN: 0-226-11488-0 (paperback)

Library of Congress Cataloging-in-Publication Data

Conley, John M.
    Just words : law, language, and power / John M. Conley and William M. O'Barr.—
2nd ed.
        p.   cm.
    Includes bibliographical references and index.
    ISBN 0-226-11488-0 (pbk. : alk. paper)
    1. Law—Language. 2. Equality before the law. 3. English language—Rhetoric—
Sex differences. I. O'Barr, William M. II. Title.
    K213.c658 2005
    340'.14—dc22

                                                                    2005002710

♾ The paper used in this publication meets the minimum requirements of the American
National Standard for Information Sciences—Permanence of Paper for Printed
Library Materials, ANSI z39.48-1992.

To Ernestine Friedl, who, seeing the promise of studying the language
of the law, encouraged our original collaboration

ACKNOWLEDGMENTS

Our primary debt is to those colleagues in the field of law and language whose hard work and critical insights are the subject of this book. The contributions of many of these scholars are specifically acknowledged as we discuss their work in the course of this book, but our thanks extend to all who do law and language research.

CONTENTS

PREFACE TO THE SECOND EDITION

The first edition of *Just Words* was intended as a thematic overview of the already vibrant interdisciplinary field of law and language studies. It was not our goal to write a comprehensive review of the expansive literature that comprised the field in 1998. Rather, we set out to highlight certain issues that lie at the heart of many investigations of the relation between language and law. We felt that we could do this best by following the themes of justice, equality, and fairness through the web of legal entanglements that real people encounter as they make their way through lawyers' offices, courts, and other legal venues. We tried to illuminate the role that language plays in the law's frequent failure to deliver on its basic promise of equal treatment. The single issue that emerged over and over was the centrality of language in the production, exercise, and subversion of legal power.

The reception of the first edition has gratified us, suggesting that others who read the book or use it in teaching share its underlying concerns. The study of law and language was not one of the foundational issues in the law and society movement, but it is now a major topic of books and journal articles and appears prominently in conference programs and course curricula. It is this very growth that has occasioned a second edition: more scholars exploring the law/language relationship in ever-more innovative and provocative ways.

This edition includes the original chapters plus two new ones. The new chapters focus on three developments in law and language scholarship that have become especially significant in the six years since we completed the first edition: the increasing attention to language ideology in legal contexts, the expansion of law and language research beyond the Anglo-American world, and the dramatic growth in the field of forensic linguistics.

Chapter 9 deals with the ideologies of language that permeate the law. It asks how the law itself and the actors within the legal system conceive of language and its instrumental role in law. We show how a body of newer research and writing has focused on language ideology to further our understanding of the ways in which the law's power plays itself out in practice. After explaining language ideology as a theoretical concept, we examine research that illuminates the role it plays in the American legal system. We then discuss a project that illustrates the use of language ideology to expose power relations in a very different cultural, linguistic, and legal setting.

Chapter 10 presents a survey and critique of the now large and rapidly growing field of forensic linguistics, defined as the use of linguistic expertise in legal proceedings. We assess the contributions that linguists are making to law and ask as well about the effect of their work on linguistics itself. While we applaud the role that linguists have often played in advancing the interests of justice, we ask whether forensic linguistics has become a discipline in which application drives theory rather than vice-versa. We are particularly concerned about the diversion of scholarly time and energy away from fundamental critique of the law in favor of responding to an agenda that the law sets.

The emergence of such issues is evidence of health and vitality within the law and language community. There is productive debate over what the issues should be, how time should be allocated, what really matters, and the like. As members of the community we have our views about those topics. But as the debate unfolds, let us not lose sight of the goal of understanding how law works, how it often fails to deliver on its promises, and what we, as researchers and scholars, can do to illuminate its processes and thereby promote the values of democracy, open access, and fundamental fairness in an increasingly globalized world. To accomplish this we will need to move beyond our own societies, especially those of North America and Europe, into other areas of the world where other languages are spoken and where language itself may be understood in different ways. We must also be attentive to the political significance of the choices we make in allocating our time and selecting the questions that we study. The issues and the stakes are large, while the resources of our research community are finite.

Chapel Hill, NC
September 2004

PREFACE

Law and language emerged as a field of scholarship in the 1970s as sociolegal scholars incorporated the language of the law into their studies and as linguists began to concern themselves with language in legal arenas. Although there are now several edited volumes that focus on law and language (e.g., Levi and Walker 1990, Grimshaw 1990, Papke 1991), there is no book-length overview that attempts to assess the field and its contributions to sociolegal scholarship. What exists are primarily articles, book chapters, and monographs that take up one or another problem at the intersection of law and language.

The idea for a more comprehensive assessment of the field emerged from our teaching of general courses on law and social science and on legal anthropology, as well as more specialized topical seminars within these two fields. We have prominently featured law and language concerns in such courses because we believe that they make an important contribution to our understanding of the intersection of law and society, particularly of how law actually works in such everyday contexts as courtrooms, lawyers' offices, and even disputes outside specifically legal arenas. Moreover, law and language issues invariably generate a high level of student interest, whether the students are undergraduates, social science graduate students, or professional students in law or business. However, in bringing these materials into our teaching, we have often had to choose one monograph over another (because of issues of length, availability, and cost) and have seldom managed to cover as broad a set of law and language issues as we would have liked.

Another consequence of the scattered nature of publications about law and language has been the lack of an integrating perspective. In particular, there is no single source that canvasses a broad spectrum of the published research to develop a critical argument for the importance of studying the linguistic details of daily legal practice. We have tried to put that case forward here. In the pages that follow, we show how some of the most fundamental questions in sociolegal scholarship—issues such as unequal treatment by the law, the law's relationship to patriarchy, and gender discrimination within legal processes—play themselves out linguistically. Indeed, we argue, it is within the details of the talk that constitutes legal practice that discrimination occurs, that patriarchy manifests itself, and that the power of the law is realized. Thus, the microdynamics of the legal process and the broadest questions of justice are revealed to be two aspects of the same issue.

We hope this book will serve to encourage others to adopt the methods and perspectives of law and language. Much has been learned about law through studies of language and discourse. Language and law research has sometimes been able to clarify the details of thorny issues that have seemed resistant to other methods of analysis—questions such as what it is about rape trials that causes such great anguish for the victims, why women may not fare as well in divorce mediation as they do in adversarial litigation, and why the law accords some witnesses and litigants greater credence than others. Yet much more remains to be done, and we are hopeful that an assessment of what has been learned over the past two decades will be a stimulant to future work.

A Note about Authorship

This book is a joint project. We alternate priority of authorship in our publications in order to emphasize our common voice. We have brought different backgrounds and perspectives to the endeavor, and we believe that neither of us would have conceived of or carried out the project singly in the manner that has emerged from our collaboration. We have worked together throughout and deserve jointly whatever blame or credit our readers accord.

NOTE ON TRANSCRIPT CONVENTIONS

We have made an effort in this book to standardize the linguistic texts we use as examples. We have drawn these texts from various sources, published and unpublished, including some of our own current and previously published work. We have found that the transcription conventions of different authors can be highly variable. Some try to approximate standard English; others attempt to render complex features of spoken language not noted in the conventions of standard orthography (pauses, coughs, overlapping speech, etc.). In devising a format for this book, we elected to simplify many of the transcripts. First, we have rendered most of the speech in standard English. For example, where an original transcript contains attempts at phonetic renderings such as *werenchu* and *you c'n get,* we have changed them to the standard *weren't you* and *you can get.* Second, we have eliminated many nonstandard-English features of the original transcripts that are not relevant to the issues that we are discussing. Thus, our texts do not note pause lengths except where that information is specifically relevant. We have taken these steps in order to make the texts accessible to readers with little or no background in linguistics or conversation analysis.

In simplifying and standardizing the texts in this book, we realize that we may be eliminating linguistic features that some readers may find useful in further analyses of the texts they might wish to undertake on their own. We refer such readers to the original sources (clearly referenced in each instance), where more detailed transcripts may be available. We believe that the inconvenience that may be caused to a few readers by this decision is outweighed by the argument for greater accessibility for all readers.

The following conventions are used in this book:

(2.5)	A silence whose length is specified in seconds (here 2.5 seconds)
CAPITALS	Loud speech
[ ]	Speech that overlaps with that of another speaker
italics	Stressed words or phrases
— —	An interrupted utterance and its resumption, as in

WITNESS: They did mention—
LAWYER: Then did—
WITNESS: —did mention that . . .

[*italicized words*]	Editorial comments
( )	The material contained within was not fully audible

CHAPTER ONE

The Politics of Law and
the Science of Talk

I t is almost twenty-five years since we began our own collaborative work at the intersection of law and language, and there is little in the field that is much older. The body of work that we consider here is not the product of some theoretical master plan. Rather, it has coalesced as scholars of diverse intellectual backgrounds have arrived from many directions at the common realization that the language of the law is profoundly important. Some whose primary interest is the law have been struck by the centrality of language in almost every legal event, while others whose main interest is language have discovered the law as an extraordinary research setting. Collectively—if often unaware of each other—the members of this accidental alliance have produced the subject matter of this book.

When we first turned our attention to the subject in the mid-1970s, most scholarship that considered law and language focused on written legal language, especially the arcane language of statutes and legal documents. Although we found many articles and books that noted in passing the importance of the linguistic base of the law, we found only a single source that dealt with law and language in any real depth. This was David Mellinkoff's monumental *The Language of Law* (1963), which analyzed the structure of written legal language and explained the Latin, French, and Anglo-Saxon origins of contemporary usages. It took a new generation of language-oriented fieldworkers with sociological, anthropological, and sociolinguistic backgrounds to initiate a broader study of the language of the law as it operates in the many venues of daily practice. Beginning about 1970, this new generation of researchers went to the places where people actually talk about their troubles and express their claims and began to study what happens there. It is their scholarship that provides the foundation for our argument about the importance of language and discourse in understanding law and legal processes.

Those who have studied law and language in this latter way can be grouped in three general categories. One group has focused explicitly and self-consciously on language as the medium through which law does most of its work. Research in this category is exemplified by Brenda Danet's (1980a) demonstration of the strategic significance of alternative ways of naming and categorizing objects and actions,[1] as well as our own investigation of the practical legal consequences of differences in courtroom speech styles (Conley et al. 1978; O'Barr 1982). A second category consists of people interested primarily in language itself who have found that legal and quasi-legal settings are a rich linguistic resource. Important examples include two ethnomethodologists: Gail Jefferson (1980, 1985, 1988), who began to study talk about troubles in everyday contexts as a part of a more general investigation of conversation, and Anita Pomerantz (1978), some of whose early research focused on how blame is managed in conversation. Researchers who comprise the third group have been less self-conscious in their focus on linguistic issues but have ended up paying close attention to the language of legal processes in order to explain the workings of the legal system. For example, in Susan Silbey and Sally Merry's (1986) ethnographic study of community mediation, language emerged as a central issue even though the researchers themselves had little formal background in linguistics.

The particular body of work that is our focus here introduces another important variable into the law-language equation: power. This research looks at the law's language in order to understand the law's power. Its premise is that power is not a distant abstraction but rather an everyday reality. For most people, the law's power manifests itself less in Supreme Court decisions and legislative pronouncements than in the details of legal practice, in the thousands of mini-dramas reenacted every day in lawyers' offices, police stations, and courthouses around the country. The dominant element in almost every one of these mini-dramas is language. To the extent that power is realized, exercised, abused, or challenged in such events, the means are primarily linguistic. This book is a search for those linguistic means.

Focusing simultaneously on law, language, and power can give us a new insight into what has been the fundamental question in American legal history: how a legal system that aspires to equality can produce such a pervasive sense of unfair treatment. In the one hundred thirty years since the ratification of the Fourteenth Amendment to the Constitution and its guarantee of equal protection, normative legal reform has succeeded, at least on some levels, in eradicating the most blatant forms of discrimination. The law permits all citizens to vote and hold public office. Federal and state laws prohibit employment discrimination on grounds of race, religion, gender, disability, age, and sometimes sexual orientation. No one may be excluded from public benefits for discriminatory reasons. In the courtroom, all criminal defendants are entitled to be represented by counsel. All citizens are eligible for jury duty, and lawyers may not rely on race or gender in selecting jurors for particular cases. Race is not a legitimate factor for judges to consider in sentencing.

Yet in the face of such undeniable progress in the law's ideals, there is still widespread unease about the fairness of the law's application. One can sense the problem just by spending time in a courthouse and paying attention to the daily routine. Listen to the way that police officers and judges speak to women seeking domestic violence restraining orders. Listen to the way that mediators interact with husbands and wives in divorce cases. Observe the reactions of judges and jurors to the testimony of different kinds of witnesses. Talk to small claims magistrates about what constitutes a persuasive case. Nobody is doing anything that the Supreme Court would condemn as a violation of equal protection. But it is hard to escape the feeling that the law's power is more accessible to some people than to others.

What is it that gives rise to this feeling? Why do many people continue to think that the law does not treat them fairly? The answer cannot be found just in the study of legal norms. The law no longer returns fugitive slaves, treats women as the property of their husbands, or excludes African American citizens from juries. If the law is failing to live up to its ideals, the failure must lie in the details of everyday legal practice—details that consist almost entirely of language.

In the chapters that follow, we take up a number of compelling instances in which linguistic analysis[2] has shed new light on the nature of the law's power and the inequality of its application. In chapter 2, we address the frequently asserted claim that rape trials revictimize women who attempt to prosecute their assailants. We argue that the feeling of revictimization has little to do with the rules about introducing the victim's prior sexual history, which so-called rape shield laws have attempted to reform. Rather, the reality of revictimization is to be found in the linguistic details of common cross-examination strategies that are taken for granted in the adversary system. Reformers, we conclude, have been looking in the wrong places, and the prospect for real improvement is uncertain.

In chapter 3, we focus not on a substantive area of the law (such as rape) but on a legal *process* that is brought to bear on a wide range of disputes: mediation. We look specifically at the current trend of resolving divorce cases through mediation rather than traditional adversary trials. According to the legal literature, this change is having two apparently contradictory effects: women tend to prefer mediation, but from a financial standpoint, they do not do as well as they did under the adversary system. Collecting linguistic data from a variety of legal and social science sources, we attempt to discover the precise mechanisms through which these effects might be produced.

Building on the details of the previous two chapters, chapter 4 poses a more general question: is there any linguistic substance to the claim that the law is fundamentally patriarchal? Legal writers often cite the revictimization phenomenon and the allegedly unfair treatment of women in divorce as evidence that the values of the legal system are the values of a historically male power structure; as a result, they argue, the law is insensitive to the social reality of women's lives. We assess this claim linguistically. Going beyond the examples of rape and divorce, we reanalyze some of our own earlier work to make the case that law displays a deep gender bias in the way it performs such basic tasks as judging credibility and defining narrative coherence.

The subject of chapter 5 is the natural history of disputes. We draw on research about individual components of the disputing process, from initial injury to trial, to create a linguistic model of the evolution of a dispute. The theme of power emerges again, in a subtle yet significant way. As they progress from wrong to resolution, disputes undergo multiple transformations. Each transformation is interactive, the product of negotiation between a disputant and another person—the adversary, a friend, a lawyer, a court clerk, a judge. And every such negotiation is in large part a contest for power whose outcome will shape the rest of the dispute.

Chapters 6 and 7 extend the basic argument of the book across place and time. In chapter 6, we argue for the importance of a linguistic orientation in the comparative study of law. We introduce recent work in legal anthropology to make the point that some of our most venerable assumptions about the law of non-Western societies may derive from inadequate attention to linguistic detail. In chapter 7, we extend the argument historically. It is often said that modern linguistic research did not become possible until about 1945, when the invention of the mechanical tape recorder allowed repeated hearings of linguistic evidence. But research into the legal archives of medieval France and imperial Rome shows the potential of a linguistic approach to the study of legal power in the distant past. Finally, in chapter 8, we offer some thoughts about the future of law and language scholarship.

Why We Wrote This Book

We were motivated to write this book by a growing sense of need. We believed that the law and language field, as theoretically diverse as it was, was sending a coherent message about law, language, and power. But this message had to be dug out of individual books and articles scattered here and there across the scholarly spectrum. We decided that the time had come for a single accessible source that organized some of the most significant law and language research around a unifying theme.

There are a number of useful review articles and collections. Brenda Danet (1980b) and Don Brenneis (1988) have written comprehensive review essays about law and language, but both are now out of date; Elizabeth Mertz (1994) has done a more recent survey. Judith Levi (1994) has published a comprehensive bibliography of the field in pamphlet form, but it lacks critical commentary. Among the anthologies, the most helpful are Allen Grimshaw's *Conflict Talk* (1990), Judith Levi and Anne Graffam Walker's *Language in the Judicial Process* (1990), and David Papke's *Narrative and the Legal Discourse* (1991). Grimshaw collects linguistic analyses of disputes and arguments from a variety of interesting cultural settings, including American and Italian nursery schools, psychiatric examinations, and labor-management negotiations. In Levi and Walker's book, a set of conference papers, the contributions all endeavor to show the value of linguistic methods in understanding the American legal process. In Papke's book, as the title indicates, the organizing theme is narrative, which the contributors study in contexts ranging from legal education to appellate opinions. None of these, however, is organized so as to tell what we believe to be the emerging theoretical story of the field.

The inadequacy of the current literature has been especially evident in the dozens of courses that, between us, we have taught under the general rubric of law and society. In most instances, we have brought together students from law schools and social science departments. Law and language has been the exclusive topic of many of these courses; in the others, it has been one of a few major topics. In both cases it has been very difficult to find materials suitable for a class of students from varied disciplines. Much of the best work is in monograph form, substantial books devoted to a single, relatively narrow research project. (Moreover, some are available only at exorbitant cost.) The teacher thus faces a Hobson's choice: take an excerpt short enough to pass copyright clearance, which will probably be insufficient to convey the point of the book, or make the students buy the book and devote a major segment of the course to a single topic. In addition, much of the important writing in the field is highly technical. This slows the progress of the course to a crawl, if it does not cause the students to give up entirely.

For reasons such as these, we have long felt a need for a book that lays out the major issues in the field in a readable form. Our objective here is to capture the theoretical import of the work we discuss, while reducing the technical aspects to what is absolutely essential. We strive for accessibility in every sense of the word: a readily available book of reasonable length that uses a minimum of jargon and makes few assumptions about the prior knowledge of readers.

Our hope is that the entire book can serve as the core of a law and language course, while individual chapters may prove useful as freestanding linguistic readings in broader law and society courses.

In explaining how we selected the research we have discussed, it is important to be explicit about what this book is *not*. It is intended to be neither a textbook nor a comprehensive survey of the field. The fact that we do not mention some body of work does not mean that we do not think it is important. This is rather a book organized around what is, in our judgment, the most important theoretical issue in law and language: the use of linguistic methods to understand the nature of law and legal power. We chose the items that we have included primarily because each combines rich linguistic analysis with an interest in broader social issues. Taken together, they make the strongest possible case for the importance of law and language research to both the social sciences and the law.

In the remainder of this chapter, we introduce some background issues that are essential to an appreciation of the work that we discuss in the substantive chapters. First we examine three concepts that are at the core of law and language research: language, discourse, and power. We then review in some detail the intellectual traditions from which the field of law and language has emerged.

Basic Concepts: Language, Discourse, and Power

Many scholars use the terms *language* and *discourse* without explaining what they mean by them. This can be confusing because these related terms have multiple meanings in the academic world; they are synonymous for some purposes but distinct in other significant ways. Language is the more straightforward of the two. Language includes sounds, units of meaning, and grammatical structures, as well as the contexts in which they occur. Events that count as law in people's lives—making a will; getting a divorce; going to small claims court; serving as a juror, witness, or defendant—consist primarily of language. In a practical, everyday way, law is language, in either its spoken or its written variety. Language is the stuff of contracts, statutes, judicial opinions, and other legal documents, as well as the essence of the daily dramas that unfold in trial courtrooms, lawyers' offices, and mediation centers.[3]

The term *discourse* has two senses, one linguistic and one social. The former sense, which overlaps with *language,* is illustrated by phrases such as *everyday discourse* and *courtroom discourse,* the latter by phrases such as the *discourse of psychoanalysis* and the *discourse of human rights.* In the linguistic sense, discourse refers to connected segments of speech or writing, in fact to any chunk of speech or writing larger than a single utterance.[4] It thus includes conversations, sermons, stories, question-answer sequences, and so forth. Discourse analysis is the study of how such segments, or texts, are structured and how they are used in communication. In the context of law, discourse in the linguistic sense refers to the talk that constitutes courtroom testimony, closing arguments, lawyer-client interviews, arguments between disputants, mediation sessions, and the like. In the two last decades, a number of researchers have turned their analytic attention to the linguistic structure of these events and have attempted to understand how they accomplish the legal work that they do. That body of scholarship forms the basis for many of the arguments that we make in this book.

The use of *discourse* to refer to more abstract social phenomena owes its currency to the influence of Michel Foucault. In *The Order of Things* (1970) and *The Archaeology of Knowledge and the Discourse of Language* (1972), Foucault lays out his notion of discourse as the broad range of discussion that takes place within a society about an issue or a set of issues. Examples include the *discourse of punishment* and the *discourse of sexuality,* which became, respectively, the subjects of two of his later works, *Discipline and Punish* (Foucault 1977) and *The History of Sexuality* (Foucault 1978, 1985a, 1985b). We will sometimes refer to discourse in the more abstract, Foucaultian sense as *macrodiscourse,* to distinguish it from discourse in the linguistic sense, which we will call *microdiscourse.*

Discourse in Foucault's sense is not simply talk itself, but also the way that something gets talked about. Logically, the way that people talk about an issue is intimately related to the way that they think about it and ultimately act with respect to it. Discourse is thus a locus of power. Different discourses compete for ascendancy in the social world; one is dominant for a time and then may be challenged and perhaps replaced by another. The dominance of a particular discourse inevitably reflects the power structure of society. At the same time, however, the repeated playing out of the dominant discourse reinforces that structure. Discourse, as Foucault put it in *The History of Sexuality,* "can be both an instrument and an effect of power" (1978:101). In the end, though, because dominance is the product of competition and negotiation, dominant discourse plants the seeds of its own undoing. In effect, as people talk about an issue over and over again, they learn too much. Even as the participants in the social discussion are being constrained by the dominant framework, they are acquiring the resources to subvert it. In Foucault's words, "Discourse transmits and produces power; it reinforces it, but also undermines and exposes it, renders it fragile and makes it possible to thwart it" (1978:101).

Foucault's theory of discourse has shaped research in a variety of disciplines where scholars have to come to share his concern with specific historical processes and the connection of discourse to power. Although Foucault does not present a unified theory of law, his concept of discourse has influenced contemporary legal scholarship profoundly. His principal contribution has been to emphasize the multiplicity and complexity of legal discourses (Hunt and Wickham 1994:39–49). Whereas traditional scholarship has tended to treat "the law" as a single, coherent entity, Foucault analyzes it as "a multiple and mobile field of force relations, wherein far-reaching, but never completely stable, effects of domination are produced" (1980:102). Law works both in opposition to and in concert with such "disciplines" as penology, psychology, and education, which operate " 'on the underside of the law' to 'naturalize' the legal power to punish at the same time they 'legalize' the technical power to discipline" (Hunt and Wickham 1994:46, quoting Foucault 1977:223). Foucault thus encourages legal scholars to seek power in practice, to construct meaning from the bottom up rather than the top down.

As we have examined the varied uses of the term *discourse*, we have come to understand a fundamental relationship between its two principal meanings. We have become convinced that the linguistic and social notions of discourse are merely different aspects of one and the same process of expressing social power. In fact, the central argument of this book is that the concrete linguistic technique of discourse analysis is an indispensable tool for explaining discourse in the more abstract, sociological sense. For example, we argue in the pages that follow that the claim that law is patriarchal—a statement about dominant legal discourse—can only be fully evaluated by examining the details of talk in the courtroom. Discourse at the macrolevel—discourse as Foucault understands it—must manifest itself at the microlevel, as talk. It is only through talk, after all, that dominance can be expressed, reproduced, and challenged. Seen from this perspective, the multiple meanings of discourse are quite natural, indeed inevitable, and a resource rather than a source of confusion.

Finally, *power* itself—although its meaning is in some respects self-evident—also requires some explanation. Harold Lasswell (1936) once defined politics as "who gets what, when, how." *Power* is the answer to the question of *why* some people get things, while others do not—why, in other words, the haves have what they do. Stated in this way, the study of power must deal with the fundamental issue of inequality, asking why it exists and how it is maintained. This sense of power is encompassed in the notion of *hegemony*, which means preponderant power in a political context, the ability of some groups to subordinate others. We are concerned here with power in legal contexts. Legal power, like other forms of power, has an intimate relationship with inequality, but it is an ambiguous and sometimes ironic one. Throughout history, the power of the law has been a two-edged sword, simultaneously enabling some people to attack social inequalities and enabling others to defend them. People have used the law's resources in order to undermine a status quo that the same law has created and maintained. Thus, during the American civil rights struggle of the 1950s and 1960s, both opponents and defenders of segregation claimed the law's protection.

The work of Foucault is again helpful in sorting out the complex relationship between legal power and inequality. He reminds us that power involves more than the authority of the state. Indeed, the modern world is characterized by the importance of power exercised locally at myriad sites far removed from political centers (Hunt and Wickham 1994:16–17). Foucault (1977:12) emphasizes the need for attention to the mechanics or "microphysics" of this dispersed power. When we examine the exercise of power in detail, we discover that it not only excludes and prohibits, but also produces: "it produces reality, it produces domains of objects and rituals of truth" (Foucault 1977:194). The very exercise of power thus reinforces it. Inevitably, however, power also produces resistance to itself. Power may exclude, but those who are excluded remain on the scene, ready to turn local-level episodes of oppression into moments of resistance. This resistance is not the large-scale revolution promoted by Marx, but rather the occasional yet still significant hijacking of local power by individuals who are usually on the receiving end. It is thus in the details of daily practice that the nature, the maintenance, and the subversion of power are all to be understood.

Foucault's ideas are especially relevant to the concept of legal power. Legal power occasionally manifests itself as the power of the state, as when Congress legislates or the Constitution is amended. But the manifestations of legal power that have the most direct impact on individuals are usually local: decisions by prosecutors to bring charges, jury verdicts, sentences handed down by judges, and so on. In Foucaultian terms, the purpose of this book is to explore the microphysics of legal power by examining such events at the microlinguistic level.

The Origins of Law and Language Research

As we noted earlier, in the 1970s and 1980s the findings of a variety of researchers from different backgrounds began to converge in that area of scholarship we term law and language. The resulting body of work has contributed much to our understanding of the linguistic enactment of law's power. In looking back over more than two decades of research, two preexisting fields—sociolinguistics and law and society—stand out as having set the stage on which the joint study of law and language could proceed. Although each developed independently, their convergence helped produce the body of research on which this book is based. It is perhaps appropriate to consider each field individually before asking how their combined interests gave rise to our present concerns.

Sociolinguistics

Many contemporary linguists are concerned in one way or another with the fact that language is a social phenomenon. In contrast to earlier generations of linguists, they do not study the structure of language in isolation from society. Sentences do not exist in the abstract, they argue, nor are words usually spoken without a purpose. *Sociolinguistics* is the branch of linguistics that studies the relationship between language and its social context.[5]

It is perhaps not too great a simplification to say that the major impetus to the development of sociolinguistics was an effort to expand upon the linguistics practiced in the 1950s. The primary concern of sociolinguistics has always been the integration of social variables into theories of language. Until the 1960s, it was common for theories of the structure of language to be based on ideal, perfectly formed utterances,[6] which typically existed only in the imaginations of linguists. The nonideal utterances[7] that real people actually speak (and write) were downplayed or ignored. Actual language is filled with sentences that seem to change their direction in the process of production and with variable forms of pronunciation and modes of expression. The very variation that was seen as a complicating factor in structural linguistics became the primary focus of sociolinguistics.

William Labov did some of the earliest significant work in sociolinguistics and remains one of the most prominent names in the field. He was able to show that social factors such as age, race, ethnicity, gender, and context are integral parts of language and its use. For example, he demonstrated that speech variations among New Yorkers correlate with class and social setting (Labov 1966). Although Labov's stated interest has always been in explaining how language works, rather than how society works, he has been convinced from the outset that social factors must play a central role in such explanations. This orientation has enabled Labov and others who share his vision to expand the understanding of language significantly beyond the limits of classical theory.

This concern of linguists with the language-society relationship has had parallels in other academic fields. For example, sociologist Erving Goffman (1959) initiated the study of how members of a society negotiate their way through everyday interactions—the field later named *ethnomethodology*. Some of Goffman's followers began to focus specifically on linguistic interactions, or conversations, and the field of *conversation analysis* developed. Its major premise is that, since conversation is one of the most basic human activities, the rules for organizing it must be among the most fundamental principles of social organization. Abjuring such abstract questions as why people *really* do things, conversation analysts search within the details of actual conversations for evidence of the rules that participants appear to "attend to" or "orient toward." We describe conversation analysis in considerable detail in chapter 2;

we mention it here as a variant on the fundamental sociolinguistic concern with the concrete analysis of language in real-world contexts.

Similarly, in the 1960s, more and more anthropologists began to include language as a topic of study, rather than merely treating it as the medium through which culture can be studied. Dell Hymes captured this emerging concern in the phrase "the ethnography of speaking," which he defined as the concern with "the situations and uses, the patterns and functions, of speaking as an activity in its own right" (1968:101). Inspired by Hymes, anthropologists turned increasingly to questions of who speaks particular varieties of language when, where, and to whom.[8]

Taken in conjunction with the new social orientation of many linguists, these developments meant that a great deal more attention began to be paid to language in social context than previously had been the case. The pervasiveness of communication in social life meant that every discipline concerned with society would have to come to terms with language. As in the early days of cultural anthropology, there was a world of language use and variation to be documented and explained. But the very success of the sociolinguistic agenda gave rise to a new problem. As more and more observations were made about the social contexts of language, critics began to ask, So what?

Before we examine some of the answers that law and language researchers have given to this question, let us first consider some aspects of the parallel development of law and society scholarship from the 1960s to the present.

Law and Society

Law and society is an interdisciplinary field that attempts to understand the connections between law and its social context. Researchers who identify themselves with this label come from a wide variety of fields—every one of the social sciences, many humanistic disciplines (especially history and philosophy), and academic law. Despite the diversity inherent in so broad a sweep of the academic world, law and society scholars seem united about their basic concern—showing how law really works in practice. For these scholars, deviation from the ideals of the law is the primary object of study, not something to be dismissed as mere noise in the system. Despite this shared interest in law in action, law and society is characterized more by a general research orientation than by a specific research agenda. In a recently published collection of some of the most influential papers in the field, Roger Cotterrell noted:

> In legal studies in the English-speaking world "law and society" does not designate a unified field of scholarship, a distinct subject or an academic discipline. It is a label for very varied researches which need to be categorized in this special way only because of pervasive failures of imagination in traditional legal scholarship. (1994:xi)

Law and society researchers look skeptically on law's claim of equal treatment for all. They ask questions about who gets arrested and why (Black 1971). They seek to understand the gender biases that may result from the legal regulation of domestic and work relationships (Fineman 1991; McCann 1994). And they are interested in whether concerns about the process of making a legal decision can overshadow the outcome (Lind and Tyler 1988). Investigating these issues often means turning taken-for-granted assumptions on their heads in order to understand how law is complicated by the social context in which legal principles must be realized.

Like sociolinguistics, the law and society field developed its momentum in the 1960s, although skepticism about the law living up to its ideals dates back at least to the legal realist movement in the early decades of this century. Many of the founding members of the Law and Society Association were sociologists, but they were soon joined by anthropologists, historians, philosophers, political scientists, and some legal scholars. The association's journal, *Law and Society Review,* began publication in 1967. From the outset, law and society has not prescribed a particular theory, method, or application of its findings. Rather, the field has existed as an area of scholarship united by a concern with law and the complications caused by the social context in which law always exists. More than three decades after the founding of the Law and Society Association and the *Review,* the field retains its interest in the law's failures to live up to its ideals. But at this point, the movement has been so successful in its basic objectives that additional instances of biases and shortcomings often serve more to underscore what has come to be general knowledge than to produce genuinely new insights about how law works.

Shortcomings of the Fields in Isolation

Despite the success of the research programs of both sociolinguistics and law and society, each field has, when working on its own, ultimately failed to address a fundamental issue. For sociolinguistics, the problem is this: after a generation of empirical studies, it is now well known that language variation is not unsystematic, as some earlier linguists had assumed, but rather socially patterned. In fact, we now know a great deal about how social differences are encoded within language. What the field has often neglected to do is to connect the variation it has documented with broader issues. Much sociolinguistic research has failed to ask whether language variation is truly consequential in social life, as opposed to being merely an interesting curiosity. Some question how productive it is to continue to document instance after instance of socially patterned variation. Since the basic principle of sociolinguistics was established, many people outside the field (and even some within it) have felt that we have been learning more and more about less and less.

In conversation analysis in particular, researchers and theorists have frequently shied away from making a connection between conversational organization and the dynamics of power. The great strength of conversation analysis has been its attention to ordinary people speaking in everyday contexts: friends on the telephone, people around the dinner table, and the like. The product of this research—the preeminent achievement of conversation analysis—has been a grammar of conversational interaction. It is appropriate to call it a grammar because it explains the strategies that people employ in a conversation solely by reference to other events within the conversation. External factors, such as status inequalities or preexisting relationships among the parties, have rarely been taken into account.

But this focus on the ordinary, necessary as it was, has had a constraining effect. Most important, it has resulted in an overwhelming concentration on interactions between people who are (or are assumed to be) of roughly equal social status. To be fair, conversation analysts have not been unaware of such factors as status and power, but have chosen not to consider anything external to the language of the conversation itself. Nonetheless, the fact is that there are few conversations in which status and power are not relevant; think, for example, of exchanges between parents and children, senior and junior co-workers, or even men and women. Far from being the norm, relationships of true equality are so rare as to be treasured. Although some recent work on gender issues in language has dealt with power and its consequences,[9] for most of its history conversation analysis has excluded this elemental issue from consideration. Even the research that has been done in institutional settings where power imbalances are explicit has been modest to the point of diffidence in dealing with the question.[10]

The problem with law and society scholarship is one of methods rather than goals. The primary objective of sociolegal scholars has been to document the law's failure to deliver on its biggest promises, especially the equal treatment of all citizens. Where the field has sometimes come up short is in its explanation of how such failures occur. For example, we have known for a long time that the haves come out ahead and that race and gender can make a difference in legal access and outcome. But law and society scholarship has been less successful in exposing the mechanisms that produce these inequalities. What is it exactly that the haves do for themselves or to others that results in their greater success before the law?[11] What happens to women and minorities in legal contexts that results in their positions being undervalued and underrewarded?

Conclusion: Combining Concerns

For more than twenty years, it has been evident that the most effective way to overcome the weaknesses of the two fields is to merge their strengths. Sociolinguistics can benefit from law and society's focus on who gets what and when, whereas law and society can turn to sociolinguistics for a deeper understanding of how they get it. The two disciplines already share a common concern with social divisions along lines of class, race, ethnicity, and gender. Sociolinguistics explores how language variation correlates with these variables, while sociolegal scholarship argues that they influence access to justice. Nothing could be more logical than to investigate the places where language and justice converge. From a sociolinguistic perspective, the question is whether language variation has social consequences in legal settings. The sociolegal version of this question asks whether we can discover in language the precise mechanisms—Foucault's microphysics—through which injustice happens. Since law-in-action consists almost exclusively of linguistic events—trials, agreements, conferences with lawyers, and the like—the two disciplines have always had ample ground on which to meet.

The advocacy of this merger is a fundamental motivation for this book. By analyzing a number of instances in which it has already occurred and greatly benefited our understanding of both language and law, we make the case for even deeper collaboration in the future. Our objective is to discover how the power of the law actually operates in everyday legal settings. Drawing on the work of an intellectually diverse group of law and language scholars, as well as some of our own research, we seek to identify the linguistic mechanisms through which power is realized, exercised, sometimes abused, and occasionally subverted. In the course of answering questions such as these, we also learn a great deal about the nature of power itself. We see, for example, how the linguistic details of particular legal events can simultaneously reflect and reinforce power relations that cut across society. We also discover the critical role of language in resisting and reforming existing power arrangements.

At the end, we reach the conclusion that language is not merely the vehicle though which legal power operates: in many vital respects, language *is* legal power. The abstraction we call power is at once the cause and the effect of countless linguistic interactions taking place every day at every level of the legal system. Power is thus determinative of and determined by the linguistic details of legal practice, and it is those details that are the subject of this book.

CHAPTER TWO

The Revictimization of Rape Victims

I n this chapter, we begin the detailed examination of the linguistic mechanisms through which legal power is realized and reproduced. We focus on
the prosecution of the crime of rape and attempt to understand what it is
about rape trials that leads to claims that rape victims are revictimized by the
legal process. First we review the legal, political, and scholarly discourse about
rape, paying particular attention to the issues of power and domination. We
then examine the actual language of rape prosecutions in an effort to connect
abstract ideas about power with the day-to-day realities of courtroom practice.
Here, as in subsequent chapters, our objective is to understand how discourse
practices reflect, ratify, and sometimes challenge social hierarchies.

Rape and Power

Over the past twenty-five years, few legal issues have been the focus of such intense political, social, and scholarly debate as the crime of rape. This debate
has proceeded on several levels. Criminologists have argued about the incidence of the crime. Whereas FBI reports and other "official" statistics indicate
that 4 or 5 women per 1,000 are raped each year (Koss 1994:161–63), a number of investigators have produced data indicating that rapes are least ten times
more common than that (Koss 1994:163–72; Koss 1988; Russell 1984). Others debate the causes. Explanations range from pervasive male pathology (Koss
1994:19–34; Koss 1988; Briere and Malamuth 1983) to the structure and values of society (MacKinnon 1989:182; Koss 1994:4–16).

Two aspects of the debate are particularly relevant to the concerns of this
book. The first is its focus on rape as an exercise in *power.* At the physical level,
this claim is obvious: rape is a crime in which a man overpowers a woman,

using actual or threatened force to take sexual advantage of her. But rape also involves power in other ways that are less obvious but equally significant. In particular, the abuse of power that occurs during the act of rape has been seen to reflect, indeed to be an instance of, broader abuses of power that society condones or even promotes (MacKinnon 1989:176).

Historical analyses, for example, have chronicled the changing definitions of the crime of rape. At any point in history, the definition of rape has included only a limited subset of all possible acts of nonconsensual sex. Forced sex with slaves, for example, did not constitute rape;[1] and until very recently, married women could not complain of rape by their husbands.[2] The historical trend has been to expand the area defined as criminal (Koss 1994:158–59, 223–24; Spohn and Horney 1992; see, e.g., N.C. General Statutes §§14-27.3–14-27.10). Nonetheless, the fact that society has tolerated *any* forms of forced sex makes a statement about power relations and the sexualization of violence (MacKinnon 1989:145–46; Caputi and Russell 1992:18–19). If particular acts of forced sex have to be specially defined as criminal, then the unstated premise is that women are presumed to be subject to the power of men (MacKinnon 1989:169).

The second and related point is that the power politics of rape do not end with the commission of the crime. Critics of the legal system point out that rape is grossly underreported (Warshaw 1988; Russell 1984). When it is reported, they argue, it is not prosecuted vigorously, and convictions are rarely obtained (Matoesian 1993:14–15). All of this is particularly true with respect to acquaintance rape, which is said to be far more common than rape by strangers (Koss 1994:163–65; Estrich 1987) and which, in many states, is defined as a less serious offense than stranger rape.[3]

The analysis of rape leads inevitably to power relations between men and women. One problem is the law itself. The elements of the crime are defined in male terms, it is argued, as is consent, which is the principal defense in acquaintance rape cases (MacKinnon 1989:169, 181–82; Estrich 1987:82). The law, in other words, is patriarchal, because it is written and applied from a male point of view. It takes for granted the idea that women are subordinate to men. Because of the law's patriarchal perspective, the critics contend, a woman who did not actively, indeed aggressively, resist will be seen as having consented to sex. District attorneys look at the allegations from the same patriarchal perspective when deciding when to prosecute, as do jurors when judging guilt or innocence (Matoesian 1993:15, 1995:693–94). Thus, in the prosecution of rape—just as in the act itself—male domination is realized in social action.

Some of the strongest criticism of the system focuses on what happens when a rape case finally gets to the courtroom. What happens is commonly described as "revictimization" or "rape of the second kind" (Matoesian 1995:676). The victim is, of course, forced to relive the rape in her courtroom testimony and is revictimized in this literal sense. But all too often, it is argued, the courtroom reenactment results in the victim being blamed for the crime. Defense lawyers exploit male-biased legal definitions of consent to badger the victim about ambiguous signals she might have sent to the perpetrator (Estrich 1987:18). The vigor of her resistance will probably be questioned, again by male standards (Estrich 1987:65; MacKinnon 1989:177). Trivial inconsistencies in her testimony will be blown out of proportion to suggest a faulty memory, if not mendacity. She will also be attacked if any aspects of her post-rape behavior fail to conform to male notions of logical response to a crime—for example, if she did not flee the scene and report the crime as soon as physically possible.[4]

Perhaps the most controversial mechanism of revictimization is the common defense tactic of cross-examining the victim about her prior sexual history (Bohmer 1991:320–25; Spohn and Horney 1992:20–28; Allison and Wrightsman 1993). Previous sexual relations with the perpetrator will be highlighted to imply consent on the occasion in question. The defense lawyer may also draw on the victim's sexual experiences with others to portray her as a "loose woman," improving the odds for the consent defense.[5]

Efforts to reform rape prosecution have concentrated on these issues (Koss 1994:249–54). Some states, for example, have done away with requirements that the victim prove active physical resistance in order to defeat the consent defense (Bohmer 1991:323; Goldberg-Ambrose 1992). Specially trained rape units, often staffed by women, have become ubiquitous in police departments and district attorneys' offices.[6] Some jurisdictions have experimented with closing courtrooms and protecting the identities of rape victims from the press.[7] And in what is widely viewed as the most significant reform, many states have enacted "rape shield" laws, which prevent defense lawyers from putting the victim's prior sexual history before the jury.[8]

Despite the vigor with which these reforms were advocated, many scholars who have evaluated them have concluded that they are having little tangible impact on the incidence of rape, the rate of reporting, or the outcomes of rape prosecutions (Matoesian 1995:671). Although these new laws appear to make a different ideological statement about gender relations than did their patriarchal predecessors, the realities of men's power over women seem little changed. Why?

One answer to this question has come from sociologist Gregory Matoesian. In his 1993 book, *Reproducing Rape,* Matoesian argues convincingly that rape reformers have been looking for solutions in the wrong places. The reformers, Matoesian contends, have assumed that the power imbalances inherent in rape prosecution derive from defects in the *structure* of the process—such things as evidentiary rules about what information can be used to attack the victim's credibility. Matoesian's essential point is that the realities of power are far more complex. Power is more than an abstraction that is made concrete through the operation of simple rules. Rather, the concepts of power and domination and their real-world manifestations are two sides of the same coin. On the one hand, *power* is an underlying reality that helps shape the rules by which those conflicts are waged and their outcomes determined: men are able to dominate rape prosecutions because they have power. On the other hand, *power* is the label we apply to the pattern we observe in the outcomes of innumerable daily social conflicts: men seem to dominate rape prosecutions, so they must have power. The thing we call power is thus both cause and effect. If this is true, then efforts to change the distribution of power by tinkering with the structures through which it is exercised are doomed to failure.

The key to unlocking the conundrum of power, according to Matoesian, is to understand the minute details, in particular the microlinguistic details, of the interactions in which power is exercised. It is widely accepted, for example, that defense lawyers revictimize rape victims through their cross-examination techniques. But just what is it that lawyers *do* that causes people to have this reaction? Is it something as simple as the power to mention the victim's prior sexual history? Or does the lawyer's apparent power over the victim depend on far subtler rules of interaction? Structural reforms, such as rape shield laws, assume the adequacy of the former class of explanations; their apparent inefficacy may be the best evidence that much more is going on.

Understanding the microlinguistics—the microphysics, to use Foucault's term—of power may lead to more effective rape reform by exposing the futility of current efforts. Conversely, it may ultimately lead to the conclusion that the problem is too complicated for the law to solve. More important, Matoesian argues, linguistic analysis can help us to understand the nature of power itself. Language is the primary mechanism by which we act out the power relations in our society. It is also a means by which we reaffirm those power relations. Our shared understandings of power give meaning to the way we talk, but at the same time, the way we talk helps to shape our understandings.

Another way to understand this linguistic approach to power is through the concept of *discourse,* which we introduced in chapter 1. To recapitulate, this multidimensional term has two meanings that are especially relevant here: *discourse* in the concrete linguistic sense of connected sequences of speech or writing and *discourse* in the more abstract sense of "a way of talking about actions and relationships" (Merry 1990:9). Discourse at its various levels is not mere talk, however; it is intimately connected to both thought and action. A way of talking about something is also a way of thinking about it, since what we say both reflects what we think and helps to shape what we and others will think in the future. And by structuring the way that actions get talked and thought about, discourse ultimately suggests and limits the possibilities for future actions.

We can think of the law of rape together with the talk that occurs in and around the prosecution of rape cases as comprising a multilevel discourse. This discourse is the dominant discourse about rape in our society: the dominant way of talking, thinking, and acting with respect to those actions and relationships that rape implicates. Feminists and others who would reform rape law and its application contest this dominance and seek to substitute a discourse of their own. Both are discourses about power, specifically the power of men over women. The dominant discourse, its critics contend, both reflects and perpetuates that power, while the alternative seeks to reverse it.

Research such as Matoesian's seeks to connect the linguistic and the more abstract notions of discourse. It asks how the higher-order discourse about the power dynamics of rape is inscribed in the realities of day-to-day talk. In one sense, such work is a search for the mechanisms through which the power of the dominant discourse is exercised. But it is equally a search for the source of that power. The flow of influence is in both directions: higher-order discourse informs day-to-day talk, but the latter also shapes the former. And, significantly, changing daily discourse may be the most efficient way of subverting dominant ways of thinking. In the instance of rape, reform of normative legal rules seems to have had little impact on the experiences of rape victims with the criminal justice system. Perhaps the answer lies in understanding the day-to-day talk that goes on in the courthouse.

To investigate the daily discourse of rape, Matoesian draws on the methods of *conversation analysis*. The original inspiration for this method was the work of sociologist Erving Goffman. In a series of works bearing such revealing titles as *The Presentation of Self in Everyday Life* (Goffman 1959; see also Goffman 1963, 1967), Goffman argued that sociology should pay less attention to searching for the grand "rules" that govern social behavior and more attention to understanding the logic of mundane social interactions. Society is, after all, the sum of a countless number of such interactions. Conversation analysts have taken Goffman's fundamental insight and applied it to a particular sort of social interaction: conversations that occur in everyday contexts. They have marveled at the orderliness of conversation that we, as members of society, take for granted, and have sought to discover the resources that we use to maintain that order. The essence of their technique is the fine-grained, qualitative analysis of everyday conversations.

Although he employs its method, Matoesian deviates from the conversation analysis tradition in two significant ways. First, he joins a growing number of recent conversation analysts who have studied conversations in institutional rather than everyday settings (e.g., Atkinson and Drew 1979; Maynard 1984; Heritage and Greatbatch 1986; Mertz 1996, n.d.; Philips 1990; O'Donnell 1990). Second, he seeks to do more than discover the logic of conversation itself. Most conversation analysts have limited themselves to the study of *how* people manage conversations, prescinding from such questions as *why* they do what they do (Atkinson and Drew 1979:20–21). The focus has been on the mechanics of conversation rather than on the social and political objectives the parties may be pursuing. Matoesian, however, studies courtroom conversation not as an end in itself but in order to understand the power dynamics of rape.

In the rest of this chapter, we will examine and evaluate several of Matoesian's specific claims about the revictimization process, drawing on excerpts of trial transcripts published in *Reproducing Rape* and in Matoesian's (1995) article about the William Kennedy Smith rape trial. We will also introduce some additional issues that have arisen in our own study of that trial. To lay the groundwork for this material, in the next section we introduce some basic principles of conversation analysis that must be understood in order to follow the arguments.[9]

Principles of Conversation Analysis

Verbal interaction is the central and defining feature of human social life. Whether at home, at work, or at leisure, we spend an enormous amount of time talking to one another. Over the past three decades, conversation analysis has grown up around the study of this most human of activities. Its method is straightforward: record everyday conversations, transcribe them, and then dissect the transcripts in an effort to discern the resources that people employ to maintain order and coherence in social discourse. The most important discovery about talk in everyday contexts is its orderly and highly structured nature. Without external supervision or any conscious awareness of how they are doing it, participants in a conversation come to instantaneous tacit agreement on such complex questions as whose turn it is to speak and how long a speaking turn should last.

Conversation analysts tell us that conversations are governed by a structure that is as fundamental to talk as are the sounds of a language and its rules for constructing meaningful expressions. This structure is the grammar of turn-taking. We learn as children how to have orderly conversations, just as we learn how to construct meaningful utterances. Among other things, the grammar of conversation specifies the following:

- A person who is speaking can expect to finish a syntactically complete utterance before the issue arises of who gets to talk next. (For example, "I was getting ready to" is not syntactically complete, whereas "I was getting ready to leave" is.)
- A speaker who reaches a syntactically complete point in the utterance (or one that another speaker considers complete) must either relinquish the turn or attempt to continue speaking.

- A person who is speaking can influence who the next speaker will be. (For example, "What do you think, John?" attempts to select John to talk next, whereas "Do you know what I think?" is an attempt at self-selection.)
- When speaker overlaps do occur (usually at points when speaker change is relevant), one speaker normally continues as others drop out. The speaker who continues usually recycles what was uttered during the period of overlapping speech.[10]

Basic structural rules such as these allow us to communicate efficiently in everyday discourse. They enable ordinary conversations to take place with an alternation of speakers and minimal gaps and overlaps, and without referees or advance plans that state who will talk, what will be said, and how long a conversation will last.

Institutional environments such as the courtroom employ these basic rules, but modify them in important ways. The special rules governing courtroom interactions specify, for example, that lawyers ask questions and that witnesses answer them. In addition, the courtroom environment has a distinctive feature not present in everyday conversations—namely a judge who acts as referee to oversee the system of turn-taking, monitor the substance of what is discussed, and resolve complex interactional problems when they arise.

The special rules of the courtroom are highly unusual from a conversational point of view. From an everyday perspective, it would be very peculiar to limit some speakers so that their only type of turn is asking questions, while restricting others to giving answers to whatever questions they are asked. Such institutional constraints introduce into courtroom interactions a degree of rigidity not found in everyday contexts and thereby help the court do its assigned task of trying cases. But, in addition, these courtroom-specific rules have the consequence of empowering lawyers linguistically over the witnesses they examine. For example, if a witness strays in answering a question, the lawyer has considerable leeway to interrupt and bring the witness back to the point of the question. And if the witness proves unresponsive despite such efforts, the lawyer may ask the judge to instruct the witness to answer the question. Witnesses, however, have no comparable power to demand that lawyers ask questions that they deem relevant to the issue at hand. From the outset, the structural arrangements for talking in court do not privilege all speakers in the same way.

This imbalance of power is present in all courtroom dialogue. However, its consequences are most extreme during cross-examination, when lawyers examine the opposition's witnesses. When lawyers question their own witnesses on direct examination, they typically do so in a supportive manner, allowing friendly witnesses leeway in the form and substance of their answers. By contrast, the cross-examination is a hostile environment for both the lawyer and the witness. The lawyer's objective is to discredit opposition witnesses and minimize the impact of their testimony. And it is in such contexts that lawyers make maximal use of the linguistic power accorded to them.

The Conversation Analysis of Rape Trials

We turn now to the linguistic features of the rape trial that may contribute to the process of revictimization. Using Matoesian's data from *Reproducing Rape*, [11] we examine five features that lawyers manipulate to control witnesses: silence, question form, topic management, evaluative commentary, and challenges to the witness's capacity for knowledge. We conclude, in agreement with Matoesian, that these five features are indeed important strategies whereby cross-examining lawyers can dominate witnesses. We question, however, whether we have learned anything specific to rape trials or rather something about the general nature of the adversary system. The answer lies in the interaction between the commonplace details of adversary discourse and the unique context of rape, and it is there that we discover the reality of revictimization.

Silence

One linguistic feature that lawyers manipulate to exert control over witnesses is *silence*. Although, as we shall see, witnesses are sometimes reticent in court, the use of silence for strategic purposes is almost exclusively in the hands of the lawyer. The examining lawyer has the power to decide when the witness's turn begins by simply ending a question. If the lawyer chooses to be silent before asking a question or to punctuate a question with an interval of silence, there is little the witness can do, since it is not the witness's turn to speak and any effort to seize the turn would be out of order. The witness has no comparable opportunities to use silence. He or she cannot, for example, use silence as an answer to a question. The lawyer can ask the judge to instruct the witness to answer, and the judge will usually do so. Alternatively, the lawyer can end the witness's silence by repeating or rephrasing the question or by asking a new one. In either case, the lawyer's action may have the effect of adverse commentary on the witness's failure to respond.

Lawyers' control over silence allows them to accomplish two important strategic objectives. First, they can manipulate the law's question-and-answer format in ways not usually permitted by the turn-taking rules of the courtroom. Second, they can comment critically on a witness's credibility, a practice nominally forbidden by the rules of evidence and procedure. Several excerpts from the cross-examinations of rape victims by defense lawyers illustrate these uses of silence.

The basic rules of courtroom turn-taking are these: the lawyer begins the dialogue by asking a question; when the question is complete, the witness answers; when the answer is syntactically complete, it is the lawyer's turn to ask a new question; and so on. However, silence on the part of the witness at any point before or during an answer may give the lawyer an opportunity to evade these normal rules of give and take. The cross-examining lawyer has almost unfettered power to declare particular silences appropriate or inappropriate and to respond accordingly. In everyday conversations, there are rules for interpreting and dealing with silences on the part of a speaker who holds a turn. For example, a person who has been asked a question has a brief but well-understood interval to begin answering before someone else will interpret the silence as a refusal to respond. And even if that happens, there will then be a limited range of things that are understood to be appropriate: in some contexts, the question will be repeated or rephrased; in others, someone will move the conversation on to a new topic.

Under similar circumstances in the courtroom, however, cross-examining lawyers can do essentially whatever they want. In Text 2.1, the witness does not respond immediately to the question. The lawyer cuts off the witness's silence after 2.5 seconds and repeats the end of his question, loudly. The silence, followed by the emphatic restatement of the question, suggests to the audience that the witness knows the answer, but is unwilling to speak it.

Text 2.1 (Matoesian 1993:143)

> Lawyer: Then they're not in substantially the same condition, are they?
> (2.5)
> ARE THEY?

In Text 2.2, the lawyer allows the silence to continue for more than 6 seconds, finally resuming by disparaging the witness's apparent failure of memory.

Text 2.2 (Matoesian 1993:143)

> Lawyer: Well WHAT were the items that you hadn't remembered when you—remember as of Friday?
> (6.2)
> Or don't you remember that?

Finally, silence following an answer before a lawyer asks another question can serve as an all-but-explicit commentary by the lawyer on the credibility of preceding utterances—what several investigators have called the "pin-drop effect" (Matoesian 1993:144).

Text 2.3 (Matoesian 1993:145)

> LAWYER: Is it your sworn testimony (1.0) under sworn, SWORN oath (0.8) that in four hours at the Grainary you had only two drinks?
> (1.2)
> WITNESS: Yes.
> (45.0)
> LAWYER: Linda . . .

Note that the witness is powerless to resist this tactic. She has given an obviously complete yes/no answer, thus ending her turn. To begin speaking again would be to violate the lawyer's control over turn allocation, likely to earn a rebuke from the judge. The only constraint on the lawyer—and it is a minimal one—is the possibility that the judge may get irritated and tell him to get on with the cross-examination.

Thus, silence is a tool for lawyers in their management and control of courtroom discourse. It is available for them to use in the ways demonstrated here, with the consequences that witnesses are impugned and their credibility challenged. Witnesses lack any practical countervailing resource.

Question Form

Lawyers control not only the timing of questions but also their form. This is significant because the form of a question can limit the range of permissible answers available to the witness. Some kinds of questions can also serve as statements of blame that stand irrespective of the witness's answer.

Question forms differ radically in the extent to which they constrain the witness's answer. At the two ends of the continuum of control are the WH question and the tag question. The former is the open-ended why, where, when, which, who, what, how question. The latter consists of a statement followed by a question such as "isn't that true?" or "correct?" or "didn't you?"—as in "You drove the car into the parking lot, didn't you?" Among the numerous question forms available to a lawyer,[12] the WH question is the least controlling and coercive because it imposes no particular form on the answer, whereas the tag question, with its implicit insistence on a yes/no answer, is the most controlling.

All of this is common knowledge among trial lawyers. The techniques of question-form management are taught to law students in trial practice courses. As one widely used trial advocacy text advises, "Open-ended questions are disastrous on cross-examinations. Hostile witnesses are always looking for an opening to slip in a damaging answer. Questions that ask 'what', 'how', or 'why' or elicit explanations of any kind invite disaster. These kinds of questions are best avoided altogether" (Mauet 1992:216).

The management of question form is illustrated by Text 2.4, in which a defense attorney initially uses WH questions to seek a definition of "partying" and then switches to tag questions to imply that the witness had an unhealthy interest in sex, drugs, and alcohol.

TEXT 2.4 (Matoesian 1993:151–52)

LAWYER: What's meant by partying? You, you're what? Nineteen? Were you nineteen at that time?
WITNESS: Yes.
LAWYER: What's meant among youthful people, people your age,
5   Brian's age, by partying?
WITNESS: Some take it just to go and, with some friends, people, and have a few drinks, and some do smoke, some do take the pills.
LAWYER: Partying.
10   WITNESS: (Drugs.)
LAWYER: Is it not true, partying among people your age, does not mean to go to a party?
WITNESS: That's true.
LAWYER: It implies to many people that, implies sexual activity,
15   doesn't it?
[*An objection by prosecuting attorney at this point is overruled by judge.*]
LAWYER: To many people your age that means sexual activity, does it not?
20   WITNESS: To some, yes, I guess.
LAWYER: And at the very least it means the use of intoxicants?
WITNESS: Yes.
LAWYER: So, when they suggested, who suggested that you go partying?
25   WITNESS: I don't know who first brought it up. They [did mention]—
LAWYER: [Then did—]
WITNESS: —did mention that, uh, there would be friends who had the apartment who would be having a party.
30   LAWYER: So the word partying, let's go party, some like that, (inaudible) not just go to a party?
WITNESS: Mmhmm.
LAWYER: Correct?
WITNESS: Mmhmm.

As is apparent from the question-and-answer sequences in lines 4–8 and 23–29, the WH form invites a narrative from the witness.[13] The tag form (lines 14–19)[14] demands a yes/no answer. But because each of the tag questions is preceded by a statement that is damaging to the witness, the answers are almost irrelevant. Even if the witness answers in the negative, the denial may be lost in the flow of the lawyer's polemic. By controlling question form, the lawyer is thus able to transform the cross-examination from dialogue into self-serving monologue.

Topic Management

Another linguistic resource available to a cross-examining lawyer is the ability to manage the topic under discussion. On the simplest level, this is an obvious consequence of the fact that lawyers ask questions and witnesses answer them. By posing a particular question, one might assume, the lawyer determines the topic of the answer.

The reality of topic management is a good deal more complex, however. A cross-examination is not simply a series of questions followed by topically parallel answers. Instead, a witness may employ a variety of strategies to evade the lawyer's preferred answer. The lawyer may then seek to regain control by repeating, rephrasing, or elaborating on questions that have failed to elicit the desired answers.

Text 2.4 illustrates these points. The lawyer moves the witness toward acquiescence in a definition of "partying" that includes consensual sex. As discussed above, the lawyer succeeds in part through his manipulation of question forms. But his ability to maintain topic control is equally important. He begins by asking for the witness's definition of partying; she volunteers the elements of alcohol and drugs (lines 6–8). The lawyer pursues the theme, pinning down the distinction between partying as understood by the witness and her peers and partying as understood by others—middle-aged jurors perhaps (lines 11–13). He then expands on the topic by suggesting that sex is another routine party activity (lines 14–19). When the witness's answer is mildly evasive (line 20), he returns to the intoxication theme (line 21). When the witness gives her unqualified assent to this proposition (line 22), the lawyer has closed the circle, linking the witness and her friends to a party scene that unequivocally includes drugs and alcohol, and very probably consensual sex as well.

The lawyer then executes a subtle and highly significant topic shift. Having defined the category "partying" to include drugs, alcohol, and sex, he moves to include within that category the behavior of the witness on the night of the alleged rape (lines 23–24). The witness is initially silent and then offers an answer that evades the full force of the question (note her phrase "having a party" rather than the lawyer's "go partying") (lines 25–29). The lawyer does not let the evasion stand, however. Instead, he presses the point in two final questions (lines 30–33), which insist that the night's activities came within the agreed-upon definition of partying.

In the preceding example, the witness ultimately yields to the lawyer's topic management strategy. Far from advancing her cause, she becomes an unwitting collaborator in defining her activities on the night in question in a way that undermines, perhaps fatally, her contention that she was raped. She, like other witnesses, was not entirely without resources to resist such linguistic domination, however. Witnesses often decline to provide the kind of answer that the question presupposes. For example, as the following text illustrates, a witness may refuse to give an expected yes/no answer, instead challenging the question by deviating from its specific topic.

TEXT 2.5 (Matoesian 1993:154)

> LAWYER: You were attracted to Brian, weren't you?
> WITNESS: I thought he was a nice clean-looking man.
> LAWYER: He was attractive-looking, correct?
> WITNESS: Yeah.
> 5 LAWYER: And basically when you left that parking lot all you
> knew about him was that he was a good-lookin' man, isn't that true?
> WITNESS: Yeah.

As Text 2.5 also suggests, however, witness resistance is likely to be short-lived. When the witness sidesteps a pejorative question, the lawyer can use elements of the answer to frame another question that is almost equally damaging. In this instance, when the witness hears her own topic, and indeed her own key word (*looking*), in the follow-up question, she finally acquiesces in the lawyer's suggestion that she willingly went off with a man—the defendant—to whom she was attracted. The linguistic resources available to the lawyer are simply too many and those available to the witness too few.

Commentary

Another source of domination available to the cross-examining lawyer is the opportunity to make covert evaluative comments on the witness's behavior. Such comments may concern the witness's behavior during the trial (or other associated legal proceedings) or in the course of the events outside the trial that constitute the substance of the case. Such comments are not stated directly, but are embedded in questions. This allows the lawyer to stay within the bounds of the courtroom's prescribed question-and-answer format. The following two questions are examples of such covert commentary.

TEXT 2.6 (Matoesian 1993:164)

> LAWYER: Isn't it true that on direct examination by Mrs. Roberts you never once answered a question with "I don't know" or "I don't remember"?

TEXT 2.7 (Matoesian 1993:164)

> LAWYER: Isn't it true that on cross-examination by Mr. Billings you, on numerous occasions, indicated you didn't know or didn't remember?

Although these utterances are couched in the required question form and do not constitute the sort of explicit commentary that is permitted only in closing argument,[15] they nonetheless contain clear negative evaluations of the witness's behavior. In each instance, the rhetorical force of the question is to comment critically on a discrepancy between what the witness now claims to remember and what she remembered during a previous examination. Significantly, the lawyer structures the question so as both to offer an evaluative comment and to demand that the witness confirm his evaluation in her answer.

In another example, a lawyer expresses his contention that the witness planned, or even fabricated, her testimony in a way that she believed would enhance the probability of winning. What the lawyer's questioning strategy does in this instance is to raise, via implication, the issue of whether the witness is to be trusted.

TEXT 2.8 (Matoesian 1993:163–64)

> LAWYER: Did you ever say that three people got into your car?
> WITNESS: Yes, I did.
> LAWYER: How often did you say that?
> WITNESS: A few times.
> 5   LAWYER: Before you talked to the prosecutor in this case?
> WITNESS: Yes.
> LAWYER: Was that because you thought that made your story sound better?

The lawyer is not permitted to state directly that he suspects that the witness may have fabricated details of her story. However, when couched as a question, such an assessment may be made indirectly.

Although it is logical to assume that a witness might in turn offer parallel commentary on the questions asked (such as "I don't think that's an appropriate question," "You're trying to put words into my mouth," or "I don't see where you're going with that question"), such instances are rare in court. When a witness does not answer the question directly within the constraints imposed by the lawyer, the lawyer may object on the grounds that the answer is not responsive to the question. The fact that witnesses have no resource parallel to the objections permitted to lawyers further underscores the imbalance of power under which witnesses must face examination.[16]

Notwithstanding the resources that are disproportionately available to the lawyer, a witness will sometimes offer resistance to a lawyer's assessment of her conduct by *downgrading* it. In the example that follows, the general topic is crossing the border from Missouri to Illinois. In his first two questions, the lawyer attempts to impose a damaging assessment on the witness's border-crossing behavior: that she goes to Illinois in order to take advantage of the lower drinking age. In answering the second question, the witness attempts to downgrade the lawyer's original assessment ("That's not the sole purpose") and thereby to diminish the significance of her action. Because the lawyer can follow up with another question, the witness's downgrade does not stand. In framing his follow-up question, the lawyer upgrades the previous downgrade by insisting that alcohol consumption was at least a partial motive for crossing into Illinois, and the witness is compelled to assent. Once again, the structure of courtroom interaction gives the lawyer an insurmountable advantage.

TEXT 2.9 (Matoesian 1993:180–81)

> LAWYER: Can you drink over at Saint Louis?
> WITNESS: No.
> LAWYER: So you come over here so you can get some alcohol, is that correct?
> 5   WITNESS: That's not the sole purpose, no.
> LAWYER: That's one of the purposes, is it not?
> WITNESS: Yeah.

The Witness's Capacity for Knowledge

A final linguistic strategy used by cross-examining lawyers to achieve and maintain domination involves direct challenges to knowledge claimed by the witness. Matoesian calls these challenges "epistemological filters" (1993:184). Epistemology is the study of knowledge: how we acquire it and how we decide what is really known. The lawyers' challenges described below are epistemological in that they call into question not only the specific facts the witness claims to know, but also the sources of the claimed knowledge, and ultimately whether the witness is capable of knowing anything at all.

In the cross-examination excerpt in Text 2.10, the subject is the location to which the defendant drove the alleged victim on the night of the rape. The witness has previously identified the place as Glen Carbon. The lawyer now probes the source of her knowledge (line 4), and the witness responds in a way that would certainly be adequate by the standards of everyday conversation (lines 5–7, identifying the inscription on the water tank). But the lawyer continues the challenge, deprecating the certainty of her knowledge (line 8) and then positing an alternative epistemological theory: that the police planted the idea in her head (line 17).

TEXT 2.10 (Matoesian 1993:184–85)

LAWYER: You say that Brian's car led the way over to this Glen Carbon area?
WITNESS: Mmhmm.
LAWYER: How do you know that was Glen Carbon?
5   WITNESS: There's a water tank? Maybe? A big silver [bubble]—
LAWYER: [(What?)]
WITNESS: —thing that says Glen Carb–, Glen Carbon.
LAWYER: (Okay) but you don't actually know whether or not you were in Glen Carbon, or had you been told you were in Glen Car-
10   bon at that point in time?
WITNESS: I was told that was a part of Glen Carbon.
LAWYER: By the police officers?
WITNESS: Mmhmm.
LAWYER: (Okay), so you don't actually know it was Glen Carbon
15   of your own personal knowledge.
WITNESS: No I assumed it when I'd seen [(that big)]—
LAWYER: [And when] the police officers told you.

Two further aspects of this exchange are significant. First, because of the lawyer's control over turn-taking and the form of questions, it is very difficult for the witness to contest the epistemological challenge. When the lawyer's "how" question elicits an ostensibly satisfactory response (lines 4–7), he pursues the point with a series of questions—in effect, statements—that exert progressively more control over the witness's response (lines 8–end). Because his final question (lines 14–15) calls for a yes/no answer, he is able to treat her initial "No" as a complete answer and cut off her developing explanation.[17] Despite the plausibility of that explanation (that she had seen the Glen Carbon water tank, assumed that was where she was, and then had her assumption verified by the police), the lawyer is able to interrupt it and conclude the exchange with a damaging evaluative comment.

Second, the genders of the lawyer and the witness seem highly relevant to the power dynamics of this exchange. The other methods of linguistic domination described thus far occur regularly in all kinds of cases and irrespective of the gender of the protagonists. As we shall see, the relationship between these devices and the politics of male domination is discoverable only at deeper levels of analysis. In the case of epistemological challenges, however, that relationship seems closer to the surface. Could a lawyer so readily challenge a *male* witness's ability to draw factual inferences from his observations? Or does the challenge depend on the cultural stereotype of women as being incapable of logical deduction and having diminished capacity for knowledge generally? We turn to these issues in the next section.

Is It Really about Rape?

In reviewing various linguistic strategies by which lawyers dominate witnesses, we have said very little about rape. In fact, until we reached the last of these strategies—epistemological challenge—we did not make a single argument that even depended on gender dynamics. On the contrary, anyone with any exposure to the adversary system will recognize that all but the last are staples of cross-examination, used without regard to the subject matter of the case or the genders of lawyer and witness. And with respect to epistemological challenge, even if it is far more likely in the cross-examination of a female witness by a male lawyer, there is no reason to believe that its use is limited to rape trials or more prevalent there than in other contexts.

These unremarkable observations give rise to an important question: From a linguistic perspective, is there really anything unique about rape trials? Or does the revictimization process consist simply of generic cross-examination strategies?[18] Perhaps we think we see something unique because the adversarial treatment of rape victims is particularly offensive to our moral and political sensibilities.[19]

Matoesian has recognized the problem. In *Reproducing Rape,* he asks, "Could it not be that the relevant moral inferential work being transacted [in rape trials] represents instead mundane, gender-neutral categorizations: doing credible or incredible testimony; doing honesty or dishonesty; doing consistency or inconsistency, etc.?" (Matoesian 1993:163). In other words, is revictimization just ordinary cross-examination?

Matoesian's answer to this question seems oddly out of place in a work that aspires to rigorous linguistic empiricism. He acknowledges that the processes of reproducing rape are gender-neutral, "but only at a surface level!" (1993: 163; exclamation his). "On a deeper level of social organization," he argues, ostensibly neutral linguistic practices are inseparably bound up with patriarchal values. Matoesian seems to be asking the reader to accept an argument about the meaning of linguistic behavior on the basis of an a priori assessment of the nature of society.

One need not rely on assumptions about social organization to demonstrate the uniqueness of rape trials, however. First, the appropriate background against which we should interpret the use of apparently generic cross-examination strategies is not some "deeper level of social organization" but the crime of rape itself. In judging a case of acquaintance rape, the jury's task is to assign social meaning to a commonplace behavior—sexual intercourse—that is in itself neither right nor wrong. In particular, the jury must decide whether the behavior in question was an act of *domination.* It is hard to think of another crime that has precisely these qualities. Although legal culpability may ultimately depend on the state of mind of the perpetrator, shooting another human being, hot-wiring someone else's car, and failing to file an income tax return are all presumptively pathological actions in and of themselves.[20]

With this point in mind, recall the various linguistic strategies we have reviewed: they are all strategies of domination. When used in a rape trial, they are strategies of domination employed in the service of one accused of domination. Thus, while these strategies may not be unique to rape trials, they have a poignancy in the rape context that is unmatched elsewhere. A woman telling a story of physical domination by one man is subjected to linguistic domination by another.[21] In this sense, revictimization is real, and its mechanism is linguistic.

There is also abundant direct evidence that rape trials are unique linguistic events. Matoesian (1995) develops some of this evidence in a more recent article in which he analyzes the 1991 William Kennedy Smith rape trial. He discusses two linguistic phenomena that are of major strategic importance in rape trials and that would be inappropriate in any other context: the "double bind" of sexual logic and the covert exploitation of the witness's prior sexual history (1995:686).

The Sexual Double Bind

The double bind is the dilemma that an acquaintance rape victim finds herself in when she tries to explain her interaction with the defendant. In such cases, the victim is usually called upon to explain how a normal social engagement evolved into a crime of violence. A critical element of the explanation is how the witness describes her state of mind at various points before and after the alleged rape. If she describes herself as having been emotional, the lawyer may play on the stereotype of the flighty woman to suggest that she is irrational and thus not credible, and perhaps now vengeful as well. If, on the other hand, she portrays herself as having been calm and in control, the lawyer may emphasize that she does *not* fit the stereotype, implying that an unusually logical woman would not have allowed herself to be dominated. When the defendant is a wealthy man like William Kennedy Smith, the calm, logical woman also becomes a target for accusations of gold-digging. The woman is thus in a double bind: she loses, whichever approach she takes.

In Text 2.11, Roy Black, Smith's defense lawyer, is cross-examining Patricia Bowman, the alleged victim. Black picks up on Bowman's evaluation of Smith's demeanor ("very smug") and upgrades it ("And arrogant?") in order to develop the theme of a woman scorned, perhaps driven to seek revenge by Smith's unwillingness to connect with her emotionally. Bowman falls into the trap: in denying the charge of anger, she admits to confusion.

TEXT 2.11 (Matoesian 1995:684)

> LAWYER: And he was sitting there, and I think you said, with his legs crossed?
> WITNESS: He had his ankle up on his knee.
> LAWYER: And you say that he was very calm at that time?
> 5   WITNESS: And very smug.
> LAWYER: And arrogant? Made you madder than you were?
> WITNESS: It didn't make me mad. It confused me.

Elsewhere in the cross-examination, Black does the same thing in a slightly different way. Once again, he exploits Bowman's characterizations of Smith to sharpen his portrait of her as a scorned woman whose emotionally charged story is not worthy of belief. He adopts Bowman's assessment of Smith ("indifference") and upgrades it ("cold and indifferent"). She acquiesces, accepting Black's now-enhanced description of her dismay at Smith's attitude.

TEXT 2.12 (Matoesian 1995:684)

> LAWYER: He was calm and arrogant, you say?
> WITNESS: Yes sir.
> LAWYER: He was certainly not being very nice to you.
> WITNESS: It was more an indifference.
> 5   LAWYER: He was cold and indifferent?
> WITNESS: Yes sir.

Patricia Bowman and other rape victims cannot win. They are either too illogical or too logical. When Bowman elsewhere characterizes portions of her interaction with Smith as calm and rational, Black pursues the topic to suggest that she had a serious interest in him. The implication, of course, is that she was a calculating pursuer rather than a helpless victim.

TEXT 2.13 (Matoesian 1995:686)

> LAWYER: He told you he was in medical school?
> WITNESS: Yes he did.
> LAWYER: Of course, that got you more interested in him, didn't it?

WITNESS: I was interested in any other outlooks he could have
5   on my daughter's problem . . .
. . .
LAWYER: And you talked to him about medical matters involving
your daughter, isn't that right?
WITNESS: Yes sir.
10   LAWYER: You became more interested in him as you found out
that he had this kind of background?
WITNESS: I became more interested in what he had to say.

Rape victims are not allowed to negotiate a middle course between emotion and reason. Defense lawyers push them to extremes. At one moment, the lawyer portrays the woman as so emotional that she probably consented to sex, regretted it, and then brought charges to get revenge; at the next, he depicts her as too rational and controlling to have been lured into domination by another. The woman is not permitted to be simultaneously competent and vulnerable. In Text 2.14, Bowman suggests that her initial feeling toward Smith was mild affection that stopped well short of sexual abandon. Black immediately challenges that possibility with negative assessments.

TEXT 2.14 (Matoesian 1995:680)

LAWYER: Yesterday you told us that when you arrived in the parking lot in the car you kissed Will. Is that correct?
WITNESS: I testified that when we arrived at the estate, he gave me a goodnight peck.
5   . . .
LAWYER: That's all it was?
WITNESS: Yes sir.
LAWYER: Nothing of any—, nothing more than that?
WITNESS: No.

Sexual History

Rape victims are also subject to attack on the basis of their sexual history with men other than the defendants. Many states, including Florida, the site of the Smith trial, have enacted rape shield laws, which prohibit explicit questions about the victim's sexual history. Nonetheless, skillful defense lawyers can accomplish the same thing by innuendo. In Text 2.15, Black asks Bowman a series of apparently sympathetic questions about her meeting with Smith. But he subtly connects her to "the bar scene," with all its tawdry connotations, by suggesting that Smith rescued her from it. Then, by the device of abandoning his own question in midsentence ("You were no longer—"), Black implies that

Smith's arrival interrupted the unspecified bar-scene activities in which she had been engaged. The rapist is thus transformed into a missionary to fallen women.

TEXT 2.15 (Matoesian 1995:679)

> LAWYER: You had an engrossing conversation?
> WITNESS: Yes sir.
> LAWYER: You didn't have to be involved in the rest of the bar scene?
> 5   WITNESS: Yes sir.
> LAWYER: You were happy to have found that?
> WITNESS: It was nice.
> LAWYER: You were no longer—, in fact you were with him almost exclusively?
> 10   WITNESS: I don't know.

In these examples from the William Kennedy Smith trial, it is not the basic linguistic devices that are unique. On the contrary, Black accomplishes his objectives through such familiar devices as control over question form, topic management, and commentary disguised as questions. What is unique is the effect of these devices in the rape context. The double bind strategy, for example, would have no saliency in other kinds of cases. One can imagine a lawyer suggesting that a woman who had witnessed an auto accident was emotional and flighty, but what sense would it make to imply in the next breath that she was too logical? Even more obviously, covert references to a woman's sexual history would be out of place in a case where her sexuality was not squarely before the jury.

It is also hard to imagine a man being subjected to this kind of cross-examination. On the one hand, imputing emotional instability to a man requires specific evidence, since it does not evoke a stereotype. On the other hand, what is to be gained by imputing a calculating, logical mindset to a man—even in matters of sexual conquest—since that is what everyone expects? The point is well illustrated by an excerpt from prosecutor Moira Lasch's cross-examination of Smith. When she accuses him of a lack of emotional involvement in the events of the evening, he simply acquiesces, and the attack goes nowhere.

TEXT 2.16 (Matoesian 1995:684)

> LAWYER: So you have this conversation—, well you had this act, then you ejaculate and then you say, "Well I'm going into the water and take a swim now."
> WITNESS: Yes.

5   LAWYER: That sounds not too romantic, Mr. Smith.
WITNESS: I don't know how to respond to that.[22]

A final illustration of the uniqueness of rape trials comes from our own study of the Smith case. Here, Black cross-examines Bowman about her pantyhose, which she earlier testified she had removed at some point on the night of the rape.

TEXT 2.17 (Authors' transcription from videotape of trial)

LAWYER: Did you take off your pantyhose at Au Bar?
WITNESS: I don't remember doing that.
LAWYER: Did you have your pantyhose on when you left the bar?
WITNESS: I'm, I think I did.
5   LAWYER: Did you have your pantyhose on when you drove your car from Au Bar [with Smith as her passenger]?
WITNESS: Yes.
LAWYER: Did you have your pantyhose on when you got to the parking lot at the Kennedy home?
10   WITNESS: Yes.
LAWYER: Did you have your pantyhose on in the car in the, in the parking lot?
WITNESS: Yes.
LAWYER: Did you have your pantyhose on when you got out of
15   your car?
WITNESS: I'm not sure.
LAWYER: Did you have your pantyhose on when you went into the house?
WITNESS: I'm not sure.
20   LAWYER: Did you have your pantyhose on in the kitchen?
WITNESS: I don't remember.
LAWYER: Did you have your pantyhose on when you walked through the house?
WITNESS: I don't remember.
25   LAWYER: Did you have your pantyhose on when you walked across the lawn?
WITNESS: I don't remember.
LAWYER: Did you have your pantyhose on going down the stairs?
30   WITNESS: I don't remember.
LAWYER: Did you have them on while you were standing on the beach?
WITNESS: I don't remember.
LAWYER: Did you have them on when you were going up the
35   stairs?
WITNESS: I don't remember.

In this sequence, Black uses an ordinary cross-examination technique—the repetitive question form—to extraordinary effect. The form of the questions is within Black's exclusive control. The law of evidence does prohibit repetitive questioning, but Black skillfully avoids that prohibition by a subtle shift from question to question. Each question hammers home the identical point but in reference to a moment in time slightly later than that in the previous question.

In an effort to understand the effect, we have asked many of our students to analyze this testimony. The students continually focus on Black's ability to manipulate gender differences in the classification of clothing. From a male perspective, the students contend, there are two principal classes of clothing: clothes and underwear. Pantyhose constitute underwear because they are never fully exposed in public. One's underwear is exposed to the opposite sex only in circumstances of intimacy. Decent people do not lose track of their underwear when in mixed company. Patricia Bowman, by contrast, cannot remember what happened to her underwear during her evening with William Kennedy Smith. How, Black's questions imply, can a man be held responsible for his actions toward such a woman?

By contrast, the students argue, pantyhose are interstitial from a female perspective. They are underwear in the sense that they are worn beneath something else, but their removal does not always imply intimacy. Indeed, removing one's pantyhose in the dark before walking on the sandy beach is a perfectly ordinary act. From this perspective, the status of Bowman's pantyhose at various times during the evening is irrelevant to the issue of Bowman's consent to sex. Because of Black's control over the questions, however, this perspective is never expressed.

This line of questioning could occur only in the cross-examination of a rape victim. Black has identified and exploited a topic that has no male counterpart. It is meaningful only because the sexuality of a woman is at issue.

Conclusion: Rape and the Power of Discourse

The microdiscourse of the rape trial is a compelling example of how power is realized through linguistic practice. Rape victims are indeed revictimized, but not by any legal rules or practices peculiar to rape. Instead, it is the ordinary mechanics of cross-examination that, in this extraordinary context, simultaneously reflect and reaffirm men's power over women. The basic linguistic strategies of cross-examination are methods of domination and control. When used against the background of the rape victim's experience, they can bring about a subtle yet powerful reenactment of that experience.

The linguistic analysis of rape also yields convincing evidence of the inseparability of the multiple meanings of discourse. The discourse of rape is multifaceted; it comprises, at a minimum, the talk that transpires between rapist and victim, the statements contained in the law of rape, the largely linguistic practice of lawyers and witnesses involved in applying that law, and the cultural commentary on all of the foregoing. At every level of the discourse of rape, important social values concerning women, men, and their relationships are evident. The fine-grained analysis of the discourse of legal practice, however, affords insights that are not available at higher levels of abstraction. We see how the law translates social values into social action, as well as the role that law can play in either strengthening or subverting those values. In the words of Alan Hunt and Gary Wickham, "Discourses have real effects; they are not just the ways that social issues get talked and thought about" (1994:8). Analysis such as this enables us to understand what those effects are and how they come about.

CHAPTER THREE

The Language of Mediation

I n this chapter, we undertake another case study of the relationship between
political claims about legal power and the linguistic means through which
that power is exercised. Here, however, we focus not on a substantive area
of the law (such as rape) but on a legal *process* that is brought to bear on a wide
range of disputes: mediation. In general terms, mediation is any conciliatory,
nonbinding process in which disputants, with the aid of a neutral facilitator, try
to reach a mutually acceptable resolution of their problem (Hughes 1995:566).
Mediation is conciliatory in the sense that the parties talk to each other in an
effort to compromise, rather than presenting competing evidence, as they
would in a formal trial. It is nonbinding in that the facilitator has no power to
enter a final judgment, as a judge or arbitrator can.

The past ten years have seen a phenomenal growth in the popularity of mediation (e.g., Grillo 1991:1551–55). Many courts require it before certain kinds
of cases can go to trial (e.g., Clarke et al. 1989). Community mediation centers
have proliferated, and thousands of lawyers, social workers, business people,
and others are now holding themselves out as mediation professionals. Significantly, numerous published accounts report widespread consumer satisfaction
with mediation as a less expensive, faster, and more satisfying alternative to
litigation (see Hughes 1995:568–69; Bohmer and Ray 1994:224–25; Grillo
1991:1548–49; Clarke et al. 1989:53–66; Kelly 1989). The disputants' sense
of control over the outcome seems to promote both satisfaction and compliance
with mediated agreements (Garcia 1995:40; Friedman 1993:17).[1] Even lawyers are reported to like mediation, despite the fact that it might be seen as a
threat to their historical monopoly over dispute resolution.[2]

The reviews have not been uniformly positive, however. Critics charge that
the very user-friendly qualities that have made mediation so popular also make

it dangerous (e.g., Bryan 1992:453–54; Hughes 1995:573–73; Grillo 1991: 1601–5). That is, in the cooperative ambience of the mediation session, people with strong legal and moral claims may be induced to let down their guard and make concessions that are neither required by the law nor consistent with their interests. Moreover, the critique continues, these effects are not randomly distributed but work almost invariably to support powerful interests and reinforce the political and economic status quo.

Our purpose in this chapter is to assess the mediation phenomenon from a microlinguistic perspective. What is it about the mediation process that prompts such strong reactions, both positive and negative? First we address the seemingly incontrovertible fact that mediation "works": by all accounts, it resolves many disputes in a way that is satisfactory to the disputants. How does it do so? What are the mechanisms through which angry people on the brink of litigation are led to talk to each other and agree on an outcome? Then we consider the practical consequences of mediation's apparent success in resolving disputes. We test the claim that mediation is subject to political manipulation by searching for the linguistic processes through which that might happen. Through the examination of microdiscourse, we seek to assess whether mediation reflects and reaffirms the dominant macrodiscourse. We begin with a brief overview of the mediation process.

What a Mediation Session Is Like

People often talk about mediation as though it were a unitary phenomenon. In fact, there are many kinds of mediation structures, and they differ from each other in significant ways.[3] Many community-based mediation centers, for example, have clients who seek mediation voluntarily, whereas court-annexed programs provide mandatory mediation for people who have been diverted from the judicial system. Some court-annexed programs offer mediation as an alternative to the formal prosecution of minor crimes, while others require that certain kinds of civil litigants (parties to divorce cases, for example) go through mediation before their cases can go to trial. Procedurally, some programs use a single mediator, and others have two or more; programs also vary in the amount of talk between the parties and the way the interaction is structured. It is therefore difficult to describe mediation in terms of any universal features. Nonetheless, to set the stage for our discussion of how mediation works on a linguistic level, we offer the following description of mediation as it operates in a community mediation center where one of us has worked as a mediator (compare Friedman 1993:33–59; Grillo 1991:1589; Hughes 1995:566–69).

Before a session begins, civil discourse between the parties has broken down. Something has happened; they have disagreed; perhaps the dispute has escalated to the point where they are not even speaking to one another.

Mediation enters the picture as a possible mechanism for settling the conflict through talking things out. Some parties come to this community mediation center on their own. Others are referred by the local criminal court with the promise of having their cases dropped if working agreements can be reached. Although some are thus coerced into mediation by the threat of prosecution, many who enter mediation are voluntarily seeking a way to mend social relationships that have failed.

When the disputants arrive at the mediation center, they are often angry. They are ushered into separate rooms to wait for the session to begin. When they are called in by one of the two co-mediators, the first order of business is to lay out the rules that will be followed. Each side will present its version of the dispute, beginning with the complainant. There will be no interruptions. Each party will get to tell its story while the other listens. There will eventually be time for questions and discussion, but during the initial presentations, they are to listen respectfully.

An unstated goal of the mediators is to work as impartial and supportive listeners, a technique in which they have been extensively trained. Ideally, this means that they will not take sides or show any partiality. Regardless of who is speaking, they should demonstrate through both gestures and linguistic behaviors that they are listening actively. They are encouraged, for example, to sit up in their chairs, to indicate understanding by nodding frequently, and to affirm the stories and positions of each side by repeating back what they have heard, using such introductory phrases as "What I hear you saying is . . . ," "Let me see if I understand you correctly," and "You seem to be saying that . . ." In addition to providing support and encouragement to the speaker, these techniques have the important effect of making the mediators the addressees of each speaker's story, with the other party cast in the role of overhearer.

Beyond active listening, the mediators will work to structure the substance of the talk so as to promote the overriding goal of the mediation center: reaching an agreement that the parties can promise to follow. What this means in practice is that the mediators will help the parties separate the issues that seem amenable to some sort of resolution from those on which they are hopelessly deadlocked. If successful, the mediation session will result in a written agreement that both parties assent to and promise to follow. It will state in simple, everyday language what they have agreed to and what they will do to ensure that the terms work. It is supposed to be up to the parties to fashion the specific terms, with the mediators serving as nonjudgmental scribes and editors. This often results in agreements whose details might strike an observer (who incidentally would never be allowed in the room due to the mediation center's overriding concern with confidentiality) as odd ("X agrees not to let his dog out anymore at 3 A.M.," or "Y will pick up any garbage that spills on the walk in front of the apartment building where he lives"). But when the process works, the parties take a proprietary interest in the agreement and, for that reason, strive to live up to its terms. In the best of circumstances, the climate of civility that mediation fosters spills over into daily life, enabling the former adversaries to regenerate at least some of their social connections.

Restoring Civility

We turn next to the linguistic analysis of how mediation manages to restore communication and promote agreement between a pair of antagonists. The research of sociologist Angela Garcia is particularly helpful in understanding the microlinguistic phenomena that produce such effects. Using the methods of conversation analysis, Garcia (1991, 1995) focuses on the differences between mediation talk and everyday arguments. She points to details in the linguistic structure of mediation that serve to suppress some essential features of arguments. The result is the conciliatory environment that is the hallmark of mediation.

In her 1991 article, Garcia adheres to the traditions of conversation analysis, concerning herself with questions of *how* rather than *why*. She does not, for example, ask whether suppressing arguments is a good or a bad thing, nor does she assess the effects of doing so in particular contexts. Similarly, she is content to show how mediators acknowledge disputants' stories without addressing the issue of why they acknowledge them as they do. Nonetheless, her detailed data and fine-grained description allow her readers to extend the analysis to other, more explicitly political issues—as Garcia (1995) has done in her more recent work, and as we shall do later in this chapter.[4]

The Structure of Mediation

Accusations, counteraccusations, blamings, denials, raised voices, and hurt feelings make up the stuff of arguments in daily life. Once started, arguments easily escalate to a point where civility seems irretrievably lost. Driving this all-too-familiar pattern are the interactional mechanics of arguing.

Most arguments begin when one party accuses or blames another. The accused or blamed person retorts. There follows a counterretort, and on it goes. Whether it is the you-did/no-I-didn't/yes-you-did of children's arguments or some more elaborate adult version, almost all arguments have this basic structure. Mediation alters the rules of conversational exchange in such a way as to mitigate argumentation and facilitate the regeneration of nonargumentative talk. A look into the linguistic details of mediation reveals just how this happens.

According to Garcia, two structural features are critical to the linguistic distinctiveness of mediation. First, mediation sessions usually allow each disputant to tell his or her story, while requiring the other to wait quietly for his or her turn to speak. In everyday conversation, by contrast—and especially in arguments—overlapping speech and competition for speaking turns are commonplace. Second, mediation sessions, unlike ordinary conversations, include a third party—the mediator—who is expressly empowered to enforce conversational etiquette and referee interactional disputes.

As a result of these structural features, Garcia contends, mediation suppresses arguments in several related ways. First, the accusations and denials/counteraccusations that occur in quick succession in everyday contexts are separated from one another temporally. This disrupts the back-and-forth rhythm of argument by imposing a cooling-off period before a retort can be issued. This decoupling can cause retorts to be less vehement, and in some cases to be omitted altogether. The fewer the contested accusations, the less there is to be resolved.

Second, accusations and denials between the disputing parties are addressed to the mediator rather than the other disputant. Instead of being confronted in the first person, the respondent is the subject of a less threatening third-person reference. Such an accusation is more easily ignored without loss of face. Finally, the normative order of mediation encourages mitigated rather than aggravated accusations and denials. This ethos of understatement prevents many of the escalations that occur in ordinary argument.

Garcia documents these processes with detailed examples drawn from mediation sessions. In Text 3.1, for example, the complainant accuses the respondent of verbally abusing her. We can readily imagine an everyday situation in which such an accusation, phrased in the confrontational second person, would elicit an immediate retort and continue to escalate. Here, however, the accusation is directed to the mediator and framed in the third person, and the respondent says nothing. Indeed, when the complainant solicits a minimal response (the final "you know?"), it is the mediator, not the respondent, who replies.

TEXT 3.1 (Garcia 1991:829)

> COMPLAINANT: The first knowledge I had of her dislike, aggravation with me, one time she, I was coming from the car, with my child who was about two at the time. And her daughter came up to me and said "Get her out of the way" or something and she
> 5   said, you know, she just hurled a lot of accusations. I don't know how much detail it's worth going into. But it was a lot of you know, rather vile obscenities that I only use if I'm furi–, you know?
> MEDIATOR: Um-hmh, yeah.

Contrast this with an instance in which the disputants violate mediation's special rules of turn-taking. Text 3.2 is taken from a child custody mediation.

The ex-husband is explaining why he is unwilling to give up visitation time. His ex-wife breaks two of the fundamental linguistic rules of mediation. First, she interrupts the ex-husband with a response and an accusation, rather than waiting her turn; and second, she addresses her remarks directly *to* her ex-husband (note her use of "you"), rather than speaking to the mediator *about* him. The exchange that ensues sounds like an everyday argument. It continues until the mediator loudly and forcefully reasserts control.

TEXT 3.2 (Garcia 1991:829)

> Ex-HUSBAND: YEAH, I, you know? I still don't feel good about
> it, because like this is my flesh and blood! You know? And you
> know, uh, I['m yeah—]
> Ex-WIFE: [But] *you* shouted abortion, for nine months [with
> 5   Sharon.]
> MEDIATOR: [Listen, we] are not—
> Ex-HUSBAND: Hey—
> MEDIATOR: —talking a[bout]—
> Ex-HUSBAND: —[WHO] had the abortion? Y[ou want to get]
> 10   SMART?
> MEDIATOR: [Wait a minute!]
> Ex-HUSBAND: DIDN'T SH[E JUST] HAVE ONE?
> MEDIATOR: [Hey wait!] HOLD IT! WE'RE NOT IN HERE TO
> TALK ABOUT THAT. I DIDN'T TALK ABOUT MY PROB-
> 15   LEMS, OR WHATEVER. WE'VE ALL GOT A STORY. That's
> no one's business.

The Moral Order of Mediation

In addition to these structural effects, the moral order of mediation sessions also facilitates agreement. By emphasizing at the outset the goals of compromise and noncompetitiveness, the mediator sets the stage for nonadversarial talk. Disputants' linguistic behavior appears to take the norms of mediation into account. They talk more about what happened than whose fault it is, and they employ linguistic devices that soften, or downgrade, the accusations that they make. For example, in Text 3.3 (Garcia 1991:831), the complainant states the problem in a far less confrontational way than he might have in an everyday argument.

TEXT 3.3 (Garcia 1991:831)

> COMPLAINANT: A lot of the, uh, the la–, the labor that was, uh,
> conducted in the motor home was, was not done in a, in a profes-
> sional, uh, way. I mean, basically, it wasn't completed profession-

ally. It wasn't, it is my, uh, in my estimation, it wasn't, uh, com-
5   pleted at all.

This complaint is constructed so as to focus on the problem rather than on the person accused of failing to complete the work. The talk is about *what* rather than *who;* the action is named but not the agent. Contrast this with another possible statement of the problem in which the complainant named the person he believed to be at fault, used pejorative adjectives to describe the person, and then linked that person with the problematic action—and in a raised voice. That kind of highly charged, accusatory statement of the problem is just what might occur in everyday argument. In mediation, Garcia argues, people rarely make direct accusations, instead mitigating them in a variety of ways, including, as here, by deleting the agent.[5]

Even when the accused party is named, the accuser may still downgrade the accusation by assuming some of the blame. For example, instead of saying simply that the other party has caused the problem, the accuser may use the inclusive pronoun *we* to describe what happened, as in Text 3.4.

TEXT 3.4 (Garcia 1991:832)

> COMPLAINANT: Since the beginning of this year, we've been harassing each other . . .

Such a statement seems calculated to promote conciliation rather than argumentation. By including himself as a causal agent, the speaker accepts a share of the blame for the problematic action, thus making a significant concession.

Finally, the accuser may downgrade the accusation itself. In Text 3.5, the complainant divides the problematic action into two components. Even though the mediator has explicitly asked for a statement of the *im*proper work, the complainant mentions first the component that was not blameworthy. This is indeed a gentle accusation.

TEXT 3.5 (Garcia 1991:832)

> MEDIATOR: Okay. Improper mechanical work?
> COMPLAINANT: Yeah, improper, uh, work completed by the
> mechanic. I would imagine part of it was done, uh okay, but
> there were two or three things that were, that weren't completed
> 5   properly.

Summary

Garcia's work presents a compelling linguistic picture of how mediation manages to move disputants toward agreement. By altering the conversational structure and moral environment of everyday argument, mediation defuses confrontation. Such devices as decoupling accusations and denials and forcing the parties to speak to the mediator rather than each other are the linguistic equivalent of a referee separating two boxers and sending them to their respective corners. And when the disputants do state their charges and counter-charges, the normative order of the mediation session exerts a moderating influence on both the content and the tone of the accusations.

We thus begin to understand the linguistic processes through which mediation restructures communication, promotes agreement, and produces consumer satisfaction. The next question is whether the same kind of microlinguistic analysis can help us to evaluate the larger political claims that have been made about mediation. Can linguistics help us decide whether, as its proponents claim, mediation is a neutral and benign process or, as the critics assert, it is subject to subtle manipulation by the powerful? We must first review in greater detail just what the critics have said.

The Macrodiscourse of Mediation

The search for an answer to this question leads us once again to the concept of discourse. There is an extensive literature that treats mediation as a discourse in the sense of a way of talking about disputes. This body of work focuses on the ongoing contest between the discourses of mediation and adversarial adjudication for dominance in the field of dispute resolution. Since dominant discourses are translated into social action, this literature emphasizes, the outcome of the contest is not a mere theoretical concern. On the contrary, the ascendancy of one discourse over the other influences not only the process by which disputes are resolved, but also who wins and who loses.

The idea of mediation as a way of talking about disputes has been perhaps best developed by feminist legal scholar Martha Albertson Fineman in her work on divorce. In a series of writings culminating in her book *The Illusion of Equality: The Rhetoric and Reality of Divorce Reform* (Fineman 1991), Fineman characterizes the recent history of divorce law as a successful struggle by the "helping professions" (social workers and various kinds of therapists) to substitute their discourse for that of the law. Prior to the 1960s, divorce and custody cases turned on such traditional legal concepts as rights, responsibility, and fault (Fineman 1991 : 19). One spouse obtained a divorce by proving that the other had been at fault in destroying the marriage. The legal grounds for divorce were such things as adultery, desertion, nonsupport, and abuse; when husband and wife simply did not want to remain married, the conventional strategy was for the wife to complain of "mental cruelty" and for the husband not to contest the charge. Findings of fault influenced the distribution of property. Adulterous husbands could expect more onerous alimony assessments than those guilty only of unspecified mental cruelty. Fault, or its absence, was also an essential criterion in child custody cases. Judges were supposed to decide custody disputes "in the best interests of the child." However, the law presumed that children of "tender years" belonged with their mothers. This presumption could be overcome only by a showing that the wife was an "unfit mother."

Divorce and custody law underwent radical change in the 1960s and 1970s. In pursuit of what Fineman calls "the equality ideal" (1991:20), liberal reformers attacked the existing regime as gender-biased. It presumed, they argued, that women were dependent on men and that women were inevitably homemakers, while men were breadwinners. "No fault" divorce was introduced, meaning that spouses could divorce by choice, without the need to persuade a court that one of them had done something wrong. (Note the revealing use of *divorce* as an intransitive verb: in the 1950s and 1960s, people said things like "A is divorcing B"; it is now much more common to hear "A and B are divorcing.") When the inquiry into fault was dispensed with, the old guidelines for distributing property and awarding custody became unworkable.

Under the current law, the starting point for adjudicating divorce and custody cases is Fineman's "illusion of equality." The law now presumes that men and women are equal: equal in their capacities to earn a living and to reconstruct their lives after the divorce, and in their willingness and ability to care for their children. This, of course, is fantasy. Despite recent gains in opportunity, women on average earn less than comparably qualified men. Women are far more likely than men to sacrifice career advancement to nurture children. And with rare exceptions, mothers are more likely than fathers to sacrifice post-divorce autonomy in order to minimize the effect of the breakup on the children. Much research now indicates that, at least in economic terms, women and children are significantly worse off than before all of the "reform" began (Fineman 1991: 36–38). More so than ever before, divorce impoverishes women.

How did all this happen? Social conservatives blame the moral relativism of the sixties. Many contemporary feminists, Fineman (1991:26–28) included, point to their liberal forebears' exaltation of symbolic equality over economic reality. Almost everyone sees the law of unintended consequences at work.

Fineman's most original contribution is to identify the role of the helping professions. As the legal climate began to change, therapists presented the courts, the state legislatures, and the public with a discourse more in tune with the new environment. The adoption of this perspective in turn facilitated a change in divorce procedures. And the adoption of new procedures has had subtle yet significant effects on the social reality of divorce.

Originally, by Fineman's account, social workers and other helpers viewed divorce as pathological, something to be avoided if possible through counseling aimed at reconciliation. When divorce did occur, the helpers assisted the lawyers with expert advice on such issues as the best interests of the child. With the coming of no-fault divorce, the helping professions' attitude changed dramatically. Divorce came to be viewed not as the pathological termination of a marriage but rather as a "situational crisis" within the "family system" (Fineman 1991:152). Significantly, divorce did not end the former spouses' relationship; instead, it required the development of a new relationship as the family sought to establish a "post-dissolution organization." Where children were involved, the focus was no longer on a binary-choice custody decision. The new ideal was ongoing "co-parenting." Talk of "physical custody" and "visitation" gave way to a rhetoric of "shared parenting" and "periods of physical placement" (Fineman 1991:150).

This change in the helping professions' discourse about divorce itself was paralleled by the development of a new discourse about divorce procedure. In the early 1970s, social workers and therapists began to criticize the adversarial model of divorce and the lawyers who managed it. In the no-fault era, the legal aspects of the divorce were reduced to a mere formality. The critical task was managing the "emotional divorce," and this required the skills of the therapist, not the win-at-all-costs advocate (Fineman 1991:153). When the divorcing spouses fought over custody, the law's adversarial approach was worse than useless. All it could do was pick a winner. What was needed was a therapist who could make the parents realize that they were fighting over custody not to advance the child's best interests but rather to serve their own "profound psychological needs" (Fineman 1991:156).

To turn their theory into social reality, the helping professions offered the courts a procedural alternative to adversarial litigation—mediation, which would be directed not by lawyers and judges but by therapists. They backed up the offer with a pair of contrasting narratives about divorce. These narratives are pervasive in the literature and rhetoric of the helping professions. The first is the "horror story" of the adversarial divorce: both spouses employ lawyers who counsel them to fight over everything, there is a winner and a loser, and the children are deeply hurt by the specter of their parents fighting and the reality of "losing" the parent who loses the custody dispute (Fineman 1991:159–60). The second narrative is the "fairy tale" of the mediated divorce: rather than the spouses taking sides, "the family" enters the divorce process as a unit; the husband and wife consult one mediator rather than two lawyers; the mediator leads them through a caring, cooperative, and nonadversarial process; and everyone lives happily every after (and saves a lot of money, too) (Fineman 1991:160–61).

The process offered by the mediators has proved attractive to the legal system. Judges do not like to decide custody disputes. They are messy and time-consuming, particularly since the abolition of the old presumption in favor of the mother, and one party usually comes away embittered. Many divorce lawyers also find the new procedures attractive. They can escape their longtime image as the legal profession's bottom-feeders and hold themselves out as caring counselors.

As a result of all these factors, some kind of mediation is now the norm in most states, and the discourse of the helping professions is now the dominant discourse of divorce. Fineman (1991:144–69) argues persuasively that this has had disastrous consequences for women. The helpers are interested not in finding fault in past behavior but in shaping a workable relationship for the future. Everyone is presumed to be equally willing and able to share in that relationship. The problem is that the way people have acted in the past is often a good predictor of how they will behave in the future. Why should a father who defaulted on his parental obligations during the marriage suddenly be given equal standing with his ex-wife? Why should a woman be forced to continue a relationship with a man who has already shown himself to be an unfit partner?

The newly dominant discourse of divorce is one of neutrality. The helping professions talk of engaging in a process, of replacing confrontation with cooperation. Their rhetoric avoids mention of the power struggles between men and women, or of taking sides in those struggles. But, according to Fineman, that is exactly what they have done. By dispensing with the quest for fault and presuming both spouses to be equally fit to participate in family life, the helpers have denied women the moral high ground they formerly occupied in divorce litigation. Taking lawyers out of the process has also had a different impact on men and women: because women are typically less experienced in financial negotiations, they need lawyers more. Finally, women may be more inclined than men to seek agreement for the sake of agreement, even if it is disadvantageous. As a result of culturally based gender differences in self-definition, a woman "may feel compelled to maintain her connection with the other, even to her own detriment" (Grillo 1991:1550).

Fineman thus tells a story of two narratives competing for dominance. When the new supplants the old, the result is a change in the generally accepted modes of talking and thinking about divorce. These new modes of talking and thinking are eventually, and very subtly, inscribed in social action, with important consequences for the power structure of our society. What remains to be uncovered is the mechanics of the inscription process, the specific ways in which the dominance that Fineman describes is realized in the day-to-day talk of divorce practice.

The Microdiscourse of Mediation

We begin the search for specifics with the work of law professor Trina Grillo (1991), who is also an experienced divorce mediator. Although her terminology differs, Grillo says many of the same things as Fineman about divorce mediation and its implications for the disempowerment of women. She argues that mandatory divorce mediation "can be destructive to many women and some men because it requires them to speak in a setting they have not chosen and often imposes a rigid orthodoxy as to how they should speak, make decisions, and be" (Grillo 1991:1550). The ascendancy of the narrative of mediated divorce over that of adversarial divorce is reproduced on the level of talk.

Drawing on her own mediation experience, Grillo (1991:1556) provides several instances of how this process works. For example, under the norms of mediation, a "good" woman is one who is ready to cooperate, is rational, and does not wish to hurt her husband. Her "bad" counterpart is bitter, vengeful, and irrationally angry. How do mediators enforce these norms? By their responses to what they hear: they may criticize a woman for not putting her children first or instruct her to stay away from a particular topic. Though these "punishments" might seem trivial, they are, in Grillo's experience, quite powerful. Women hear them clearly and reform their own behavior accordingly.

The sanctioning of particular topics is not random, Grillo argues. On the contrary, it is often done in ways that directly disempower women. Thus, mediators typically make accusations about past behavior off-limits; the effect is often to deprive a woman's argument of its primary moral force (Grillo 1991:1563). Mediators are similarly dismissive of women's expressions of anger. Although they are trained to let the parties "vent," mediators do not listen for long. They denigrate the anger as counterproductive squabbling and insist that the parties move on to a more rational search for solutions. By refusing to take anger seriously, Grillo contends (1991:1574–75), mediators may demoralize women whose anger is righteous, perhaps born of a history of abuse. Such women may conclude that the process is hopelessly stacked against them and acquiesce in an unfair agreement just to be done with it.

A final example is the tendency of mediators to deflect talk about individual rights, insisting instead on "the language of interdependent relationships" (Grillo 1991:1560). Many women are culturally more comfortable with the language of relationships. For such women, discovering that they may have rights and bringing themselves to claim them may be a long, difficult, but ultimately empowering process. That power is tenuously held, however, and even a mild expression of disapproval by a mediator can prove devastating.

Through examples such as these, Grillo moves us closer to an understanding of how the power of the macrodiscourses of divorce is realized or inhibited in the microlinguistics of mediation practice. But can we find detailed real-life examples of precisely how the biases of which Grillo complains intrude into the mediation process?

Additional evidence from the research of Angela Garcia (1995) can help us to understand bias as a linguistic process. As we noted earlier, mediators are trained in "active listening." That is, they not only listen when someone is speaking, but also say things to the speaker to indicate that they are hearing and understanding what is being said. From time to time, they also summarize the parties' remarks, using such prefatory phrases as "what I hear you saying is . . ." Garcia (1995:31) calls this latter tactic "mediator representation," meaning that the mediator is speaking for, or representing, one of the parties. She argues that representation is often more than a verbatim playback: instead, the mediator may alter or extend what the party has said in subtle but potentially significant ways.

Text 3.6 illustrates the representation process. The ex-husband in a custody mediation offers a compromise solution, and the mediator later "repeats" the offer to his ex-wife.

Text 3.6 (Garcia 1995:32)

EX-HUSBAND: The twins said, "Well what happened to Thursdays?" They, you know they, you know they specifically brought that up to me and I said, "Well, it looks like Mom wants to spend more time with you two. So if you know you want to do Thursday, Friday one week, and then just a Friday the next week, that's compromising a little bit . . ."

[*A few minutes pass.*]

MEDIATOR: And then what I hear, is the last month or so, it's been every other Thursday, and then the next week is uh for the Friday, and you're not willing—

EX-WIFE: Uh—

MEDIATOR: —to he's willing to relinquish! He used the word. Uh one of those Fridays.

EX-HUSBAND: No—

MEDIATOR: Instead of making it cons[iste]nt I MEAN THURSDAYS!

EX-HUSBAND: [No] Thursdays right.

MEDIATOR: Instead of [mak]ing it I just

EX-HUSBAND: [I]

EX-HUSBAND: I'm willing to go along with the schedule that she said just to keep the status quo and keep her happy that she's you know,

MEDIATOR: Um hmh. He's offering the two Thursday night.

Garcia notes two important ways in which the mediator's representation of the ex-husband differs from the latter's earlier representation of himself. First, she states his position directly to the ex-wife (e.g., "you're not willing"), whereas he had spoken to the mediator and had referred to the ex-wife only in the third person. Second, the mediator significantly upgrades the characterization of the ex-husband's offer. He had described himself as "compromising," but the mediator describes him as "willing to relinquish," implying an outright concession. (She emphasizes the point in an ironic way by saying, "He used the word" *relinquish,* even though he did not.) Clearly attentive to the mediator's tactics, the respondent seizes the opportunity to inject a self-serving statement of his motivation ("to . . . keep her happy"). The net effect of the mediator's representation would seem to be to make the offer far more difficult to refuse.

This effect is realized a few minutes later, in Text 3.7, when the mediator restates the offer in yet another way and the ex-wife acquiesces.

TEXT 3.7 (Garcia 1995:33)

> MEDIATOR: And he is willing to give up two of those Thursdays.
> EX-WIFE: I know.
> MEDIATOR: Number one I heard it to make it consistent for the children, and that that would please you!
> 5   EX-WIFE: I'll just do it, just to meet him half way, . . .

At times, a mediator may go beyond simply restating or paraphrasing a disputant's position and actually develop new arguments in favor of one of the parties. In Text 3.8, for example, drawn from the same custody dispute, the ex-wife argues that the children should spend more time at her house because they are spending too much time away from the "home base." The ex-husband attempts to interrupt to argue the point. The mediator silences him, but then goes on to make an argument on his behalf.

TEXT 3.8 (Garcia 1995:34)

> EX-WIFE: That I got the base, the home, family, and I feel that Thursday, Friday, and Saturday without them being, consistently at home, is too much. I feel that it's too much. Even though you don't get to see them, they're not at home, and they're at school,
> 5   and they're on the road,—
> EX-HUSBAND: They're home seventy five percent of the time.
> MEDIATOR: Stan wait.
> EX-HUSBAND: Okay.
> MEDIATOR: That's your feeling.
> 10   EX-WIFE: Right.
> MEDIATOR: And you have every right to that. That is not his feeling, a[nd that's] not how he sees his home base.
> EX-WIFE: [I know] I know.
> MEDIATOR: You know he sees it very loving, very whole, very
> 15   consistent, very disciplined.
> EX-WIFE: I know!
> MEDIATOR: Okay. For him that's what he sees and what we have to discuss.
> EX-WIFE: I know.

20   MEDIATOR: And he's fifty percent a parent, and you're fifty percent a parent.

Significantly, Garcia points out, the "home base" argument that the mediator makes on behalf of the ex-husband is one that he has never made for himself. Likewise, the laudatory characterization of his home as "very loving, very whole, very consistent" is the mediator's, not his.[6] The mediator's words are "fair" in the sense that they are consistent with the ex-husband's position. But the mediator's strategy of extending and elaborating on his position surely has consequences for the balance of power in this mediation session. To prove the point, we need look no further than the mother's litany of resigned *I know*s.

In a final example from Garcia's work, two mediators take the even more radical step of "replacing" a disputant. Rather than merely restating or extending arguments in ways that are consistent with positions already stated, in Text 3.9 the mediators "negotiate instead of the disputant." When the respondent in a property dispute proposes that the complainant compensate him for benefits that he has conferred on the complainant's property, both mediators attack the proposal in a way that has nothing to do with what the complainant has actually said.

TEXT 3.9 (Garcia 1995:36)

RESPONDENT: Damned for my troubles that I went through, and the money that I paid the county to improve his property and getting the base rock fill, and everything else, that he should compensate me for part of my expenses.

5   MEDIATOR B: Let's try to understand one thing, Mister Cartel, the work and the money that you expended in putting in this culvert, and actually rescuing this property from destruction, you did it, for your sake.

RESPONDENT: I went for a compromise with the county.

10   MEDIATOR A: Yes.

MEDIATOR B: Yes.

RESPONDENT: That I would take my fences and they would accept the—

MEDIATOR A: You went with the compromise with the county, not

15   these folks. *You* went there. *You* did it.

RESPONDENT: They wouldn't have done it—

MEDIATOR A: *You* decided it was worth it to you to do it, otherwise you wouldn't [have]—

RESPONDENT: [It's not] only to my advantage, though I'm pro-

20   tecting my neighbor's advantage also.

MEDIATOR A: THAT is something you were giving your neighbors unwittingly. You were between a rock and a hard place. I will agree! But you can not, you could not have committed them

to something they didn't agree to. Now, if you feel that equity is
25   on your side. Then you can after the fact sue them for their share.
If you feel that you want to do arbitration on that you can do that.
But we're talking about something else here. Remember we
defined the area. You put five thousand dollars in there but that
wasn't his statement of the problem.

Note carefully how this interaction develops. The respondent opens with a proposal. Mediator B, without any prompting from the other party, attacks the logic of the proposal (*Why should he pay when you did it for yourself?*) and, at least by implication, the credibility of the respondent (*It's not really true that you did it for your neighbor's benefit.*). When the respondent tries to fight back, mediator A jumps in and joins the attack. In his final statement, mediator A summarizes the argument and concludes with a new point: that the respondent's claim is out of order procedurally. As if to underscore how far he has strayed from the role of neutral conciliator, mediator A says, "I will agree!"—agreeing is the job of the parties, not the mediators. Text 3.9 looks less like a cooperative, conciliatory mediation session than some kind of tag-team cross-examination.

Garcia's observations are corroborated by those of David Greatbatch and Robert Dingwall (1989), who have studied the strategies that British divorce mediators may use to favor one party's interests over the other's. They frame their research as an empirical assessment of the claim by mediation critics "that the process may be used to press weaker parties into accepting less than they could have expected had their case gone through traditional adversarial channels" (Greatbatch and Dingwall 1989:613). Using conversation analysis, they, like Garcia, find that a number of linguistic techniques employed by mediators have the effect of facilitating the presentation and discussion of one side's interests, while minimizing parallel consideration of the other side's position.

In a case that Greatbatch and Dingwall examine at great length, a husband and wife are discussing possible ways to divide their common property. Because he would prefer having cash, the husband proposes to sell the two houses that the couple now owns and divide the proceeds. The wife prefers to keep the house she is presently living in and to let the husband have the other. What happens in the session is that the mediator's management strategies operate to maximize discussion of the wife's position and minimize the attention given to the husband's proposal. The mediator does this in a variety of ways: by selecting the wife's plan for full discussion when the two possibilities are first introduced, by moving away from full consideration of the husband's plan when it is reintroduced, and by reintroducing and recycling the wife's plan for further consideration.

The alliance of the mediator with the wife's plan is seen in a number of specific ways. In Text 3.10, for example, the mediator focuses on the wife's plan as a possible solution to the couple's dilemma. The husband is objecting on the grounds that the second house is presently occupied by tenants. The mediator and the wife repeatedly urge the husband to consider possible ways around the problem.

TEXT 3.10 (Greatbatch and Dingwall 1989:621–22)

> MEDIATOR: You can't live in the house in Britvale?
> HUSBAND: Er, no it's let. Um, well there is one room, one vacant at the minute and um . . .
> MEDIATOR: You can't get them to leave then?
> 5 HUSBAND: No, it's tenanted. It's difficult to get the tenants out.
> WIFE: Well, I'm [not sure] if we really wanted to before.
> HUSBAND: [It was never—] set up to, to, sort of, it was set up to produce money for insurances for the next twenty years and that's exactly what it's doing, basically.
> 10 WIFE: It's very underlet.
> HUSBAND: It's underlet. It's not managed properly, or hasn't been for a number of years. [And it needs some work done on it.]
> MEDIATOR: [You're sure you couldn't get the] tenant, tenancy back? I mean if you needed it as your home.
> 15 HUSBAND: That was one possibility that did crop up. Um, you can apply to evict somebody if you require it as a home.
> MEDIATOR: That's right. It's what I thought.

This attention to the wife's proposal is one-sided: there is no comparable exploration of the husband's preference for selling the houses and dividing the proceeds. On the contrary, as in Text 3.11, when the husband tries to assert his concerns, the mediator responds by reasserting the wife's plan as a solution.

TEXT 3.11 (Greatbatch and Dingwall 1989:634–35)

> HUSBAND: But it's a question of point of view, but it's traumatic from my point of view. I've got nowhere to live.
> MEDIATOR: W[ell, can you]—
> WIFE: [No.]
> 5 HUSBAND: Really, I mean I have got my sister's place to live, I've got a [room]—
> MEDIATOR: [Yes.]
> HUSBAND: —but I've nowhere that's mine to live. If I wanted somewhere to live [right now]—
> 10 MEDIATOR: [Yes.]
> HUSBAND: —I mean I'm—
> WIFE: But you say you wouldn't want to live on your own anyway, so—
> HUSBAND: (Laughs.) A general hobo, running around.

15   MEDIATOR: Well I must say if, er, it seems to me worth trying the,
the Britvale property once again.
HUSBAND: Mhm.
MEDIATOR: Seeing how, uh, as like Hazel, um, my understanding
is that if you needed it for yourself [you]—
20   HUSBAND: [Yeah.]
MEDIATOR: —have a far better chance of regaining possession.
And you have every reason to say "I need it as my home."

The most important implication of such texts is, once again, that the ostensible neutrality of mediators may disappear when their behavior is subjected to detailed linguistic scrutiny. There is probably nothing in these texts, or in Garcia's, that a lawyer would point to as evidence of overt bias. The mediator lets both parties speak, she speaks respectfully to both, and she neither praises nor criticizes either party on a personal level. The parties themselves provide no evidence that they are aware of any bias on the mediator's part. But the texts leave us with little doubt that the mediator is subtly yet effectively steering the talk toward a preferred outcome.

By showing how mediators can covertly influence outcomes, researchers such as Garcia and Greatbatch and Dingwall demonstrate the plausibility of the claim that mediation can systematically disadvantage one side or the other. But do they shed significant light on the truth of the claim that mediation works to the disadvantage of women?

Conclusion: Is Mediator Bias Systematic?

We have now seen in very concrete terms that the neutrality of mediators is sometimes more of an ideal than a reality. Mediators can and do employ a variety of language strategies to shape both the process and the outcome of mediation sessions. Significantly, these strategies seem transparent to all but the most intensive kinds of scrutiny. The final question is whether these strategies have political consequences. That is, are mediators indulging their biases in purely idiosyncratic ways, or is there something systematic in the way that mediators employ their subtle power?

Both Garcia and Greatbatch and Dingwall claim to have proved conclusively the possibility of mediator bias by discovering some of its linguistic pathways. Neither project, however, claims to prove whether mediator bias is exercised in any consistent way.[7] Indeed, a comparison of the two demonstrates the extraordinary difficulty of using microlinguistic analysis to address such a question. Garcia's published examples tend to illustrate mediator activism working to the disadvantage of women, but in Greatbatch and Dingwall's extended single case, it is the husband, not the wife, who is the victim of the mediator's power.

In theory, what is needed is a broader sampling of how potentially biasing linguistic tactics are distributed. This is much easier said than done, however. In the first place, it is difficult to get statistically meaningful samples when doing intensive linguistic research. As we know from firsthand experience, access to mediation sessions is hard to get. Many mediation centers will not let researchers in the door because of confidentiality concerns; even when general permission is given, the specific consent of all parties to a mediation must be obtained. As a result, randomization is all but impossible. In addition, it takes an enormous amount of time to watch, record, transcribe, and analyze even a single mediation session—in our experience, a single hour of field observation requires dozens of hours of data preparation and study. To do quantitatively significant amounts of the kind of analysis that, for example, Garcia has done would be a superhuman task.

The second problem is one of principle rather than logistics. The work that conversation analysts do is interpretive and necessarily judgmental. We may find their interpretations and judgments highly persuasive, but conversation analysis will never be experimental physics. As the work discussed in this chapter and in chapter 2 illustrates, some of the most insightful interpretations are also the subtlest. Is it appropriate to reduce these insights to coding conventions that are both simple enough and absolute enough to feed into a formula? We suspect that in many cases this would imply a degree of precision that is not there and thus would mislead more than it would inform.[8]

At this point, we believe that it will be all but impossible to establish exactly how mediator biasing tactics are distributed. Nonetheless, there are a number of independent reasons to believe that mediator bias systematically disadvantages women and that the most important mechanisms of such bias are linguistic.

First, there is some empirical evidence—thus far limited and equivocal—that women in fact do less well in divorce mediation than in divorce litigation. A recent two-state study of divorce mediation by Carol Bohmer and Marilyn L. Ray (1994) yielded complex and inconsistent findings. In New York, they found that mediation significantly disadvantages women with respect to child support and the burden of child caretaking, but in Georgia, they concluded that "the well-being of women, and the children for whom they care, is not adversely affected by the method they select for resolving their dispute" (Bohmer and Ray 1994:232, 245).

Other researchers advance reasons why women are *likely* to be disadvantaged in mediation. Penelope Bryan (1992), for example, argues that men usually come to divorce mediation with a set of resources that their wives often lack. In the economic sphere, "the husband's greater tangible resources will grant him the lion's share of power in divorce negotiations, particularly over critical financial issues" (Bryan 1992:456). Men also control such intangible resources as status, self-esteem, dominance, and higher aspirations, all of which are logical correlates of success in mediation.

In an elegant case study, Scott Hughes (1995) illustrates these and other prejudicial factors at work in a divorce mediation. He puts particular emphasis on the tendency to be competitive versus a propensity for cooperation: in mediation, "[t]he unconditionally cooperative bargainer will cooperate at every turn, even if this results in her own destruction. She will collapse in the face of a competitive bargainer" (Hughes 1995:583). Competitiveness and cooperativeness do not seem to be randomly distributed. In Grillo's apt phrasing, "[I]t is clear that those who operate in a 'female mode'—whether biologically male or female—will respond more 'selflessly' to the demands of mediation" (1991: 1602). In litigation, such people have their positions argued—competitively—by their lawyers. But in mediation, where there are no lawyers and where cooperation is the highest normative value, they may be especially vulnerable.

Substantial linguistic evidence corroborates this suspicion. Research on gender differences in language socialization has shown that women are more likely than men to do the work of facilitating communication, of engaging in supportive listening, and of actively seeking consensus.[9] These behaviors converge with the demands of mediation. Therefore, this reasoning suggests, women, simply by virtue of the way they talk, may be more likely than men to pursue agreement as an end in itself. Consequently, they may not do as well (in tangible terms) as they might have if their cases had been handled by aggressive lawyers in an adversarial context.

We thus have a convergence of circumstantial evidence in support of the claim that mediation disadvantages women. Conversation analysis has demonstrated the existence of linguistic strategies through which ostensibly neutral mediators can exert subtle but significant influence on the process. We cannot say with certainty that this influence works against women in a systematic way, but this is a plausible suspicion. A number of things we know about gender differences in social behavior suggest that women are more likely than men to compromise for the sake of compromise, often in ways that are adverse to their material interests. Since the mediator strategies that the conversation analysts have identified can all be categorized as devices calculated to facilitate compromise, it is reasonable to suppose that, more often than not, their effects are felt by women.

We have moved in this chapter from the examination of mediation as a neutral process to an assessment of the charge that it is in fact a tool for oppressing women. On the basis of linguistic and other evidence, we have concluded that the charge, if not proved, is at least one that should be taken seriously. If we ultimately decide that the feminist critique of mediation is accurate, we will be faced with a wrenching irony: a process advocated largely because of its solicitude for women's sensibilities becoming a weapon used against them. We may also find some compelling analogies between the mediation process and the rape trial.

Grillo has commented that "[w]omen who have been through mandatory mediation often describe it as an experience of sexual domination, comparing mandatory mediation to rape" (1991:1605). This feeling may derive from the similar ways in which power is exercised in the two settings. In rape trials, we observed in chapter 2, the language strategies used in cross-examining the victim (some generic, some unique to rape cases) both reflect and reinforce men's power to dominate women. The same may be true in mediation. The language strategies of mediators may be effective precisely because they take advantage of certain social tendencies that contribute to women's relative powerlessness. As mediation becomes more and more entrenched—as it is increasingly perceived to "work"—the result will be to reinforce that powerlessness. Once again, the pattern is one of simultaneous reflection and reproduction of society's power dynamics. And, once again, it will be the detailed analysis of microdiscourse that reveals the working of power in the macrodiscourse of the legal process.

CHAPTER FOUR

Speaking of Patriarchy

The claim that the law is patriarchal has become so widely accepted in legal scholarship that its validity now goes almost without saying. Specifically, the claim is that "law and legal institutions in a number of cultures (if not all) have played a significant role in maintaining systems that subordinate and oppress female human beings, and the law continues to do so" (Henderson 1991:411). The patriarchy of the law is seen as working on multiple levels. In the most direct sense, law is patriarchal because it is powerful and men control it. Law has been described as the means for deciding "who does what to whom and gets away with it" (MacKinnon 1989:139). In every society, men largely control this decision-making mechanism. Thus, men get to decide who gets away with what. Historically, they have exercised this power to further their own interests at the expense of women. Even in the liberal democracies of the West, men denied women the right to vote until the first quarter of this century. The subordination of women is also evident in the history of marriage and property law (Henderson 1991:411–12). Male control over divorce trapped women in abusive marriages, while married women surrendered control over their property and were not allowed to enter into contracts.

Legal reform movements have eradicated the most overt sources of patriarchal power. In 1920, the Nineteenth Amendment to the Constitution finally enfranchised American women. Title VII of the Civil Rights Act of 1964 prohibits employment discrimination on the basis of sex; the Equal Employment Opportunity Commission and the courts have gradually expanded its reach to prohibit such forms of sexual harassment as the maintenance of a hostile environment in the workplace (Henderson 1991:413–14). Recent changes in family law—no-fault divorce in particular—have made divorce more readily available to women (although, as we discussed in chapter 3, some feminists contend that these "reforms" have done more harm than good) (Bartlett 1994).

Gender and Equality

The elimination of discriminatory legal rules may not have changed the law's essentially patriarchal character, however. The reason, it is argued, is that laws that appear to be evenhanded still embody a distinctively male point of view. To begin with, the very notion of evenhandedness is a male concept (MacKinnon 1989:40–43; Bartlett 1994:1261–62). To the law, "equality" traditionally has meant allowing everyone to assert rights without regard to race, sex, religion, or other status markers. For this concept of equality to work, "rights" must mean the same thing to different kinds of people. That is, the rights that the law protects must be recognized as significant all across society. In addition, people in all elements of society must have a realistic opportunity to assert those rights.

Many feminists, however, drawing on the work of Carol Gilligan (1982), have pointed out that the rights the law recognizes are, for the most part, rights to be separated from other human beings (West 1988:4–7; Bartlett 1994: 1260–61). A quick look at the Bill of Rights confirms this insight. The First Amendment, for example, protects freedom of speech and of the press. Free speech claims usually involve people who are asserting the right to offend someone: neo-Nazis who want to march through a predominantly Jewish town, "adult" bookstore owners who are contemptuous of community moral standards, or journalists who attack public figures. Similarly, the First Amendment's freedom of religion has been invoked most often to protect the right to be different. Even some of the less prominent constitutional rights place a comparable emphasis on separation: we can keep and bear arms, presumably to protect ourselves against tyrannical governments and threatening fellow citizens (Second Amendment); we do not have to quarter soldiers in our homes in time of peace (Third Amendment); and we need not tolerate unreasonable government searches of our persons, homes, or effects (Fourth Amendment).

Freedom from unwanted connection to others, it is argued, is a male concern. According to Gilligan and others, women, because of their socialization, tend to seek and value the very connections against which men seek legal protection (West 1988:13–18). From this perspective, the Bill of Rights is a male document with no female counterpart. Where, for example, is the constitutional counterpoise to the freedom of speech, the legal requirement that we assume responsibility for the offense that we give to others? Why does the law value the pornographer's right to be offensively different over the interests of the women whom his work dehumanizes? Why does there often seem to be such an imbalance between an accused criminal's right to due process and a community's right to security?

Other areas of the law will support a similar argument. For example, Anglo-American law has long exalted the contract as the ideal way to manage a relationship, whether between spouses or between strangers conducting an anonymous business transaction. A written contract is preferred over an oral one; the more specific its provisions, the better. From the law's perspective, the ideal contracting party is a person who fears entanglement with others. Before entering a relationship, such a person thinks through everything that might go wrong. The ultimate objective of the contract is to identify every sort of misconduct that might occur and specify the consequences if it does. Through this logic, the law of contract treats separation as the basic human condition and connection as an aberration requiring careful advance preparation.

The point of these examples is that the ideal of equal rights may be illusory in the sense that the rights being offered are not equally relevant to the different social circumstances of men and women. Although this was originally a feminist argument, many feminists now reject it (see, for example, West 1988; Fineman 1991). Opponents contend that it "essentializes" women's nature in a misleading and potentially dangerous way. The characterization of rights-based thinking as male, it is said, denies women's capacity for autonomy. These critics argue that when the law is "feminized"—as, for example, when litigation, with its emphasis on confrontation, is replaced by mediation, which stresses reconciliation—the results are often even worse for women.[1] The reason seems to be that male interests dominate the "reformed" procedure just as they have historically dominated every other legal procedure, but now the fact of reform effectively deflects criticism and demands for further change. The critics' solution, much oversimplified, is for women to take control of the apparatus of rights adjudication and radically restructure it to advance women's interests.[2]

Whatever their differences, however, feminists remain united on the point that American law is patriarchal. However differently individual feminists may interpret the paths through which patriarchy works, there is general agreement that the law continues to favor identifiably male interests. Significantly, many feminist scholars speak of the law's patriarchy in terms of discourse. Political scientist Zillah Eisenstein (1985:20; see also Henderson 1991:418) has described the law as "an authorized language of the state," a "discourse" suffused with the power of the state. To the extent that the law embodies male values and advances male interests, it is an authoritative *patriarchal* discourse.

As we have observed in other chapters, not only is discourse a way of talking about something, but also it is a way of thinking and acting with respect to that subject. Thus, the patriarchal discourse of law is a way of talking and thinking about women, and acting toward them, in legal and political contexts.

As long as the dominant legal discourse is patriarchal, women will be talked about, thought about, and acted upon as subordinate to male interests.

We have also seen in the previous chapters that discourse can both reflect and reproduce dominant cultural values. The dual role of discourse, this double duty as simultaneously cause and effect, can best be appreciated by examining the linguistic practices through which it is translated into social action. Ground-level linguistic practices take the forms and have the effects that they do because of the power of the values that they enact. At the same time, the repeated use of such practices reaffirms that power.

The patriarchal discourse of law provides another demonstration of this dynamic. Recall the discussion of rape in chapter 2. We argued there that the discourse of rape remains, at every level, a discourse of subordination. We asked how that could be, in the face of repeated efforts at legal reform. The answer lay in the linguistic analysis of rape trials. Normative law reform (rape shield laws, for example) has been ineffective, we concluded, primarily because it has been inattentive to the linguistic practices that continually ratify the cultural value of subordination.

In the remainder of this chapter, we reexamine some of our own empirical work in an effort to discover additional linguistic practices that simultaneously reflect and reproduce the law's patriarchy. First we review our research on the speech styles of trial witnesses, arguing that the speech practices of the courtroom exhibit a clear preference for a distinctively male style. We then examine the way in which different kinds of witnesses structure accounts of their problems, concluding that here as well there is a strong, if subtle, male bias. The point of both examples is that efforts to modify the law's patriarchy are likely to be futile without an understanding of how it manifests itself at the most concrete linguistic level.

Stylistic Variation in Courtroom Talk

When we began our collaborative research on courtroom language in the 1970s, we were strongly influenced by sociolinguistics' then-current focus on the social conditioning of language variation. Linguists such as William Labov (1972a, 1972b) and Gillian Sankoff (1980) were demonstrating through careful research that people do not simply speak differently, but that variation in language reflects such social dimensions as class, race, ethnicity, and age. In 1975, Robin Lakoff published her influential book, *Language and Woman's Place,* in which she added gender to the list of social variables that influence language. All of this work, with its common goal of illuminating the social conditioning of language variation, represented a major break with earlier generations of linguists, who had emphasized the universal aspects of language to the point of ignoring variation or treating it as insignificant.[3]

Importantly, the influence of these ground-breaking sociolinguistic studies reached beyond the disciplinary bounds of linguistics. Anthropologists, sociologists, and others began to appreciate the significance of language variation as a window on the complexity of social organization. We found ourselves in this camp as we began to investigate the dynamics of the courtroom. We were motivated to ask such questions as these: What kinds of variation are there in the ways that witnesses present their testimony? To what degree does this variation reflect social differences among witnesses (i.e., do men and women, blacks and whites, or well-educated and poorly educated people talk differently in court)? And if people do talk differently when they testify, do these differences have practical consequences?

To answer questions such as these, we undertook an empirical study of language in the courtroom.[4] First, we spent several weeks in court observing and listening. Although we could imagine some of the possible dimensions of language variation, we wanted to specify exactly what happens when different kinds of people talk in court. Some of the topics we ultimately studied had not occurred to us in advance but emerged only from the process of repeated observations. We noticed, for example, that lawyers and hostile witnesses interrupted each other regularly, and in elaborately patterned ways. We then designed an experimental study of interruption, finding that jurors are attuned to subtle variations in the pattern and that these variations influence their evaluations of both lawyer and witness.[5] In addition to studying issues that emerged during our own observations of courtroom dynamics, we selected other topics that had already been identified in the literature and then developed them empirically. Our study of language and gender in the courtroom falls into this latter category.

As we began our research, Lakoff's work had heightened our awareness of the possible significance of gender differences in speaking styles. Lakoff had argued that women, as a result of their socialization, speak a language of subordination. Through such stylistic features as hedge words (*kind of, sort of*), polite forms (*sir*), tag questions appended to declarative statements (*The meeting's at three, isn't it?*), exaggerated imprecision about quantities (*It was about a mile, but I'm not very good at distances.*), and a rising, inquisitive intonation in normally declarative contexts (*Six-thirty?* in response to a question about when dinner will be ready), women project deference and uncertainty. Thus, Lakoff concluded, women's speech both reflects and reinforces their subordinate position in society.

Against this background, we paid particular attention to female witnesses. Not surprisingly, we found many who spoke what Lakoff had termed "women's language." But we also found that not every woman spoke this way and that some men did. The women who did not were usually expert witnesses such as physicians or psychologists (there were not very many female experts in the 1970s), while the men who did were typically poor and uneducated. These findings complicated our conception of women's language, but they did not diminish the fact that some witnesses spoke a language of deference, subordination, and nonassertiveness, whereas others spoke in a more rhetorically forceful style. We coined the term *powerless language* to reflect what we had actually observed: that the speech style Lakoff had identified was associated primarily with the speaker's status in society (O'Barr and Atkins 1980). Given the social realities of the 1970s, most powerless speakers were in fact women, but the correlation of powerless language with gender was not exact.

Powerlessness and Patriarchy

Once we had defined powerless language and described its occurrence in the courtroom, we set about to answer another question: does it make a difference? We conceived of the trial as a situation in which a number of people present conflicting versions of what happened. In the end, the judge charges the jury to decide (or decides him/herself if there is no jury) which of the various versions to believe. When there are competing versions, the jury cannot give equal credence to all of them; some must be believed more than others. We were specifically interested in knowing whether witnesses who presented their testimony in a powerless style were evaluated as less credible than those who spoke in a more assertive manner.

To answer this, we conducted controlled social-psychological experiments. In simulated courtroom situations, we found that language style did indeed influence the credibility of testimony. Experimental jurors were significantly more likely to believe those witnesses who spoke assertively than those who spoke powerless language. Our findings, since confirmed in many subsequent studies of powerless language in and out of court,[6] demonstrated that style is a critical factor in the courtroom and that the relative credibility of witnesses is influenced by the manner in which their testimony is presented.

Although we did not fully appreciate it at the time, this research has important implications for understanding the subtle workings of the law's patriarchy. While we had found that powerless language was not strictly a gender-based phenomenon, the fact remained that most of the witnesses who used powerless language were women and that most men did not use it. This meant that most women, most of the time, were speaking in a style that the legal system devalued; men, by and large, did not suffer this disadvantage.

When we presented this research to audiences of practicing lawyers, as we often did, they invariably jumped to the same pragmatic conclusion: *if you want to win the case, teach women to talk like men!* We initially scoffed at these comments as yet another instance of the philistinism of lawyers. Gradually, however, we began to appreciate what they were telling us about the nature of the law. Through the credibility assessments of jurors, the law was expressing a strong preference for a speech style that was, as a matter of social fact, distinctively male. We mean "distinctively male" in two senses: in the strict empirical sense that men employed it more often than women and in the sense that, at least in the 1970s, women seemed to have little opportunity to learn it. Justice was thus more accessible to men than to women. The law's patriarchy was both reflected and reproduced in the most fundamental linguistic practices of the courtroom. The jurors' credibility assessments reflected patriarchal values. The lawyers' strategic responses ensured that those values would be reproduced.[7]

There is, of course, no rule of law that requires witnesses to speak in a powerful style. Jurors are not instructed to believe powerful speakers. On the contrary, if they are instructed on credibility at all, they are simply told to rely on their general experience and common sense.[8] And that is what they do: they apply their everyday standards to the evaluation of witnesses, and those standards include the preference for powerful speech. "The law" as an institution is complicit in punishing women for their speech habits to the extent that it remains silent as jurors act on their cultural values.[9]

So is it appropriate to use the powerless speech phenomenon as linguistic evidence of *the law's* patriarchy? Or is it evidence only of the general patriarchy of society, which the law must inevitably reflect? This is a difficult question to answer. The law often looks like a conservative, reactive institution, changing only when necessary to catch up with changes in society. Recall, for example, that legal prohibitions on birth control were being litigated in the Supreme Court as late as 1972.[10] On race relations, however, beginning with *Brown v. Board of Education* in 1954 and continuing through the affirmative action era, the law has tended to be out ahead of general social values. The best one can say is that the law can be an agent of change when it (that is, the judges and legislators who determine the law's content) chooses to be.

By tolerating jurors' preferences for powerful speech, the law offers subtle but significant support for society's patriarchal values. It is subtle in the sense that it is masked by the pervasive rhetoric of equal protection and due process and by the very real protections with which the law backs up that rhetoric in many contexts.[11] It is significant, however, in that for certain witnesses the preference for powerful speech can vitiate those protections. Any judge would immediately dismiss a juror who announced before the trial that he was more likely to believe the testimony of men than of women. But how different is this from what jurors do every day when they give greater credence to powerful speech?

The Logic of Legal Accounts

During the 1980s, the focus of sociolinguistic research shifted from speech style to what was termed "discourse." In place of the former emphasis on variation in individual elements of phonology and lexicon, sociolinguists began to examine larger units of speech. There was particular interest in "narratives" in the traditional sense of self-contained stories or accounts.[12] Sociolinguists paid increasing attention to such things as how narrators structure their accounts, how they claim authority for their stories, and how they interact with their audiences.

Motivated in part by this new theoretical focus, we began to study the structure of legal accounts. But we were also stimulated by a lingering issue from our prior research on courtroom speech styles. During post-trial interviews with the witnesses we observed in the 1970s, we repeatedly heard about their sense of frustration with the legal process. A constant refrain was "I never got a chance to tell my story. If I'd only known how bad it was going to be in court, I never would have gone." When we pressed for details, it became clear that what they meant was that the structure of courtroom discourse had short-circuited their expectations about testifying—expectations we discovered to be based on everyday storytelling habits. They had been unable to structure and illustrate their accounts as they did in ordinary conversation, and that disturbed them.

This suggested a research question: what would their stories sound like if they *did* get a chance to tell them unconstrained by courtroom rules? This question in turn suggested an obvious research setting: small claims courts, where lay people can assert legal claims in a relatively informal environment, usually without the advice or assistance of lawyers. In small claims courts, people give accounts of legal problems in whatever ways they deem appropriate. In their accounts, they act out their beliefs about what kinds of problems the law should deal with, what constitutes evidence and proof, and what sorts of remedies they expect the law to provide.

As we studied litigant accounts given in more than one hundred trials in six different cities, a striking pattern emerged: there are two very different ways in which litigants structure their accounts. *Rule-oriented* accounts base claims for legal relief on violations of specific rules, duties, and obligations, such as those inscribed in contracts. They are arranged sequentially, retelling events in a straight line from beginning to end. They deal explicitly with cause and effect, as well as with the identification of the human agents responsible for events. Importantly, these accounts conform to the logic of the law and reflect an accurate understanding of the law's sense of relevance. They emphasize evidence that bears directly on the specific rule violation being asserted and exclude evidence extraneous to the claim, in particular those details that are of a personal or social nature.

Relational accounts, by contrast, base their entitlement to relief on general rules of social conduct. Their thesis is often that decent people who meet their social obligations have an entitlement to fair treatment. Because relational accounts focus on personal status and social position, they tend to be full of details about the life of the speaker, details that the law usually deems irrelevant. Issues of time and of cause and effect are often dealt with in highly idiosyncratic ways.

The Rule-Oriented Account

Text 4.1 is the paradigm of the rule-oriented account. The witness (Hogan) is a sales executive who is appearing in court on behalf of her company, the defendant in the case. The plaintiff (Webb), a former sales representative for the company, is suing over the company's refusal to pay him a commission on the sale of an expensive scientific instrument.

As she presents the company's defense, Hogan deals directly with the issues the judge must resolve to decide the case. She treats the dispute as a contractual problem between two parties and does not discuss personalities or social relationships. The description of the dispute's context is limited to what is directly relevant to the narrow contractual issue on which she believes the judge will focus. Hogan's account is given in sequential order (note how in lines 28–42 the account progresses from March 1984 to November 1986) and is highly factual (e.g., "1500 manufacturers," line 18; "60,000 products," line 18; "it was not 400 but only 200," lines 69–70). Names (note the repeated references to Mr. Harper, Mr. Webb, and Diller and Macy), dates (lines 65–67 stress the significance of November 15 and December 15, 1986), and the contents of conversations (e.g., lines 60–63) and documents (see, for example, her recapitulation of Mr. Harper's letter in lines 53–57) are reported precisely. Unlike many relational accounts, this one presumes no prior knowledge of people, places, and events on the part of the listener.

TEXT 4.1 (Conley and O'Barr 1990:63–66)

> JUDGE: We'll come back to you in just a moment. Let's turn over to you ma'am. We do need your name, business address, and connection with the uh, Instrument Supply Company.
> HOGAN: My name is Lynn Hogan. Uh, my address, do you want
> 5   my business address or—
> JUDGE: Business address is fine.
> HOGAN: 1200 Cavanaugh Street. I am the scientific sales manager for Instrument Supply, Denver.

JUDGE: As such of course you've heard everything that's been
10   stated so far. We have several exhibits. I believe in this case
you're probably familiar with all of them.
HOGAN: Yes sir, I am.
JUDGE: But if not, you're certainly free to look them all over and
your opportunity to react to what you've heard and to further de-
15   velop whatever answer or defense you may have.
HOGAN: Okay, thank you. Um, as uh Dan [the plaintiff] stated,
uh, Instrument Supply is a scientific distributor. Uh, we represent
over 1500 manufacturers and we sell over 60,000 products. Um,
we are continuously being exposed to gimmicks from our manu-
20   facturers to boost the sale of their products. Uh, the only control
that management has, um, over these prod–, over these promo-
tions, is to pick and choose the ones that uh, best support our local selling programs, where we want the local emphasis to be.
Um, then it is my responsibility, as well as the district manager,
25   to assist the sales reps in focusing on these sanctioned programs.
Uh, in order to keep track of what we have sanctioned, we have
a calculation sheet that specifically shows the sales representative
what we are sanctioning. This is one for the first half. I have highlighted that that particular promotion for spectrometers was on
30   the first half, from March until August of 1984, giving the particular payouts, and as you'll see there is a 200 dollar payout there
for 1001 Spectrometer. In the, we, uh, usually will change some
of the programs on the second half uh, PIP program. Um, we also
as sales managers, provide to the representatives, um, some sort
35   of indication that we are bombarded, our plate is full. So I put
out to them in September of 1986, a list of the sanctioned promo-
tions. You will see on there that the Diller and Macy double payout is not on there. Uh, I was unaware that this, um, letter had
gone out from D and M. Approximately October of 1986 they
40   did send this out to the sales representative. Uh, I received notification that it was out amongst the reps late October, early November, upon returning from vacation. My management told me
of his conversation with Mr. Harper and the agreement was made
between John Taylor, uh the dis–, the then district manager and
45   Mr. Harper, that there had been a, uh, an advance notification
put out on an unsanctioned program through Diller and Macy,
not sanctioned by Instrument Supply. And uh, that Mr. Harper
was more than uh, uh, uh, he was more than open to go ahead
and pay his 200 dollars, but that we would not pay the matching
50   200 dollars.
JUDGE: What is his basis for that? Which seems to be contrary to
the flier that he put out.
HOGAN: Um, Mr. Harper in a, in a letter that Mr., I asked for

Mr. Harper to write, which I believe you already have a copy but
55   here is another copy. In there it states the events. It does say that
he um, prematurely put the promotion out to the sales force without talking to local management. Um, in early, either late October, early November, I asked him, he told me at that point about
um, what was going on with Mr. Webb and I asked him at that
60   time, I said, "Would you please call Mr. Webb and tell him that
you have prematurely put a promotion out that's not sanctioned
and that you will honor your 200 dollars and that Instrument Supply will not." He told me that he had. Uh, it is true that I was
semi-aware of this 1001 from um, uh, the sale at Lakeview. Mr.
65   Webb did a quotation to Lakeview on November 15th of 1986,
uh, stating on there that this particular quote was good until December 15th, 1986 to the customer. Um, it is my job to encourage
the sales representatives to close sales. At that time I was not
aware of the fact that Dan did not know it was not 400 but only
70   200 through Diller and Macy. Upon his resignation, um, when he
came into the office the end of December, he did at that time state
the 400 dollars and I did at that time tell him that it was 200 dollars from Diller and Macy and not a matching 200 dollars from
Instrument Supply. Um, at that point, um, Dan continued to pur-
75   sue it and um, you know we, you see the answers that we have
have uh put out. So we have paid, we did pay 200 dollars out
for Diller and Macy. Diller and Macy is reimbursing us for that
200 dollars through the PIP program. And um, excuse me, if
I could just present one other thing.
80   JUDGE: Go right ahead.
HOGAN: For the second half, and this goes with that one other
thing that I gave you, this is the second half PIP calculation sheet,
and you will see on there is no Diller and Macy payout for the
second half.
85   JUDGE: Anything else before we hear again from Mr. Webb?
HOGAN: No sir.

The Relational Account

Text 4.2, by contrast, illustrates the relational account. Rawls, the ultimately
unsuccessful plaintiff, has sued her neighbor (Bennett) for removing a hedge
on her side of their shared property line, failing to control the growth of his
shrubbery onto her property, and generally harassing her. In this text, she responds to the judge's questions about how the hedge was removed. Previously,
he has asked her a series of specific questions about the location of the property line, but she has been unable to provide any useful information on that
issue.

Here, Rawls describes and analyzes her problem in terms of social relationships rather than the kinds of rules that constitute legal doctrine. She rarely responds directly to the issues raised in the judge's questions (contrast the answer that begins on line 4 with those beginning on lines 6 and 16). Instead, the questions evoke lengthy digressions about the history of her relationship with Bennett. These digressions meander through time and place (e.g., lines 6–12, where she has to "jump back" three years and describe Bennett's comings and goings), drawing her audience ever deeper into her social world but providing little information about the specific issues that are of interest to the court. Her account contains frequent references to personal status (e.g., her references to "getting crippled up," lines 33–34, and having only one trash can, line 58), items that are significant to her social agenda but irrelevant to the court's more limited and rule-centered agenda. Additionally, the account assumes that the listener shares her knowledge of background events and places. Although the assumption of shared knowledge is common and appropriate in familiar conversation, it creates difficulties in an institutional setting when a stranger is trying to extract a set of facts and apply legal rules to them.

TEXT 4.2 (Conley and O'Barr 1990:61–63)

JUDGE: You're alleging that these trees and, and the shrubs and apparently the hedge included were removed. When did this happen?
RAWLS: Oh, well now that happened this year. At, uh—
5   JUDGE: And how did it happen?
RAWLS: Well I can, well, well I have to jump back because, uh, for three years when Mr. Bennett moved back—because he was there once before and then he moved and then he come back into that house—and all the time before—I have to say this though
10   judge—because all the time before everybody took care of that hedge and they wouldn't let me take care of it. They trimmed it and I even went to Mr. Bennett when he was there before—
JUDGE: Wait a moment. Now the question that I asked you—and I would like to have you answer it—and that is how did the hedge
15   get removed?
RAWLS: Well, um, Mr. Bennett said he told me when he moved back in, uh, because I was taking care of my trees coming up through the hedge, I was cutting them off and he told me not to do that. He said, "Don't do it," he said, "I'm going to have, the
20   church is going to pay to take them out of there, because my wife wants to put a fence and plant roses on the other side." He said, "Is that alright with you?" I said, "I don't care what you do with it," you know, and I said, "If you need, uh, money for tools,

maybe I can rent a tool and help in that respect because I can't
25   dig," you know. And I said, "If you need uh, a tool to help you remove the hedge," I said, "uh, I will," well it wasn't the hedge then
it was all the stumps underneath because he wanted that removed
because he, his wife wanted the fence and she wanted roses on it.
And so then three years went by and they let these trees grow up
30   like you see the picture there. I think you've got it. And they're so
big and then when he told me to stop taking them out because he
was gonna take out that hedge, uh, the stumps, why uh, in the
meantime I called a man and I had them, because I'm getting
crippled up and I can't bend down sir, and here I was still taking
35   out those trees and he wasn't coming to help me like he said he
was. So then I had a man come—here Jim give him this—and I
paid 45 dollars. There's the bill there and he cut it right off down
level with the ground. Well, I knew that wouldn't take it but at
least it would keep me for a little bit trying to get them tree things
40   out of that shrubbery there. Well, um, Mr. Bennett, when he
finally come out he said, "You know, that isn't going to do it," and
that's when he told me, "My wife wants to put a fence," and he
said, "You know that isn't going to do it. Those stumps are going
to have to be taken out." And that's when I told him, and he said
45   he would do it, "I and the church would take them out," and I,
that's when I told him, "If you need, uh, money for a tool or
something to help you. I'll pay for the tool or whatever." And he
told, didn't do it, and so then I just had a, the Milehigh, uh, Tree
Service come uh, uh, and um, a, and Mr., I had his name here—
50   Mr., uh, Cook come and he come in the house and sat down with
me and he looked at that and he said well he surely should help in
the shrubbery in the back because there's shrubbery in the back
that was over on my line that I've got to take out and I've got pictures of that too, sir. And he said he didn't know what the man or
55   what the man was because the tree was dead why didn't he take it
out? Well all he wants to do is harass me so he leaves it there so I
have to keep taking the stuff out and bending over and using my
trashcan, you know. This is something else. I only got one can.
Why don't he pick up his own trash? And so I went ahead and
60   paid it. He told me he would come if I need. He says, "I'll cut it
when you need me." Yet I could never get this man. I tried to
have him subpoenaed, yet I could never get him because I think
Bennett got to him first. But, anyway I got the Milehigh Tree Service here for 275, and I got his mess in the backyard—if you
65   want the pictures here—that's what I took them for. Did you give
him the ones with the trees?

The rules-versus-relationships dichotomy implicates some common gender
stereotypes. The structure of the rule-oriented account reflects some defining

beliefs that many men have about themselves: men think in straight lines, they get right to the point, they emphasize "facts" rather then emotions, and they have faith in general rules that apply to everyone regardless of personal circumstances. The relational account, on the other hand, evokes a widely held male stereotype of female thought and behavior: women are imprecise in dealing with time, they wander off the point when telling stories, they let their emotions get in the way of the facts, and they get too engrossed in context to develop and apply general principles.

Our research indicates that gender does influence the distribution of the two kinds of accounts, but in an indirect way. Most of the rule-oriented litigants we observed were men, and most of the relational litigants were women, although this was not a hard-and-fast correlation.[13] Indeed, in Text 4.1, the rule-oriented litigant is a woman, while another case that we discussed elsewhere in identifying the contrasting orientations involved two men (Conley and O'Barr 1990:68). The ability to produce rule-oriented accounts seems to be an acquired skill. The crucial factor associated with this skill is exposure to the culture of business and law. Lawyers have this skill, of course; so do landlords, merchants, and other business people, big and small. Because it is still the case in our society that these roles are most often occupied by men, the ability to give rule-oriented accounts remains largely a male prerogative.

This imbalance is highly significant because the law has a strong preference for rule-oriented accounts. Although relationally oriented small-claims litigants do prevail on occasion, most legal decision makers find it far easier to deal with the structure and content of rule-oriented accounts. In interviews with us, judges described relational litigants as hard to follow, irrational, and even crazy, while praising the straightforward efficiency of rule-oriented accounts. They reported that in order to respond to a relational account, they first had to restructure it in their own minds around whatever legal rules might apply, selecting and reordering the relevant facts, while discarding the extraneous ones. This was hard work, and they often did not bother. The implication of these comments is, of course, that relational litigants—which often means women— have a harder time gaining access to justice than do their rule-oriented counterparts.

Despite what the judges say, relational accounts are not illogical. It is just that their logic differs from that of the rule-oriented accounts that the law prefers. Relational accounts tend to predicate legal entitlement on personal need and social worth: *I am a needy person. I meet my obligations to other members of the social network and help them when they are in need. Therefore, the law should help me now.* Given this outlook, the details of one's personal life and social relations are highly relevant. If one is not concerned with the deductive application of rules, there is no compelling need to present events in chronological sequence or to be precise about such things as times, dates, and quantities. As we discuss at the end of this chapter, other societies in other places have built legal systems around this kind of logic. This suggests that, at least in theory, we could, too.

We emphasize "in theory." Many would object to such a revolutionary transformation on grounds of practical utility or their own philosophy of justice. Those who would welcome the change would confront a monumental task: undoing our system's historical connection with a rule-oriented system of reasoning. If that reasoning is indeed patriarchal, then the law's preference for it both reflects and reinforces the essential patriarchy of legal discourse.

When the law, as personified by judges, reacts more favorably to rule-oriented accounts, it is granting privileged status to linguistic practices that historically have been more associated with men than women. In Gilligan's terms, the law is preferring the abstract, rule-driven logic typical of men to the more contextual reasoning that characterizes women (Gilligan 1982). In this way, the law's linguistic practice reveals its fundamental patriarchy. The details of the interactions between judges and rule-oriented litigants comprise the mechanics of translating patriarchy into social action.

As in other contexts, though, linguistic practice is both cause and effect. Every time a judge prefers the rule-oriented structure, this act sends a message to those who would interact with the law. The message is that the easiest mode of access is to conform to the logic of the system, however gender-biased that logic may be. Anyone who is in regular attendance in courtrooms and law school classrooms can attest that people respond to this message in a pragmatic way. As more and more women enter the system as lawyers, litigants, and judges, it is they who change, not the system. Opportunities for resistance are ignored as people make the practical judgment that they need to speak the language of the law. Every time the law's linguistic practice is reenacted, the patriarchy of its macrodiscourse—that is, the way things are thought about and acted upon—is reaffirmed.[14]

Conclusion: An Alternative Vision of Justice

In this chapter, we have reviewed two of our own investigations of how legal processes actually work at the microlinguistic level. The findings we have reported are at variance with the law's ideal of equal access to justice. In this regard, our results are no different from those of most other sociolegal projects. Over and over, such studies have shown the gap between the claims of law-in-theory and the realities of law-in-action.

The particular focus of our research has been on the preference of the law for certain linguistic practices. Witnesses come in all varieties—they are old and young, educated and uneducated, and from varied ethnic backgrounds, and, importantly for the argument we develop here, they differ in terms of how they talk. The legal system prefers some of these ways of talking over others, and it expresses its preferences in complex ways.

At the level of speech styles, the system gives greater credence to those who speak in a powerful and an assertive style. Conversely, those who speak in a powerless style, which is marked by deference and imprecision, are less likely to be believed. Since men are more likely to have learned a powerful speech style than women, this preference, we believe, is a manifestation of the law's patriarchy at the most elemental linguistic level.

One response to this claim is that it is inaccurate to attribute this gender bias to "the system." After all, it is not legal officials who are evaluating men and women differently, but the lay jurors, who are the law's fact finders. To the extent that the powerless phenomenon reflects a patriarchal bias, it is the bias of our society as a whole. Since a fundamental purpose of having juries is to incorporate societal values into the law, the system will never get very far ahead of society—nor should it.

This argument is largely irrelevant to our principal point. That point is that patriarchal values are inscribed in the linguistic details of the day-to-day workings of the law. Whether the law is leading or following the larger society does not alter this reality. Moreover, the law is more than a passive conduit for the values of society as expressed by jurors. As we noted earlier, it takes active measures to screen out many of the biases that jurors might bring into the courtroom, and this could be true with regard to language variation as well.

The law exhibits a similar preference for a characteristically male epistemology in the way that it responds to different kinds of account structures. In our study of small claims courts, we found that rule-oriented accounts articulate better with the logic of the law than do their relational counterparts. Small claims judges can deal relatively easily with rule-oriented accounts, with their emphasis on rule violations and their exclusion of social context. For a relational litigant to receive a comparable hearing, a judge must be willing to make the effort to listen to the account—rather than dismissing it out of hand, as often happens—and then restructure it in terms of legal rules. Litigants who are able to construct rule-oriented accounts are typically those with exposure to the culture of business and law; it is still the case in our society that men gain such exposure far more readily than women. Once again, legal patriarchy, in the sense of favoring male interests, is realized in the linguistic details of courtroom interactions.

These processes parallel other ways of inscribing patriarchal discourse in the workings of law. How else are we to understand what we saw in chapter 2 regarding rape trials? And what about mediation? Although one might expect that women would fare better in mediation, with its ideology of conciliation, than in adversarial adjudication, the evidence we reviewed suggests the opposite. Here as well, the law remains consistently patriarchal in its linguistic practice. Methodologically, these various examples all point to the critical role of linguistic analysis in understanding the mechanics of domination and privilege. Because it is at the level of language-in-action that abstractions such as patriarchy become reality, linguistic analysis is of more than academic interest. Those who would transform the law's patriarchy are probably wasting their time unless they are prepared to challenge the practices that both reflect and reproduce it.

Finally, it is worth asking what a legal system that does not favor patriarchal interests might look like. Could the law exhibit different preferences than it does at present, or might it treat different ways of saying things more equitably? Could the law have different priorities than it now does?

Take the case of Mrs. Rawls. Her difficulties with the court had to do with the fact that she was unable to structure her problems according to the template of the law. Her logic was not that of the law. She could not seem to separate the hedge, the property line, and the concept of ownership from the complexities of social relations, unneighborly neighbors, and twenty years of bad feelings. The judge described her to us as a crazy old lady whom the law could not help. Imagine for a moment the possibility of a legal system that adjusted to the logic of its constituents, rather than insisting that they make the accommodations. What would such a legal system look like?

One need not look far: the ethnographic record of legal anthropology suggests some answers. Anthropologists have described numerous legal systems that show us different ways to listen to litigants and make decisions. The village courts of the Tiv of Nigeria and the Barotse of Zimbabwe, as described, respectively, by Paul Bohannan (1989) and Max Gluckman (1955, 1965), are instructive examples. Despite major differences between the two legal systems, both Tiv and Barotse courts allow litigants to say whatever they have to say and allow those who sit in judgment to ask whatever they want to know, to call for whatever evidence they deem important, and to visit places where events occurred. They are not bound by Western-style constraints on who can talk, what speakers can say, and how talk must be structured. Far from being extraneous, social context is central. In the cases that Bohannan and Gluckman describe, judges often seek out the social context when the litigants fail to provide it. In contrast to their Western counterparts, Tiv and Barotse judges are not strangers operating in an abstract universe without reference to the social world where disputes occur and where the parties will return after the hearing. Their overriding concern seems to be to ensure that decisions reached by the law are ones that will work in society.

In these respects, the Tiv and Barotse legal systems come much closer to the everyday understanding of disputes exhibited by relational litigants like Mrs. Rawls. It is tempting to speculate on how she would fare in such environments. Those courts would be interested in the history of her relationship with her neighbor and her claim that he had violated community norms. Their solutions would look less to past violation of rules than to future compatibility. The judges would probably maintain an interest in her affairs and would be neither surprised nor displeased to see her again if changing social circumstances warranted.

We should not be too quick to romanticize this vision of Mrs. Rawls in Barotseland, however. Despite the appeal of their legal process, Tiv and Barotse societies are at least as patriarchal as our own. Indeed, many of the cases that Bohannan and Gluckman report involve women being shuttled back and forth between kin groups like livestock. And even their enlightened procedures look very much like the mediation strategies that Fineman and others have found wanting as a solution to the patriarchy of American divorce law.

Our point is simply that there *are* alternatives to the microlinguistic structure of our legal system. Radical as some of them may seem, they have worked, more or less, in other places and at other times. Some of the alternatives might subvert the law's patriarchy; others might reinforce it, perhaps in unexpected ways. But whatever form the linguistic practice of the law takes, it will interact with the law's higher-order macrodiscourse in a relationship of mutual influence, with profound implications for the distribution of power among the law's constituents.

CHAPTER FIVE

A Natural History of Disputing

How do disputes begin? What do they look (or sound) like in their earliest stages? How does an injury or wrong develop into a full-blown dispute or even a legal case? These are perplexing questions for sociolegal scholars. The obvious solution—to follow a dispute from its very beginning through its development and eventual resolution—has enormous intellectual appeal. But is it possible to do so?[1]

In this chapter, we consider the history of disputes. We ask whether different kinds of disputes tend to unfold in regular ways and, if so, what accounts for the regularities. Our starting point is a model of dispute evolution—or *transformation,* as it is usually called—that has shaped sociolegal research on disputing for almost two decades. We then review what is known linguistically about the behaviors that occur at each of the posited stages of a typical dispute. The chapter concludes with a new model of the disputing process that is built inductively from the bits and pieces of available linguistic evidence.

Naming, Blaming, and Claiming

To date, some of the best answers to questions about the history of disputes have emerged from the conceptual framework formulated by William Felstiner, Richard Abel, and Austin Sarat in their 1980 article, "The Emergence and Transformation of Disputes: Naming, Blaming, Claiming . . ." They propose a logical model of three developmental stages through which disputes pass in their early phases. In practice, the stages are complex, reactive, and unstable, making them difficult to isolate or describe fully. Nonetheless, the conceptualization of naming, blaming, and claiming as the developmental stages of a dispute has lent useful structure to the study of disputing behavior.

Naming refers to the phase in which a particular experience is understood as injurious. Until the injured person says to himself or herself, "I have been hurt or wronged; what has happened has damaged me in some way," the injury remains unperceived *as an injury*. Many of life's untoward events never move into the naming phase. Consider such examples as a health problem arising from daily labor in a hazardous workplace, the aggravation caused by a neighbor who ignores a property line and builds a corner of his garage on someone else's property, or the annoyance or trauma resulting from a coworker's unwanted sexual advances. But until these problems are perceived as injuries and named as such, they remain embryonic disputes.

Blaming marks an important transformation in the development of a dispute. In this phase, a link is made between the perceived wrong and the party believed to have caused it, whether another person or a social entity of some sort. An employer is blamed for creating the hazard in the workplace, a neighbor's building contractor is held responsible for encroaching on the property line, or a coworker is said to have sexually harassed another person by making unwanted advances. At the completion of the blaming stage, the injury has been defined and the principals in the dispute identified.

Claiming occurs when the injured party voices the grievance to the party believed to be responsible and asks for a remedy. The employer might be asked to remove the hazard from the workplace, the contractor to rebuild the garage so that it does not cross the property line, or the harasser to act in a different way. If the party believed to be responsible complies, then the problem is solved. But this is not what always happens. The party who is held responsible may resist the claim. This denial of the claim marks a final transformation of the incipient controversy. At this point, when the parties are at loggerheads and no simple resolution is in sight, a full-blown dispute emerges.

Useful as it is, the Felstiner-Abel-Sarat framework is a logical model of disputing rather than a description of what actually happens in particular instances.[2] In reality, the three stages might occur in rapid succession, or one or another of them might be recycled a few times as a person ponders the seriousness of the injury and the possibilities of whom to hold responsible. In some cases, the transformation process might extend over a very long period of time—even a lifetime—as a victim gradually perceives the wrong and begins to move toward blaming someone and seeking resolution. (Think about recent cases in which lifelong smokers have sued tobacco companies and adults have come forward with claims of childhood sexual abuse.) What this logical model of conflict cannot do is to tell us much about what happens in each of the stages or what specific events trigger the developmental transformations.

A more complex model of the emergence of disputes can be derived from microlinguistic analysis of trouble talk in everyday life. Like the Felstiner-Abel-Sarat model, this model is built up logically from what we know about how people talk about trouble in the early phases of perceiving injury and blaming others, well before disputes as such have fully developed. But what a language-based model can add is an understanding of just what it is that people say when they perceive injuries, name them, and blame others. It can thus offer an explanation of how the various transformations actually occur. As we shall see, the interactive component of the various transformations—that is, what other people do and say—is also a critical part of what happens.

In this chapter, we assemble linguistic data from a variety of sources in an effort to expand and elaborate on the naming-blaming-claiming dispute model, and thus to appreciate the microdiscourse of disputing. Our effort is twofold: to develop a fuller understanding of the language people use when they name, blame, and claim and to consider what happens when disputes go beyond the claiming stage into the realm of ongoing confrontation. At the end of the chapter, we synthesize our linguistic observations into a new model that seeks to account for all the contingencies that may ensue during the life history of a dispute.

A Language-Based Model of Naming and Blaming

Ever since we began our own study of disputes almost twenty-five years ago, we have had the fantasy of being present at the birth of a dispute, of being able to hear the first voicings of the process of naming, blaming, and claiming. Perhaps these would be words spoken to a spouse at breakfast, a friend at work, or a neighbor across a back fence. In such intimate moments, people tell significant others what has happened. They put into words their feelings and perceptions and share them with someone willing to listen. But just what is it that they say? Is there a way to study these first tellings, these embryonic narratives about troubles? Were we able to sit at the breakfast table, eavesdrop on a telephone conversation, or stand at the fence, what would we hear?

It is extremely difficult to position oneself strategically in these intimate spaces and then wait for dispute-related topics to emerge. Nonetheless, conversation analysts have managed to collect and study bits and pieces of naturally occurring conversation about troubles in everyday life. From these fragments, it is possible to build a reasonably complete linguistic model of what people say in the earliest stages of naming their troubles as injuries and blaming others for them.

Some significant insights into the earliest phases of disputing come from Anita Pomerantz's (1978) study of trouble talk in everyday contexts. She notes that "unhappy incidents" in daily life are often announced without any attribution of responsibility. It is only later, through the interactional work done by the recipients of the talk, that responsible agents are connected with the actions. What people seem to do in everyday contexts is to mention their troubles to spouses, friends, and neighbors in fairly general terms. The recipients of the talk then ask a series of follow-up questions that initiate a collaborative search for a responsible party who can be blamed for the problem.

Pomerantz gives some examples of how this works. In each case, someone announces a problem—something's hurt, something's broken, something's wrong. What follows is a response from the recipient of the talk that begins the effort to complete the equation by identifying the person responsible for the bad outcome.

Text 5.1 (Adapted from Pomerantz 1978:116–17)

(1)   Announcement: My face hurts.
       Question: Oh, what did he do to you?
(2)   Announcement: It [the car engine] blew up.
       Question: What did you do to it?
(3)   Announcement: The cat's been eating our dinner.
       Question: Did you leave it out so that he could get to it?

These examples provide a prototype of how people talk about trouble in everyday contexts. As Felstiner, Abel, and Sarat theorized, the original event in the linguistic history of a dispute is indeed the description, the noticing, the naming[3] of the problem. But as Pomerantz shows, this initial announcement of the problem often occurs without any attribution of responsibility. Blaming comes later. Significantly, her data show that the second stage of the transformation occurs collaboratively. One person names the problem; another helps affix responsibility for it.

The recipient of the trouble talk may respond with varying degrees of directness. In examples (1) and (3) in Text 5.1, the recipient moves immediately to the identification of a suspect [in (1), a "he" evidently known to both parties; in (3), "you"] and the specification of the guilty act (an all-but-explicit accusation of physical violence; a charge of leaving the dinner out). In example (2), the recipient names the agent ("you") but merely raises the question of what that agent might have done to cause the problem.[4] Moreover, it is interesting (although not remarked upon by Pomerantz) that all three examples reflect an effort not simply to find some responsible agent but also to find a responsible *human* agent. Although exceptions come readily to mind (such things as lightning bolts out of the sky, car crashes resulting from mechanical failure, and illnesses that seem to be merely a part of the human condition), collaborative searches for blame, in this culture at least, seem to exhibit a strong preference for discovering human agents.[5]

A second body of evidence about embryonic disputes comes from the work of Jefferson (1980, 1985, 1988). In a 1985 article entitled "On the Interactional Unpackaging of a 'Gloss,'" Jefferson's concern is the impact of the interactional environment on the telling of troubles. She finds that we often offer tokens of or hints about stories that we might tell (i.e., that might be unpacked more fully), but the actual form and complexity of the tellings that ensue depend on the behavior of those to whom we drop the hints. We say, for example, that something bad has happened, but a full-blown story does not get told unless the audience does its work by encouraging elaboration. Jefferson provides examples of lengthy conversations in which potential stories are offered or introduced several times, but only when the listeners affirmatively signal their willingness to hear elaborated versions do the stories actually get told in that form.

Other work by Jefferson discloses further details of the process of co-producing stories about trouble. The process is variable and often complex. The requisite audience participation can take a variety of forms. Sometimes, for example, the trouble will be announced by an unexpectedly detailed answer to a "How are you?" kind of question; the recipient may ignore the hint or, as in Text 5.2, invite elaboration of the problem.

TEXT 5.2 (Adapted from Jefferson 1988:422)

> QUESTION: How are you feeling now?
> ANSWER: Oh, pretty good I guess.
> INVITATION: How is your arthritis? You still taking shots?

In other instances, the announcement of the problem comes in the form of a statement. The recipient may then invite elaboration by what Jefferson calls *affiliation responses.* These are words, phrases, or other utterances that express the recipient's sympathy and interest in hearing more about the problem. Text 5.3 illustrates the process.

TEXT 5.3 (Adapted from Jefferson 1988:428)

> ANNOUNCEMENT: I been taking antibiotics ever since Sunday.
> AFFILIATION: Ohh.
> ELABORATION: And uh I, when I lie down or when I get up it feels like the flesh is pulling off my bones.
> 5   FURTHER AFFILIATION: How awful.
> FURTHER ELABORATION: Oh I have, listen I was in such excruciating pain yesterday . . .

Yet another possibility is that the recipient will help the telling along by offering a *second story.* The recipient will signal a willingness to hear more by responding to some detail of the unfolding story with a statement such as "Yeah, that sounds like when I tore that thing in my shoulder a couple of years ago—I thought I was gonna go crazy it hurt so much." Second stories seem to have the effect of motivating the original speaker to produce even more elaborate versions of the original problem.

Whatever their specifics, most of the features of co-produced trouble narratives discovered by Pomerantz and Jefferson share two related characteristics. First, in the instance when troubles get fully told, the recipient plays an active and a helpful role. Second, the linguistic relationship between teller and recipient moves in the direction of ever-greater intimacy as the teller offers more and more personal detail and the recipient signals a willingness to receive it. Significantly, such features require a friendly audience and an informal conversational environment. Thus, there is likely to be a stark disjunction when the aggrieved party moves beyond naming and blaming to the claiming stage and beyond. The story must now be retold to the potentially hostile responsible party. If that proves unavailing, the claimant may have to move into the professional world of lawyers and judges. In either of those environments, helpfulness and intimacy are unlikely, and a new set of linguistic issues will come into play.[6] We turn next to what is known about the linguistic details of the latter phases of the disputing process.

The Claiming Process

Claiming, as specified in the Felstiner-Abel-Sarat model, occurs when the injured person articulates the wrong to the blamed party and requests a remedy.[7] It is easy to imagine a variety of possible responses: (1) the blamed party agrees with the claim; (2) the blamed party denies the claim; or (3) some complex intermediate state emerges, and the two parties become entangled in an argument. In case (1), the controversy presumably ends; in case (2) or (3), a full-blown dispute can emerge. Let us examine these possibilities in more detail.

Recall our discussion in chapter 3 about conversational interaction. A major characteristic of verbal exchanges is that many sequences occur as *adjacency pairs* (Atkinson and Drew 1979:57–61). Questions-answers and requests-replies are common adjacency pairs. In some adjacency pairs, the first part invites only one possible response (or second part). Thus, a greeting calls for a return greeting; any other response is out of order conversationally. Other first parts may evoke alternative second parts: invitations may occasion acceptances, rejections, or counteroffers, while requests may be granted or denied. In most instances where the first part allows multiple second parts, only one is usual and anticipated—or, as conversation analysts put it, *preferred.*[8] An acceptance is the preferred response to an invitation, as compliance is to a request. Other responses—rejecting an invitation and denying a request—are said to be *dispreferred.* Linguistically, dispreferred second parts tend to be more elaborate than preferred second parts, often involving explanations or excuses. For example, an invitation may be accepted with a simple "Yes, I'll be there," whereas a rejection will typically take the form of "I'd love to come, but I have to . . ."

Claiming—that is, the actual confrontation of the accused by the accuser with a claim about responsibility—is the first part of an adjacency pair. From the perspective of the wronged party, the preferred second part would be an acceptance of the blame. But is this usually what happens?

Some evidence comes from Atkinson and Drew's (1979:112–17) discussion of accusations. They consider the possible second parts to accusations—denials, excuses, counteraccusations, admissions, apologies, and so forth—and conclude that the anticipated second part in everyday situations is one that somehow avoids self-blame.[9] Denials, excuses, and counteraccusations all function to avoid self-blame. Admissions and apologies, which involve some degree of acknowledgment of responsibility, are very infrequent. The logical conclusion of Atkinson and Drew's argument is that claiming is a structurally self-defeating process, one that is usually doomed from the outset. If we accuse someone, the likelihood is that he or she will deflect the accusation, rather than accepting blame.

Consider the following story, told to one of us in the aftermath of Hurricane Fran, which struck North Carolina in 1996. The teller reported that she had been driving her car down a familiar street known by her audience to have been blocked after the storm by a fallen tree. She made the detour through the neighborhood that had come to be everyone's way around the fallen tree in the immediate aftermath of the storm. On this occasion, she encountered linemen who were repairing downed power lines. One of them was directing traffic in the area where the crew was working. The narrator obeyed his directions, but to her dismay, as she drove through the work area, a limb fell on her car, damaging it badly. When she got out of the car to discuss the situation with the lineman, she was astonished when he immediately accepted responsibility on behalf of the power company and offered to pay for the damage to her car.

In her telling of the story, the narrator emphasized three striking ironies. First, her car had survived the hurricane itself, but then got wrecked when things had ostensibly returned to an unthreatening normalcy. Second, the damage had occurred as a result of obeying *safety* instructions given by the work crew. Third, and most remarkable, the crew had immediately accepted responsibility for the damage to her car. It was the convergence of these unusual occurrences that made the story worth telling.

From a linguistic point of view, the third irony is an exception that proves Atkinson and Drew's rule about the avoidance of blame. The lineman's immediate acceptance of responsibility was so contrary to everyone's expectations that it became the punch line of an elaborate story. While people might wish for such reactions from those against whom they make claims, they seem to understand that in most cases claiming merely sets the stage for further evolution of the dispute.

At any point in the process of naming, blaming, and claiming, the wronged party may decide to "lump it." *Lumping,* a term widely used in the sociolegal literature (see Miller and Sarat 1980–81:525–26), refers to the possibility that the injured party may decide unilaterally to give up on the dispute and just live with the wrong. The disputing process may seem daunting from the outset, or the aggrieved party may be beaten down by the respondent's attempts to avoid blame. Whatever the cause, lumping remains an option throughout the life of the dispute. When lumping occurs, overt disputing behavior ceases. Lumping may have lingering psychological effects, but the interactional aspects of the dispute come to an end.

But if the wronged party pursues the claim beyond an initial denial or deflection of blame by the accused, what happens next? Another piece of evidence helps illuminate this part of the process. The story in Text 5.4 was told by a plaintiff in a small claims court case. It relates the history of the plaintiff's efforts to assert a claim against a dry cleaner for ruining his suit. He confronted the cleaner with the problem twice. Both times the cleaner denied responsibility, ultimately seeking the support of a third party—a fabric analyst—in denying the man's claim.

TEXT 5.4 (Adapted from Conley and O'Barr 1990:37–38)

> I bought a suit around the last of May. I wore the suit once and sent it to the cleaners. When the suit came back, there was a spot on it. The man at the cleaners told me that there was a defect in the material. I took the suit home and told my wife what the cleaner had said. We agreed that I should take it back again to the cleaners the next day. He agreed to reclean the suit. When it came back a second time no different from the first, the cleaner offered to send it away to have the fabric analyzed. He promised to refund my money if the analysis proved that he was at fault. He got my suit back two weeks later with a report saying that he wasn't at fault but I don't agree.

This story provides some insight into the complexities of claiming in day-to-day contexts. The man hoped for acceptance of his claim. (Why else would he have bothered to assert it twice?) But the cleaner played his role according to the usual interactional script by denying responsibility on each occasion. Linguistically, sequences such as this one are common: claims elicit denials that elicit restated claims that elicit further denials that elicit restated claims—and so on. Through such sequences, claiming can evolve into argument, and the dispute can become hopelessly stalemated.

Some of the best evidence about the nature of argumentation is found in the work of Angela Garcia, which we discussed in chapter 3. Although her work has focused on how mediation alters argumentation, she nonetheless provides insights into the nature of the problem that mediation fixes. Arguments have the potential to continue endlessly because they consist of sequences of accusation-response adjacency pairs. Although an accuser hopes for an acceptance of blame, the usual second part is the opposite: some sort of deflection or denial of blame, often followed by a counteraccusation. When this begins, the back-and-forth of you-did/no-I-didn't/yes-you-did can continue ad infinitum, or at least until one of the parties gives up and decides to lump it. Thus, in the transformation of disputes, the linguistic evidence suggests that argumentation is a likely outcome as an accuser presses a claim. But in the end, argumentation does not solve the problem; each side just continues to restate its position. Beyond putting forth further arguments (or lumping it), one option still remains: turning to the legal system.[10]

What Happens When Disputes Reach the Legal System?

As we have seen, a dispute is likely to pass through several developmental phases before it reaches the legal system. At the very least, the wronged party has to perceive and articulate the problem. Then an equation must be formulated that links the wrong to a responsible party. The claim may be stated to the responsible party directly or through an intermediary, orally or in writing. If the accused does the usual thing and denies responsibility, the accuser must then decide whether to see a lawyer or seek a remedy in an informal, do-it-yourself legal forum such as a small claims court or community mediation center. In either case, turning to the legal system will involve further retellings of the problem to new audiences: lawyers, clerks, mediators, judges, and possibly even jurors. We look next at how the legal system itself interacts with and transforms disputes. The evidence we consider is drawn from detailed studies of the language of disputing in two very different legal environments: the small claims court and the lawyer's office, each of which represents an initial point of contact with the law.

Transformation in the Small Claims Court[11]

Some dissatisfied claimants may turn to a small claims court as their point of entry into the legal system. Although the details of what cases small claims courts can handle vary from state to state, they generally hear simple legal claims involving less than $2,000–3,000. The theory of small claims courts is that people can come to court without lawyers, state their claims in everyday language, and get relief. Consistent with the theory, small claims litigants rarely consult lawyers before coming to court. Some states do not permit lawyers to appear in court; in other states, lawyers are allowed but rarely appear. Small claims judges (who need not even be lawyers in some states) are supposed to conduct hearings in an informal atmosphere; in particular, testimony need not follow the rules of evidence that apply in higher courts.

When a person brings a dispute to a small claims court, her or she is always asked to fill out a complaint form. Although it is represented to be nothing more than a source of background information for the judge, this form, however simple it may be, results in a formalization of the dispute. In many or even most instances, this may be the first time the wronged party has written down what the dispute is about. Such a form requires that the parties be named and that a monetary claim be stated along with some sort of justification for the claim. For example, in one state, the form reads:

PLAINTIFF'S NAME AND ADDRESS

_____

_____

_____

DEFENDANT'S NAME AND ADDRESS

_____

_____

_____

PLAINTIFF'S CLAIM
The Defendant owes me $_____ for the following reasons:

_____

_____

_____

This form imposes a framing of the dispute that may or may not have occurred to the claiming party. The claiming and resisting parties are renamed as, respectively, plaintiff and defendant. The dispute must be reduced to a stated amount of money that the plaintiff claims from the defendant. And the "reasons" underlying the claim must be set out in a few lines.

Claimants respond to this demand for framing in interesting ways. In some instances, the written statement of the claim seems to capture the entirety of the dispute and is consistent with the account later given in court. For example, a North Carolina man sued a dry cleaner for $198.99: "Defendant ruined my wife's new silk dress with his cleaning procedures and he claims no responsibility in this matter." Subsequent retellings stressed the same three elements: the dress was new, it was ruined when the cleaner returned it, and the cleaner refused to accept any responsibility for the damage.

In other cases, the written statement of the claim is cryptic, barely hinting at what might be told in other environments. For example, a woman in Pennsylvania sued a local merchants' service organization for $550: "For the Juneteenth Crowning Ball, and a sponsor's fee." In later tellings in and out of court, the plaintiff explained that her daughter had won a beauty pageant sponsored by the organization and had expected to receive a scholarship as a result. The mother was suing because the organization had refused to pay the amount her daughter had expected to receive. In another case, a Colorado man demanded $750 from a real estate management company for "Rent deposit. Refused for unreasonable excuses." What emerged in court was a very complex story about responsibility—both legal and moral—for defects in an apartment and credit for repairs allegedly made by the tenant. In a third case, a long and complicated dispute between roommates in Pennsylvania was reduced on the form to a $500 claim for "payment of phone bill."

What is most significant about the complaint form is not so much what the claimant actually says, but the fact that the legal system requires him or her to say something and to do so in a specific format. Through the form, the law interacts with the claimant to co-produce an account of the dispute. The law demands a particular kind of claiming, one that reduces the dispute to dollars and cents and that briefly but explicitly states a justification for the claim. By transforming the claimant's account of the dispute in this way, the law—in this very first encounter with the claimant—has already begun to transform the dispute itself. When the case gets to court, the judge will look to the complaint form for an initial understanding of the dispute. Many litigants report that, when judges restate their understandings back to them, they no longer recognize their disputes.

In one city that we studied, the initial encounter with the legal system occurs as an interaction between the claimant and an intake clerk. In this jurisdiction, each person who comes to the courthouse to file a case has a private interview of several minutes' duration with a well-trained clerk. The clerk listens to the claimant's oral account of the dispute and then types a statement of claim in the form that he or she thinks will be most helpful to the judge. The clerk also collects and appends all relevant documents. The claimant then reads and signs the form. The result of this process is illustrated in the following account of a long and sometimes bitterly personal dispute between a homeowner and a roofing contractor.

TEXT 5.5 (From authors' files of small claims complaints)

> On 12/19/85, the pltff. contracted the defendant to put white aluminum cornice 3rd flr. frt. roof. Re-roof kitchen 10x10 ply 2nd flr. guaranteed 5 yrs. & 5 more yrs. brush coat. New eves box, barge board and down spout on 2nd flr roof rear coat $1,080.00 Plaintiff paid deft. $500.00. The deft sub-contracted job, who's [sic] men came to plain-

tiff's property put down less than $75.00 worth of materials, removed barge board, put up aluminum which fell off in a few days. Pltff. received a check from deft. for $250.00 which he did not cash. Pltff. has paid another contractor $1,410.00 to do the job correctly. Pltff. desires deft. to pay him $505.11 with interest, for mailings, $2.11, xeroxing cost, $3.00, court costs because of defendant's breach of contract, water damages, faulty workmanship, etc. See attached exhibits.

This kind of transformation, though more elaborate, is comparable to that effected by the simple complaint form. In both processes, the law exerts its power to demand a particular framing of the dispute. The blaming must be explicit, and the claiming must be monetary. The clerk-interview process ensures in addition that the reason for the blame is something that the law deems significant—in the above example, a breach of contract—and that the elements of the quantified claim are specifically enumerated and documented. The most significant difference between the two processes is that in the interview with the clerk, the interaction and ensuing transformation are more overt and apparent to the claimants. But the unassisted filling out of the form constitutes just as much of an interactive telling, and the transformation of the dispute that results is every bit as real. In both instances, the law as audience plays a critical role in determining what gets said.

The transformative work of the law continues when a small claims case goes to trial. Each litigant is called on to present an account of the dispute to the judge. Trials typically begin with the judge asking the plaintiff a question such as "Why are you bringing this case?" or "Why are you here?" In turn, the judge asks the defendant a question such as "What do you say?" or "What's your side of this?" Such invitations often leave litigants at a loss for words, perhaps because these questions are so different from the subtle techniques that listeners use to facilitate trouble-tellings in everyday contexts. As the trial moves along, however, judges may interact in more conversational ways—for example, by responding to litigants' statements, asking questions, and raising topics. The product—or, more accurately, the co-product—is an account produced jointly by the litigant and the law.

"The law," of course, is not in itself an anthropomorphic being that listens and responds. Rather, the entity we call the law manifests itself in the behavior of legal officials, such as intake clerks and small claims judges. Because these are real people, their orientations and reactions are not uniform, but rather variable in interesting and important ways. In our study of small claims judges, we found much variation in the ways that they interact with litigants and their accounts.[12] The most significant difference is between those judges who see their authority as closely circumscribed by legal rules that they must apply rigorously and those who believe that they have a broader mandate to disregard the letter of the law in pursuit of "just" outcomes.

Judges who see themselves as rule-bound often work to frame litigants' accounts within categories to which rules will apply. Such judges typically respond with interest and affirmation when litigants talk about contracts, property lines, or documents, but they react passively or negatively when litigants seek to introduce lengthy personal histories into their accounts. Rule-bound judges frequently told us that litigants who sought to mix the personal and the legal were unfocused, unintelligent, or even crazy.

Among those judges who have a broader conception of their role, some pursue personal moral agendas, whereas others see consensus-for-consensus's-sake as the highest value. Those pursuing personal agendas react to litigant accounts in unpredictable ways. For example, a single mother who was a defendant in a debt collection action began to tell of the ways in which the legal and welfare systems had failed her. The judge, who regularly decided cases on the basis of his personal moral values, deflected her account by asking why she kept having babies.[13]

Judges who seek consensus are most attentive to those aspects of litigant accounts that hold some promise of compromise regardless of whether the issues are relevant to some potential rule of decision. When a litigant expresses some ambivalence about one of his or her demands, for example, the judge may try to develop the point through expressions of support and elaborating questions. A similar reaction may be evoked when a defendant expresses agreement with a prior statement by the plaintiff. Consensus-oriented judges frequently offer to suspend the hearing so that the parties can talk privately. They may also "preview" the possible legal outcome of the case and urge the parties to settle on similar terms.

The general point is that all types of judges interact with litigants to transform the disputes before them regardless of whether the judge stresses legal rules, personal values, or the process of conciliation. Although the account of the dispute that emerges in the small claims courtroom is likely to be very different from versions told earlier in the disputing process, it will be yet another co-produced account. In this critical linguistic respect, the role of the judge is no different from that of the neighbor across the back fence or the spouse at the dinner table who might have participated in previous transformations.

Transformation in the Lawyer's Office

Another point of entry into the legal system—and therefore a potential locus of transformation—is the lawyer's office. In their recent book *Divorce Lawyers and Their Clients,* Sarat and Felstiner (1995) show that the interaction between client and lawyer is above all a contest between competing discourses. By approaching a lawyer in the first place, a lay person acknowledges that he or she wants a legal remedy for a problem. The lawyer listens and responds to what the client says through a template built of legal understandings and framing mechanisms. Whether or not the client's problem ultimately ends up in court, the encounter with a lawyer produces linguistic transformations similar to those observed in small claims courts.

For many people, this encounter with law-in-practice is a jarring experience. As they attempt to tell about the trouble that brings them to the lawyer's office, they do not always find sympathetic, affirming listeners such as those described by Jefferson. Rather, they often find themselves telling their stories to professionals who value distance over affiliation and control over support.

In a study of more than forty divorce cases, Sarat and Felstiner found two overarching ways in which lawyers transform their clients' disputes. First, whereas clients typically frame disputes in terms of moral blame and legal rights, lawyers use a variety of linguistic strategies to recast them as battles over such tangible issues as houses, support payments, and visitation schedules. Second, while clients' initial accounts usually envision cases as going to trial and being decided by judges or juries, lawyers are constantly at work in subtle ways to move clients around to the view that settlement is preferable to adjudication. Significantly, lawyers almost never tell clients that they are wrong or that they must repudiate their view of the case. Instead, they induce clients to volunteer successive new accounts of their cases until the tellings that emerge are compatible with the discourse of lawyers. By imposing changes on their clients' microdiscourse, lawyers effect a shift in the macrodiscourse of the disputes.

One linguistic strategy that the lawyer employs to change the focus of the dispute from moral to tangible issues is to offer unsupportive responses to a client's rhetoric about blame. In Text 5.6, a wife provides a poignant moral account of why the marriage failed. Her lawyer responds neutrally to this information and then changes the subject.

TEXT 5.6 (Sarat and Felstiner 1995:32)

> CLIENT: There was a harassment and verbal degradation. No
> interest at all in my furthering my education. None whatsoever.
> Sexual harassment. If there was ever any time when I did not
> want or need sex, I was subject to these long verbal whip lash-
> 5   ings. Then the Bible would be put out on the counter with pas-
> sages underlined as to what a poor wife I was. Just constant
> harassment from him.
> LAWYER: Mmn-uh.
> CLIENT: Then he undertook to lecturing me, and I'd say, "I don't
> 10   want to hear this. I don't have time right now." I could lock my-
> self in the bathroom and he would break in. And I was just to
> listen, whether I wanted to or not. And he would lecture me for

hours. Literally hours. There was no escaping him, short of getting in a car and driving away. But then he would stand outside in
15   the driveway and yell, anyhow. The man was not well.
LAWYER: Okay. Now how about any courses you took?

By contrast, in Text 5.7, when the client's talk focuses on the disposition of
common property, the lawyer's neutrality is replaced by supportive and encouraging responses.

TEXT 5.7 (Sarat and Felstiner 1995:38)

LAWYER: Have you discussed any more getting rid of the van and
getting yourself another vehicle?
CLIENT: Yes. I talked it over with him, and asked if he would be
willing to release the van if I were to find a car.
5   LAWYER: Yeah.
CLIENT: And he said, "If he thought it was a fair deal, or a decent
deal," or something. And I said, "Well, if I'm going to be making
the car payments, what does it have to do with you? All I want
from you is to release the van." He still wants that control.
10   LAWYER: He's looking at everything as dollar signs. Pretty typical
reaction. He's going to be defensive on all those things. Have you
been looking for vehicles?

Lawyers may also deflect client rhetoric about morality and blame by bringing the talk back around to the legal process. In Text 5.8, a husband refers to
his wife's character defects in an effort to explain her refusal to negotiate a
property settlement. The lawyer ignores this theme. Without commenting on
the client's assessment of the wife, the lawyer instead responds with a procedural suggestion about how to move more quickly toward settlement.

TEXT 5.8 (Sarat and Felstiner 1995:39)

LAWYER: What would happen if the two of you sat down and
started talking?
CLIENT: Well, anytime we've ever had discussions, they always
turn into arguments. There are a number of other things besides
5   the getting a job issue that I feel are inequitable in our relationship. On the rare occasions that she actually listens, she's not a
good listener. When she actually listens and senses that she'd better change her ways, that may last for a week before it's back to
the same old thing. And she's tied up with her hobbies. We were
10   really broke this winter, and I tried to discuss it with her. She
said I should go see a financial counselor. She one evening said,
"Well, when I get my inheritance I should share that with you."
And I said, "Well, that would help." But then she'd just start

ranting and raving, as if I had the nerve to consider that any of her
15   inheritance would be mine. So she doesn't mean it when she does
ever make a concession. And it's very temporary and fleeting.
LAWYER: Maybe she'd make a stronger commitment to a counselor that can listen to your two points of view.

Throughout their dealings with clients, lawyers enhance their authority by stressing their knowledge, skill, and expertise. Perhaps surprisingly, they rarely base their authority on their knowledge of legal rules. Rather, they freely admit that "official" rules almost never determine outcomes. They emphasize instead their familiarity with the pragmatic details of how the system "really" works. This doubles the client's dependency: he or she must rely on the lawyer not only to deal with the law's official rules but also to negotiate the subtle but informal practices that actually determine outcomes.

This relationship of client to lawyer is illustrated in Text 5.9, in which the lawyer counsels a wife whose husband has just obtained a restraining order keeping her away from the marital home. The wife, who is confused and outraged, asks two apparently straightforward legal questions. The lawyer's responses show off his mastery of the court's basic procedures, as well as his special access to insider knowledge.

TEXT 5.9 (Sarat and Felstiner 1995:89)

CLIENT: How often does a case like this come along—a restraining order of this nature?
LAWYER: Very common.
CLIENT: It's a very common thing. So how many other people are
5   getting the same kind of treatment I am? With what, I presume, is
very sloppily handled orders that are passed out.
LAWYER: I did talk to someone in the know—I won't go any further than that—who said that this one could have been signed
purely by accident. I mean, that the judge could have—if he
10   looked at it now—said, "I would not sign that," and it could have
been signed by accident. I said, "Well, then how does that happen?" And he said, "You've got all this stuff going; you come
back to your office, and there's a stack of documents that need
signatures. . . . There's someone else that needs your attention, so
15   you go through them, and one of the main things you look for is
the law firm or lawyer who is proposing them. And you tend to
rely on them."

By increasing the client's dependency, such assertions of authority support the lawyer's efforts to move the client's focus from moral to tangible issues. If the law as practiced is indeed an all-but-impenetrable enigma, then what basis can the client have for resisting the lawyer's reframing of the dispute? The same strategy can also help the lawyer achieve a second major objective: positioning the client to forgo an adversarial confrontation and accept settlement.

This evidence from Sarat and Felstiner's study of talk in divorce lawyers' offices provides another window on the interactional details of how disputes are transformed through encounters with the law. Lawyers' ways of responding condition and shape clients' accounts and attitudes. Subtly, the lawyers advance a particular view of rights and wrongs and of the solutions that should be effected. Clients' stories about blame and moral responsibility for marital troubles get cool receptions. Instead, lawyers encourage talk about property and settlement strategies. They also emphasize aspects of law and the legal process that make them indispensable to the solution of their clients' problems. Their discourse embodies a view of law as flexible and indeterminate and of legal processes as liable to be influenced by the personalities and prejudices of particular judges.[14] Although a sampling of interactions between divorce lawyers and their clients is hardly a basis for strong universal claims, the evidence that Sarat and Felstiner adduce is surely indicative of the kinds of transformations that occur when lay clients bring other kinds of problems to legal professionals.

Reflections on Transformations

In this chapter, we have explored the evolution of a dispute from its early phases of naming, blaming, and claiming through the further transformations that the legal system effects. It has become evident, we hope, that a dispute does not exist in isolation from the contexts in which it is expressed. Rather, the account of a dispute that is given at any point in time *is* the dispute. All the contexts in which a dispute is expressed are interactional, and each such context shapes the dispute in unique ways.

Additional evidence about how the legal system transforms disputes comes from what litigants have to say after their cases have moved through the legal process. In these moments, litigants reflect on what has happened to them and on their efforts to achieve justice. As a part of our study of small claims courts a few years ago (Conley and O'Barr 1990), we interviewed litigants after their cases were decided. We sought to understand how their actual experiences with the law differed from the expectations they had going into the legal process. What the litigants told us in these interviews[15] adds a final note to the study of dispute transformation.

First, litigants expressed surprise that the accounts given by opposing parties had managed to transform the dispute. Before going to court, they had understood their disputes only from their own points of view; indeed, many litigants had failed to imagine that there might be alternative perspectives, let alone what accounts given from those perspectives might sound like. So confident were they in the inherent truth of their own stories that they had not contemplated the possibility of counternarratives that might have their own plausibility. Only after the fact did they realize that these counternarratives had so altered the courtroom discourse as to create new disputes whose form and content were unforeseen and often unnerving. We heard the same lament again and again: "The case that came out in court wasn't the one that I filed; maybe I should've known that this would happen, but I didn't."

Second, we learned that people had not foreseen that the law itself would have a similar transforming effect, reworking their stories into disputes that were sometimes unrecognizable. When these litigants filed their cases, things had seemed straightforward: they had been wronged; the opposing parties were at fault, had failed to rectify the problems, and needed to be punished in some way. They had been unprepared for how the law would strip their stories of their emotional and evaluative dimensions. They had been equally unprepared for the way in which the courts would shift the focus of their cases from such global issues as moral probity and social responsibility to specific questions about contractual language and monetary remedies. Once again, there was a recurrent theme: "The judge didn't want to hear what I had planned to say; he kept asking about things that had nothing to do with the problem."

Third, litigants—both winners and losers—often expressed dismay about the way that judges had responded to their stories. They had imagined that the inherent veracity of their own narratives would carry the day. They had expected, it seemed, that judges would have no recourse but to affirm and agree with their stories. They had failed to appreciate that judges might sit impassively as they talked or respond neutrally to what they had to say. When it happened, as it often did, that judges sided with the opposing parties—by seeming to assist them in getting out their counternarratives or by finding in their favor at the moment of decision—they were dumbfounded. The complaint was usually along these lines : "I can't believe that the judge paid any attention to what those people were saying; it was so obviously a bunch of lies."

The litigants we interviewed thus recognized, at least after the fact, that the legal process had changed the nature of their disputes. They identified three sets of agents who had collaborated in this transformation: the opposing parties, the normative requirements of the law, and the judges. In revealing these discoveries to us, the litigants reaffirmed the fundamental principle that disputes have no life separate from their particular tellings in specific contexts.

But how do litigants explain this transformation process to themselves? In particular, how do they account for what has happened to them and deal with their failure to foresee it? One obvious response would be to blame the system, to say that the law is an oppressive institution with no concern for justice. This was not what the litigants told us, however. What they did instead was to blame themselves or the particular judges who had heard their cases. The litigants held themselves responsible for their failure to prepare for the transformations their stories had undergone. Many also criticized the judges for failing to help them, usually adding that other, "better" judges would have done more.

Whatever its therapeutic value for litigants, this personalizing reaction to adverse experiences clearly works to the benefit of the system. This focus on the microdiscourse of the dispute deflects attention away from analysis of the macrodiscourse of the legal process itself. It precludes a consciousness of law that understands such experiences as inherent in the nature of law and legal practice. Such an understanding might promote resistance to the power of the law. Instead, the litigants' personalization of the difficulties they experienced leaves the law's hegemony unchallenged.

Although the litigants' analyses may have the unintended consequence of promoting the status quo, they are in another respect unusually perceptive. By individualizing their experiences, they call attention to the fact that the law's power is realized through concrete linguistic events. And when they reconcile themselves to the system by blaming their problems on themselves, they demonstrate that those linguistic events not only reflect but also reaffirm the law's power.

Conclusion: Toward a Natural History of Disputing

We began this chapter by reviewing the *naming-blaming-claiming* model that has shaped the analysis of dispute transformation for more than fifteen years. We then considered what is known linguistically about the processes of naming, blaming, and claiming, as well as about subsequent phases of disputing not covered by the original Felstiner-Abel-Sarat model. We are now in a position to propose a model of our own. Our model, which is summarized in the figure below, is based on linguistic and ethnographic evidence. Its purpose is to

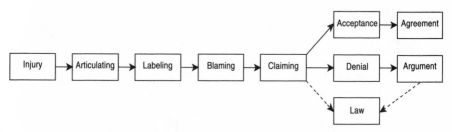

Notes: Lumping can occur at any point.
          Articulating and labeling are both included in Felstiner, Abel, and Sarat's
          (1980–81) "naming" stage.

elaborate on and extend the original: elaborate on by offering additional empirical depth, and extend by tracking a dispute past the point of claiming and through its final disposition. To emphasize its empirical derivation, we call the model a *natural history of disputing*.[16]

The naming-blaming-claiming continuum forms the core of the new model. We have added the antecedent phase *perceiving the injury* and have separated *articulating* and *labeling* from each other. We then follow the dispute beyond the claiming stage to delineate two possible outcomes: acceptance, leading to agreement, and denial, leading to argument. Recourse to law and lumping are options at various phases.

Like all models, this one has its limitations. The real world is so complex and the variations on what can and does happen are so numerous that it is impossible to account for all the possibilities. We make no claim to have covered every contingency in the life of a dispute or to have brought every relevant piece of empirical evidence into our formulation. Our more limited objective is the same one we have pursued throughout this book: to challenge existing ways of thinking about legal processes by paying closer attention to their linguistic details.

CHAPTER SIX

The Discourses of Law in Cross-Cultural Perspective

Thus far, we have considered the multiple discourses of law solely from an Anglo-American perspective. We have relied entirely on English-language evidence from American and English legal proceedings to develop the argument that the linguistic practice of the law reflects, reproduces, and sometimes challenges its dominant ideals. In this chapter, we explore the cross-cultural applicability of this approach. Specifically, we ask whether it is possible to dissect the linguistic enactment of legal power in the non-Western societies that have been the traditional concern of legal anthropology and, if so, how legal anthropology's received knowledge would hold up in the face of such analysis.

A useful starting point may be to ask, What do we think we know about legal discourse from a cross-cultural point of view? The answer is that we—that is, the sociolegal community, particularly legal anthropologists—think we know quite a bit about both the theory and the practice of non-Western law.[1] To illustrate the point, consider the contributions of five of the most important figures in the history of legal anthropology: Karl Llewellyn, E. A. Hoebel, Max Gluckman, Paul Bohannan, and Laura Nader.

In *The Cheyenne Way,* Llewellyn and Hoebel (1961, orig. 1941) tried to reconstruct the "law-ways" of a Cheyenne culture that had disappeared more than fifty years before they did their research. Their principal resource was the memories of elderly Cheyennes who had observed or, more often, heard about "cases of hitch or trouble" (Llewellyn and Hoebel 1961:26). These memories became the basis of a detailed theory of legal principles and dispute resolution. Several years later Gluckman published *The Judicial Process among the Barotse of Northern Rhodesia (Zambia)* (1955). On the basis of his own observation of contemporary cases, Gluckman claimed to have discovered the

Anglo-American concept of "the reasonable man" in the jurisprudence of a Zimbabwean society. Gluckman was subsequently taken to task by Bohannan (1969) for imposing Western legal categories on the Barotse materials, and a famous debate ensued. Drawing on his work with the Tiv of Nigeria (Bohannan 1989, orig. 1957), Bohannan argued that each society's legal categories are unique and therefore not even translatable; Gluckman (1969) continued to insist that his cross-cultural comparison was both appropriate and correct. Significantly, neither questioned the other's ability to lay claim to an understanding of the logic of a non-Western legal system. The final example, Nader's *Harmony Ideology and the Construction of the Law* (1990), explores the complex legal ideology of Mexico's Zapotec people. Her thesis is that as a legacy of colonialism, the Zapotec idealize harmony as the ultimate end of law and that this ideology defuses challenges to the status quo.

Our point in mentioning these canonical works is an epistemological one: the intellectual claims of legal anthropology are exceedingly robust. As these few examples illustrate, for more than fifty years legal anthropology has claimed insight into the principles, procedures, decision-making logic, and ideology of non-Western law. All of these topics are contentious ones in our own society, of course, the subject of never-ending debate among legal scholars. If wisdom is so elusive when we are looking at our legal system, which operates in our own language, it seems only reasonable to look critically at the basis for legal anthropology's claims. In other words, *how* does legal anthropology know what it purports to know?

The short answer is "ethnography." At least since Bronislaw Malinoswki's *Crime and Custom in Savage Society* (1985, orig. 1926), legal anthropology has relied on patient fieldwork by participant observers. Its claim to authenticity relies on the ethnographer's opportunity to see and hear disputes evolve and to watch, transcribe, and (at least in recent years) record legal proceedings. But how deep has this ethnography been? Inferences about issues such as decision-making logic and ideology are statements about the discourse of law in a particular society. Has the ethnography penetrated far enough toward the level of linguistic practice to justify such inferences? Is the ethnography linguistically rich enough to show us how the dominant discourses of law are reproduced, reaffirmed, challenged, and transformed in other societies?

To be fair, legal anthropology has always been sensitive to these questions. Back in 1926, Malinowski railed against relying on informants who "retail the Ideal of the law" (1985:120); he argued that the ethnographer must take care to test the informant's report against the evidence of actual disputes. In the 1950s and 1960s, the Gluckman-Bohannan debate took the methodological self-consciousness of legal anthropology to a more sophisticated level. Whereas Malinowski seemed to be drawing a contrast between subjective and objective knowledge of another society's law, Gluckman and Bohannan argued over the very possibility of knowledge. Gluckman, analyzing his Barotse cases, claimed to see Anglo-American tort law's "reasonable man" standard operating there as well. Bohannan, arguing from his Tiv materials, suggested that such comparisons are inevitably infected by the epistemological biases of the analyst, and therefore suspect. In other words, once we open up the possibility of comparing other societies' legal reasoning to our own, we tend to see what we want to see. According to Bohannan, it is better to leave native legal concepts untranslated, to be appreciated on their own terms.

The Gluckman-Bohannan debate has continued in updated versions (see, for example, Comaroff and Roberts 1981:6–11). Current legal ethnographies such as Nader's *Harmony Ideology* exhibit sensitivity to the full range of contemporary concerns about the contingent nature of knowledge. But even as legal anthropology has become more thoughtful in questioning the bases of what it claims to know, a gap has remained. Sociolinguist Brenda Danet put her finger on the problem in an influential review essay published in 1980. Commenting on the anthropological analysis of the role of questioning in dispute processes, she observed: "Most of the anthropological literature is insufficiently detailed to permit precise statements about the nature of the procedures" (Danet 1980a:516). In reviewing the work of a number of ethnographers, Danet (1980a:516–18) made statements such as these:

> We know little about the exact conditions under which claim construction is transformed from direct argument to some combination of direct argument and indirect claims made in response to questions.

> In Kpelle trials . . . Gibbs [1962, 1967] provides no information on the exact structure of questioning or the rules that govern turn-taking.

> Despite a wealth of materials on Lozi court cases, however, [Gluckman (1955, 1965, 1973)] does not describe the exact sequence of events in court. . . .

> Yakan litigation also combines narrative presentation of claims with questioning, though Frake (1969) gives no details on the latter.

Danet's point seems to be that as of 1980 legal anthropologists had rarely given us the kind of linguistic data necessary to evaluate their claims. An examination of a more recent legal ethnography such as Nader's suggests that not much has changed.[2] We are given rich descriptions of "cases" that state the underlying "facts" of the dispute; report the court proceedings, often with generous quotations from the principals; present the result and rationale given by the decision maker; and sometimes provide an epilogue about the subsequent relations of the disputants. However rich the description, though, there is a vast gap between the linguistic practice that constituted the actual dispute and what is made available to the reader. Most of that practice is summarized or paraphrased; the speech that is reported directly is translated into idiomatic English. The reader must put a great deal of trust in the ethnographer.

There are many reasons why the presentational style of legal anthropology has developed as it has. The case-reporting strategy described above is exactly what is found in the published decisions of Anglo-American courts. The law professor Llewellyn brought the case method to the Cheyenne materials; the legally trained Gluckman took it to Zimbabwe. It would be unfair to suggest that these and other legal anthropologists have been thoughtlessly imposing a familiar method on data from other societies. On the contrary, it has always seemed to fit. In the preface to the 1989 edition of *Justice and Judgment among the Tiv*, Bohannan captured the prevailing sentiment with characteristic eloquence:

> I used the case method first because I admired the method as it had been used by Llewellyn and Hoebel in *The Cheyenne Way*, and I had been taught it by Max Gluckman. Moreover, the Tiv drove me to the case method. My self-assigned task was to discover as much as I could about what they were interested in. They put a lot of their time and effort into cases. (1989: vii)

An additional reason for adopting the law's case-reporting conventions has to do with sample size concerns. Conventional social science wisdom holds that the more instances that can be cited in support of an interpretive argument, the more persuasive it becomes. However, publishers, teachers, and students all prefer short books. Thus, if you are going to rely on numerous cases to make your point, you must condense them. Extended transcripts are casualties in the quest for a broader base of support.

Technological limits have been another factor working in favor of the summary approach. For much of the history of legal anthropology, recording equipment was unavailable or impractical. Even when it has been available, the desirability of using it has been questioned. We turn once again to Bohannan, this time in his preface to the original edition of *Justice and Judgment among the Tiv:*

> By other techniques, such as sound recording, it would have been possible to get fuller transcriptions of the cases. I am not sure that it would be desirable, for I have found, in trying to use it, that gadgetry so absorbs the attention of the field worker that it is very easy for him to forget that he must gear his life to the people he is studying, not to his gadgets. . . . The only sensible gadget for doing anthropological research is the human understanding and a notebook. Anthropology provides an artistic impression of the original, not a photographic one. I am not a camera. (1989: xxiii, orig. 1957)

Others have made the related argument that raw transcription produces more data than the anthropologist can intelligently interpret (e.g., Epstein 1967:222).

Some scholars have refused to accept these principled defenses of legal anthropology's reliance on summary and paraphrase. In a strongly worded critique in 1975, David Turton wondered whether ethnographers of law and politics were not simply covering up the fact that they were not fluent in their subjects' languages. Considering the question of why anthropologists have given little attention to public political discussions, Turton wrote:

> I should offer some explanation as to why this whole subject has been overlooked, even by those anthropologists who have presumably had to sit through many hours of political oratory during the course of their fieldwork. It could be, of course, that after due study and consideration they came to the conclusion that this public discussion was mere window dressing, masking the underlying principles of social organisation. They may have been helped to this conclusion by observing that there is very little element of surprise in the decisions reached by public meetings—that the decisions are, more often than not, foregone conclusions. From personal experience, however, I think it is just as likely that the anthropologists concerned simply did not, and indeed could not, understand well enough what was going on in public discussions until it was too late. (1975:164)

Turton's concern cannot be lightly dismissed. Think about the difficulty that even educated lay people—native speakers of English—have following the proceedings in American courts. Now add to this inherent difficulty the problems faced by an anthropologist who may have had only a few months' experience with the radically unfamiliar language in which the court is being conducted. Bohannan wrote in 1957: "My wife and I used no interpreters among the Tiv until we had been with them for almost a year. By that time we spoke Tiv quite fluently and understood it well" (1989:xxi). How many legal anthropologists could say this? How many could claim the kind of fluency that Turton argued for? We must at least consider the possibility that some of our canonical knowledge is suspect because the researchers did not fully understand what was being said.

Whether because of conscious methodological choice or communication difficulties, the present record of legal anthropology is not one that permits much analysis of the details of the discourse of legal proceedings. The potential consequences of this state of affairs are obvious. First, our ability to evaluate the discipline's claims about law and legal procedure is impaired. Suppose, for example, that we want to ask whether there really was a "reasonable man" in Barotse jurisprudence. For all the breadth and depth of Gluckman's cases, we still cannot pursue the question with the same intensity that Gregory Matoesian brings to the issue of the revictimization of American rape victims. Even

Bohannan, with his very real concern for the authentic Tiv perspective, does not afford us this luxury. As we contemplate instance after instance, we are left wondering whether the whole field of comparative law might not look different if the data permitted us to test claims about law and legal discourse on the microlinguistic level.

The state of the ethnographic record may also have compromised legal anthropology's concept of culture. Most classic ethnographies of law suggest a cultural model wherein rules direct action. The contentions of litigants and the decisions of Tiv *jirs,* Barotse courts, and Cheyenne councils are explained in terms of the substantive principles and forms of argument that comprise part of every member's cultural literacy. There are moments of resistance and opportunities for change, but it is clear that rules direct action, and not vice versa.

The current idea of culture is considerably messier. In a study of police culture, criminologists Clifford Shearing and Richard Ericson (1991) provide a fascinating example of the application of contemporary notions of culture in a law-related context. They look closely at the stories that police officers tell about how they do their jobs. Sets of rules prove to be too simple to account for the cultural knowledge that these stories reflect. Instead, "[s]omehow competent officers know what to do" (Shearing and Ericson 1991:487). In their effort to understand what the officers know and how they know it, Shearing and Ericson ask, "What if we took police stories seriously as *stories?*" (1991:488). Some stories, they find, are merely short-lived descriptions of the world as police officers experience it. Others are told and retold until they reach mythic status as "carefully crafted poetic pieces that capture the insights and wisdom of countless officers who have, through their telling of it, embellished and polished the story" (Shearing and Ericson 1991:491). Stories are thus revealed to be both reflections of the police officers' world and resources for reproducing and sometimes transforming it.

Reflecting on what police stories suggest about the nature of culture, Shearing and Ericson reject the image of officers learning rules, which they then follow or violate. Rather, "they are active participants in the construction of action" (Shearing and Ericson 1991:500). The stories provide open-ended information to other members of the police culture—"gambits and strategies" that they can use in constructing culturally appropriate action in new and often unforeseen circumstances. Culture itself is less a set of rules than a flexible set of resources, "a poetic system that enables action through a trope and precedent based logic" (Shearing and Ericson 1991:500). Importantly, it is the stories—the linguistic practice—that enable the interpretation of culture, and not the other way around. We are left to wonder whether legal anthropology's understanding of culture may have been impoverished by the unavailability of equivalent stories.

Questioning Huli Women

Laurence Goldman is perhaps the most strident current advocate of the view that the record of legal anthropology is linguistically inadequate. Remarking caustically on Bohannan's claim a generation ago that the "literature in legal anthropology [was] small and almost all good" (1964:199), Goldman has written that "this same and now large corpus of works is, in certain critical and fundamental respects, inadequate and almost all bad" (1986:350). That inadequacy derives from "problems of legitimation and ethnographic reliability" (Goldman 1986:350)—in particular the absence of authentic discourse from case reports.

In his initial effort to prove the point, Goldman (1986) examined gender dynamics in the dispute processes of the Huli, a people of highland Papua New Guinea. His investigation begins in the informal, ad hoc public moots, where many disputes are heard and mediated. Goldman notes that the traditional ethnographic view has held that the moots are a striking instance of gender equity in a society that "in most domains is typified by a rigid role differentiation along sexual lines" (Goldman 1986:355). A preliminary analysis tends to support this view. For example, although only men can serve as mediators, women may speak as disputants, witnesses, or supporters, and the stated norms for receiving their testimony are strongly egalitarian. Moreover, the moot procedure seems unchoreographed. Litigants present their claims in many ways, and there are no preset rules for deciding who talks when. Consistent with the open-ended nature of the process, "women are not subject to any constraint on the length, locale or format of their speaking turns" (Goldman 1986:355).

In 1973, the national government created a multilevel official legal system to function alongside the moots. Village courts comprise the lowest level of the government system. Although their stated purpose is to mediate informally in the manner of the moots, the village courts have evolved into adjudicatory rather than conciliatory bodies. Significantly, village court procedure quickly moved away from the unrestricted conversation of the moots and toward the controlled question-and-answer style (Goldman calls it "ping-pong") characteristic of Western courts.

Among the questions Goldman poses are, first, whether the reputedly egalitarian norms of the moots have been carried over to the village courts and, second, whether the moots actually practice the gender equity that is conventionally attributed to them. After a study of question forms in cases involving illicit premarital sex that is strikingly similar to Matoesian's work on rape trials, Goldman answers both questions in the negative.

With respect to the first question, Goldman's data on the distributional patterns of question forms are especially compelling. He reports initially that questions in general are four times more common in village courts than in moots. This confirms the accepted view that the village courts have gravitated toward foreign procedures.[3] Goldman also finds that in the village courts almost four times as many questions are addressed to women as to men. Because so many of the questions asked of women involve "the extraction of a high degree of detail about the sexual acts committed," he concludes that they reflect an "attempt to shame women" (Goldman 1986:375). Finally, examining the use of WH questions (who, what, where, when, why, how) in village courts, Goldman (1986:377) notes that "why" questions are commonly put to women but *never* to men. The reason for this disparity, he believes, is that women are made to feel that they must explain their actions, while men are comfortable leaving their motives ambiguous: "they leave it up to their 'male' audience to construct possible reasons for their actions" (Goldman 1986:377).

Addressing the second issue—whether even the moots really are egalitarian—Goldman finds that comparable, if subtler, gender inequities are present in the linguistic practice of the moots. For example, questions that take the form of declarative statements with interrogative intonation are put to women much more often than to men. Goldman believes such questions to be coercive because "they tell more than they ask" (Goldman 1986:375). He also examines relative frequencies of "affirmative/negative" questions, which call for yes-no answers, versus types of questions that permit more discursive answers and even invite the display of rhetorical skills. The former, which are inherently more controlling and coercive, are directed at women substantially more often than at men. Goldman further notes that, when affirmative/negative questions are put to men, they are often softened or "rendered non-confrontative"; thus, the coercive form is revealed to be "the dispreferred form for soliciting responses from male addressees" (1986:375).

Having reviewed these and numerous other details of question structure, Goldman concludes that there is a "remarkable degree of fit or internal consistency . . . in terms of the hypothesis that, on the evidence of interrogative form, both moots and courts are more coercive of women" than men (1986:377). As between moots and village courts, he finds that the deferential, nonconfrontational style of the former has been carried over to the latter only in instances of interaction with men. Thus, the ideology of gender equality is an illusion in both venues, and even the egalitarian formalities have disappeared in the village courts. But the illusion can be appreciated only through the microanalysis of the actual language of disputing.

Goldman sees a relationship between these microlinguistic practices and the dominant discourse of gender relations among the Huli: "One could go on to argue that this [linguistic coercion of women] is related to male power or discriminatory ideologies typical of Highlands [New Guinea] societies. The interrogative process becomes a means of playing out inter-sex dramas, the process *is* the punitive repercussion of male power" (Goldman 1986:377). In other words, the interrogative process not only exemplifies the partiarchy of Huli society but also helps to ratify and reproduce it.

As in the Anglo-American cases we have examined, linguistic practice is both effect and cause of the dominant discourse about Huli gender relations. And as in those cases, new insights into that discourse have been made possible only by detailed linguistic analysis. This is a level of analysis, Goldman argues convincingly, that has been absent from legal ethnography, perhaps by conscious choice or perhaps because of a lack of understanding of what people are saying.

Goldman on Accident

In subsequent work on Huli law, Goldman has continued to press the point that a meaningful understanding of law needs to be based on a genuine appreciation of the discourse that constitutes it—whether that discourse takes place in English or some other language. In his recent book *The Culture of Coincidence* (Goldman 1993), Goldman uses Huli linguistic data to attack a widely accepted precept of comparative jurisprudence: the idea that non-Western people do not recognize the possibility of accident.

According to this traditional view, as Goldman describes it, the non-Western legal mind cannot accept that an injury has occurred for no reason at all, but instead insists on finding a responsible agent. Sometimes the agent is a human being who both intends and causes (in a Newtonian sense) the injury, as in the case of a person who deliberately strikes another with a rock. This kind of responsibility is compatible with Western notions of fault. In other cases, however, there is no evidence of an agent of this conventional sort. In such cases, the traditional analysis holds, non-Western legal reasoning assumes that someone must have used supernatural means to cause the harm and seeks out likely suspects. When a plausible candidate is found, that person is held responsible, regardless of whether he or she actually caused the harm through intent or negligence. The idea of accident—that is, the occurrence of misfortune without a human agent behind it—is claimed to be missing in most non-Western societies. (This is not to say that Westerners do not prefer to assign blame, but merely that they recognize cases in which accident must be the accepted explanation.)

For example, in a case reported from the Brazilian Kuikuru (Dole 1966:76), when two houses in a village burned down, there was no thought that it was just an accident. Instead, a shaman conducted a divining ceremony during which he conversed with interested members of the community and then fell into a trance. He named as the culprit a man who had left the village several years ago and never returned. Because changing residence was regarded as an admission of being a troublemaker, the shaman's explanation met with general acceptance; Sherlock Holmes–style questions about whether the suspect could really have "done it" were never raised. The traditional view thus ascribes to non-Western legal systems a theory of strict liability. Liability is strict in two senses: someone must be liable for every harm, and a suspect cannot avoid liability by saying that he did not intend the injury or was not physically responsible for it.

To set the stage for his examination of Huli legal discourse, Goldman revisits some of the great classics of anthropology and their arguments about the role of accident in non-Western law. The idea that the non-Western mind cannot accept accident dates back at least to Lucien Lévy-Bruhl's *La mentalité primitive* (1923). In a passage Goldman (1993:45) quotes at length, Lévy-Bruhl wrote:

> "[T]he very idea of accident is inconceivable to the primitive mind. . . . In fact, there is no such thing as chance. The idea of accident does not even occur to a native's mind, while on the contrary the idea of witchcraft is always present."

The most famous ethnographic explication of Lévy-Bruhl's theory is E. E. Evans-Pritchard's *Witchcraft, Oracles, and Magic among the Azande* (1937). His prototype of Azande reasoning about misfortune was the case of the falling granary. A man was sitting in the shade beside an elevated grain storage vessel. As the man leaned on the granary, one of its wooden supports broke. The heavy granary toppled over, killing the man. In such instances, how do the Azande explain what has happened? They do not, Evans-Pritchard asserted, call them accidents, as we almost certainly would. Rather, the Azande see these occurrences as manifestations of the supernatural powers of witches. Such happenings occasion searches for the human agents whose evil intentions were played out through witchcraft. In the end, every death and serious illness is someone's responsibility. Things do not just happen; people make them happen through the machinations of witchcraft.

But just how did Evans-Pritchard come to these conclusions about Azande thought? What sort of data did he collect, and how? How did he analyze the data? Asking such questions leads into the now-familiar territory of reflexive anthropology, where it is fashionable to dismiss nearly all that has come before as hopelessly biased and irretrievably useless. If we reexamine Evans-Pritchard according to those standards, we learn that much of his work was conducted on the veranda of his house or in front of his tent, through interpreters, and that he did not know much about the Azande language. It now seems clear that he did not know enough to avoid subtle misunderstandings of how the Azande talk and reason about misfortune. Perhaps the "Azande" theory of misfortune, which has become a paradigm case in the anthropological literature, would be unfamiliar to the Azande themselves.

Goldman (1993:66–67) documents the export of Evans-Pritchard's Azande model—with all its faults—to other African societies and later to the Melanesian ethnographic literature. Even the hill tribes of Papua New Guinea, the neighbors of the Huli, are said to conform to the Azande paradigm. In case after case, ethnographers report the rejection of accident in favor of strict liability. For example:

> [N]o distinction appeared to be drawn between intentional and unintentional killing, as among the Kikuyu, Kamba and certain Nigerian tribes. . . .

> [A]mong the Arusha "no jural distinction" is made between premeditated and accidental homicide. . . .

> Among the Ashanti, all accidents are understood as ultimately the result of offences against supernatural agencies. . . .

> "[T]he Melanesian view about compensation for injury caused to person or property is far more like one of absolute liability than liability based on fault" . . . .

> [T]he Jale [of New Guinea] . . . do not "distinguish between intent, negligence, inadvertence, and accident as aggravating or extenuating circumstances". . . .

Cases such as these lead to an impression of fundamental differences between *us* and *them.* They become the basis for arguing that *our* legal system is rational and fair, whereas *theirs* is magical and arbitrary. Our world view, our legal culture, our system of thought—all are different in their core from those of more "primitive" people. In short, we are not like them; we and they inhabit different worlds of thought about causality, responsibility, and blame. But, argues Goldman, the linguistic support for this conclusion is suspect. By sitting on the veranda (figuratively, if not literally) and by failing to know the local language well enough to have a real understanding of what was being said, nondiscourse-oriented anthropologists may have been imposing our linguistic, legal, and cultural templates on other societies.

To test the reliability of legal anthropology's conventional wisdom about accident, Goldman adduces further linguistic evidence from his long-term study of the Huli. This evidence suggests that the Huli do indeed distinguish between accident and intentionality, but—and this is the critical point—they do so in ways that differ fundamentally from how we do it in English. As a result, unless we understand their language in considerable depth, we run the risk of drawing an erroneous conclusion about the differences between our legal reasoning and theirs.

"In English," Goldman observes, "our notions of accident frequently discriminate between actions that are under the control of agents and happenings that are essentially non-agentive in nature" (1993:1). A primary way we indicate this difference in English is through the use of adverbs such as *intentionally, wilfully,* and *deliberately* versus *accidentally, inadvertently,* and *unintentionally.* These adverbs qualify statements such as "X hit Y." With one of the former adverbs, we blame; with one of the latter, we exonerate. Similarly, terms such as *arson* and *murder* convey intentionality, whereas *setting on fire* is ambiguous with respect to intention. But these are English-language concepts and modes of expression. It would be a great mistake to assume that their simple presence or absence in another language indicates that we do or do not share that society's approach to legal responsibility. Rather, we need to be prepared for the possibility that another society might linguistically encode similar legal concepts in other ways—ways that are so fundamentally different from our own that we may miss them altogether if we cannot hear what is being said with an almost-native ear.

The Culture of Coincidence examines a number of Huli discussions about a death that had occurred. The facts are simple; the interpretation is not. A woman named Gegai was visiting another woman. The second woman's home burned down, and Gegai died in the fire. Was this occurrence an accident, or was it someone's fault? These are the questions with which the Huli struggled. The occurrence was discussed in various ways over a period of time in Huli public life. The sum total of all that got said by all the parties involved constitutes the Huli equivalent of an inquest or a trial. It is this public talk that Goldman examines in an effort to understand how the Huli manage accident and blame.

Goldman's conclusion is that the Huli do indeed think of some occurrences as accidents, much as we do, and make no effort to assign responsibility for their occurrence to a human agent. His evidence is complex. The discussion transcripts themselves require ninety-two published pages and his analysis of them more than two hundred additional pages. We review only a small segment of that evidence here. But the following examples serve to illustrate Goldman's method and more generally to demonstrate the essential role of microlinguistic analysis in revealing Huli legal theory.

Verb Forms and Accidents

In the first example, Text 6.1, two members of the community discuss the fire and then begin to draw analogies to other events that our legal system might characterize as accidental. (In this and the following texts, each italicized Huli line is followed by Goldman's translation into idiomatic English. In most of the Huli lines in Text 6.1, one word is in Roman type. This is a *habitual* verb form, which is discussed in the paragraph following Text 6.1. The translation for the habitual verb form is in italics in the English line that follows.)

TEXT 6.1 (Goldman 1993:90–91)

SPEAKER 1

(1)   *Anda dalu* daga
(2)   When houses burnt, then people *used to get burnt.*
(3)   *Wiya dagua dedagoni*
(4)   What was there got burnt like this.

SPEAKER 2

(5)   *Iba* piaga[4]
(6)   People *used to drown.*

SPEAKER 1

(7)   *Iba* piaga
(8)   People *used to drown.*

SPEAKER 2

(9)   *Ira longai* piaga
(10) Misadventures *occur* involving trees.

SPEAKER 1

(11) *Iba longai* piaga
(12) Misadventures *occur* involving trees.

SPEAKER 2

(13) *Uli* piaga
(14) People *used to fall* into holes.

SPEAKER 1

(15) *Uli* piaga
(16) People *used to fall* into holes.
(17) *Nde kira kirali kirahowa mendego* pilaga *wiyagoni*
(18) Whilst two people were together *one used to fall* down.
(19) *O biago ale bidagoni*
(20) Like the event[s] referred to it [this one] has happened.

   None of the Huli words in Text 6.1 can be translated directly as some variant of "accident." Yet it is perfectly clear that the two speakers intend to put the present burning incident in the context of similar misfortunes that have no human cause. They accomplish this, Goldman argues, through the repeated use of the habitual verb form (the nonitalicized Huli words, translated in italics). This form indicates that the described action occurs customarily, typically, usually. The habitual form is gnomic, meaning that it is used to state timeless, proverbial truths. It is a way of showing *grammatically* the normal, unremarkable quality of what is being talked about. In English, by contrast, we usually convey the same idea *adverbially*, by our choice of words. Rather than simply changing the form of the verb, we add such words as *usually* or *customarily*.[5]

In Text 6.1, the habitual form of the verbs indicates the ordinariness of what happened in the case under consideration. Sentence (1), translated as (2) "When houses burnt, then people used to get burnt," is a statement about how things usually work in Huli. The logic is this: people live in grass houses; grass houses catch fire easily; when houses burn, people can get burned, too. Sentence (1)—like the others describing analogous misfortunes—neither identifies a human agent nor compels a search for one. When properly understood, it is clear evidence that accident as we know it is also a logical possibility in Huli. Without the detailed understanding of the habitual form that Goldman provides, however, we would probably miss the point entirely. Looking only at a literal translation into English, we might well conclude that the text has nothing to do with recognizing the possibility of accident.

This single piece of evidence might suffice to make Goldman's point, but there is much more. For example, in the following two English sentences, note that identical verb forms are used to convey very different meanings:

(1)   The man hurt.
(2)   The man hurt the woman.

In sentence (1), the verb *hurt* describes the state the man was in at some point in the past. It lacks an object of any sort. It simply describes how things were. By contrast, sentence (2) employs *hurt* to express the idea that the man did something to the woman that resulted in her being in a particular state. Outside its context, we cannot tell which meaning of *hurt* is intended; the verb form alone does not resolve the ambiguity. It is easy to imagine a person who lacks facility in English becoming confused about the logic of the two sentences.

But this is English. The Huli language does not allow for this sort of confusion. Sentences (1) and (2) could not be confused in Huli because different forms of the verb would be used to express the different ideas of state of being (1) and cause and effect (2). For example, the verb *burn* in Huli would be *da* if describing a state of being and *dela* if implying cause and effect. Thus, sentences (3) and (4), which employ identical verb forms in English, would employ the distinct forms *da* (3) and *dela* (4) in Huli (Goldman 1993:95–96).

(3)   The house burned.
(4)   X burned the house.

The point of this example is once again that Huli grammar not only permits but indeed *requires* the speaker to distinguish between an accidental burning and one caused by an agent. In talking about the case in question, Goldman emphasizes, Huli speakers and listeners were constantly attuned to this distinction—a distinction that makes sense only to people who recognize the possibility of accident. As in the example in Text 6.1, the distinction could be readily lost in the process of translating Huli into a language (such as English) that lacks separate forms for transitive and intransitive verbs. We are left to wonder, as Goldman wants us to, whether Evans-Pritchard and others might have missed such subtle encoding mechanisms in reaching the conclusion that the non-Western legal mind does not recognize accident.

Ergativity

A final illustration involves the property of *ergativity*. In languages that have this property, nouns and pronouns that are the subjects of transitive verbs—that is, they are the *agents* responsible for the action of the verbs—are grammatically marked so as to distinguish them from nouns and pronouns that are intransitive subjects (Dixon 1979). English obviously is not an ergative language in this sense.[6] When the first-person-singular pronoun is the subject of an English sentence, it is always *I*, regardless of whether the sentence is *I jumped* or *I hit the ball*. If English were ergative, the *I*'s in the two examples would be different in some way. Typically, the transitive subject carries a marker, as in *I (AGENT) hit the ball*. But since English is not ergative, the form of the word *I* does not reveal its status as an agent; we must listen for the information to be provided by additional words.

Huli, by contrast, is ergative. The two Huli sentences that follow are among Goldman's many examples of how ergativity functions to mark agency and responsibility. In each case, Goldman's English translation follows the Huli sentence (Goldman 1993:121).

(5)   *Ibu andame dene . . .*
(6)   She got burnt by means of the house.
(7)   *Kenobi one biagome inaga ainya delara*
(8)   Kenobi's wife burnt my mother.

In each of these examples, the key element is *-me,* the suffix that marks an agent or instrument. In sentence (5), *-me* is affixed to *anda-* (house) and connotes that the house is the responsible agent. *Ibu* (She), the subject of the sentence, is unmarked, meaning that *She* is not an agent. The ergative features of the sentence thus imply that the burning was an accident, in the sense that an inanimate object—the house—rather than a person is identified as the responsible agent. A more idiomatic English version of the same idea might be *She* *accidentally got killed when the house burned down.* In sentence (7), the agentive suffix is attached to part of the phrase identifying Kenobi's wife (the word for *wife* is *one; biago-* is an intensifying particle, which emphasizes the identification). The word for *mother* (*ainya*), the object of the verb, is unmarked. The agentive suffix identifies Kenobi's wife as the responsible agent. To achieve the same effect in English, we might use the adverb *intentionally,* or perhaps we would say *Kenobi's wife was responsible for burning my mother.*

The ergativity problem is a further reminder that the absence of a vocabulary of accident in a particular language does not mean that its speakers do not recognize the concept. What we do in English by using an adverb such as *accidentally* or *intentionally,* the Huli do with grammatical forms. But to know this, we have to understand the details of how Huli grammar works and how such notions are encoded within their language. If we work in another culture with a limited understanding of the local language or through an interpreter, as many anthropologists do, we run the substantial risk of missing the point of what is being said. Under such circumstances, we are likely to hear through our own linguistic template or that of an interpreter who strives to say things in ways that will make sense to the English-speaking anthropologist. If we do not hear the equivalents of such words as *accidentally* and *intentionally,* we may conclude that the other culture does not recognize the concepts that these words encode in English. The substance of what is being conveyed through the *structure* of the other language may get misunderstood or lost altogether. It is this problem, Goldman suspects, that lies at the heart of anthropology's longstanding but erroneous presumption that *they* differ from *us* in their inability to comprehend the possibility of chance occurrence. Goldman's linguistic analysis suggests an alternative presumption: that all cultures have notions of accident but use different linguistic strategies to express them.

Repairing Relationships in Weyewa

Some recent work in linguistic anthropology confirms Goldman's methodological point about the importance of detailed analysis of actual legal discourse, even as—ironically—it challenges his thesis about the prevalence of the concept of accident. In *Power in Performance: The Creation of Textual Authority in Weyewa Ritual Speech* (Kuipers 1990), Joel Kuipers reports on his extended study of ritual speech performance by the Weyewa people of eastern Indonesia.[7] Although its substantive goals are somewhat different, Kuipers's book is strikingly similar to Goldman's in the depth of its linguistic analysis and the richness of the transcript evidence that is adduced to support each argument.

Kuipers's subject is a form of ritual speech, generally constructed in poetic couplets, that is employed in all Weyewa ceremonial events. This speech is conceived of as "'words of the ancestors'" (Kuipers 1990:ix). Such words "transmit the ancestral 'voice' in formal, poetic, but intelligible monologues that narrate the history of promises, obligations, and commitments to ongoing relationships of ceremonial exchange." Their ritual purpose is to remind people of and thus restore a set of essential relationships. For the Weyewa, "complete saturation in the words of the ancestors is an important goal guiding the stages of a prolonged ritual process of atonement and exchange between the ancestors and their descendants, between wife-givers and wife-takers, and ultimately between life and death" (Kuipers 1990:1–2). Kuipers focuses on the details of the "sociolinguistic trajectory," whereby talk about some problem progresses "from a squabbling debate to an utterly unified and monologic *performance* of the words of the ancestors" (Kuipers 1990:2). He calls this process *entextualization.*

One of Kuipers's specific topics is the question of how people talk about misfortune or calamity in ritual contexts. Misfortune is typically characterized as "personal, isolating, disorienting, violating, sudden, extraordinary and 'hot'" (Kuipers 1990:38). Its personal quality is reflected in the word for misfortune itself (*podda*), which refers simultaneously to the disastrous event and the experiences of the victim. Misfortunes are reported in phrases that vividly depict the event as being aimed at the victim (for example, "*wolota mawenna/* the blowgun strikes exactly" and "*reketa manindo/*the dart hits its mark"). Such characterizations are consistent with the testimony of victims about their sense of being singled out and personally attacked by the event. For example, a man whose father died suddenly cried out, "*rudduka pandoku-ngga/*I was set down wrongly"; "*bondala pa-ndenga-ngga/*I was just placed aside" (Kuipers 1990:39).

But who or what aims misfortune at the victim? The answer often lies in "ruptured *relationships* among specific actors who participated in the event," and in particular in neglect of the bonds between the human and the spirit worlds (Kuipers 1990:42). As Kuipers's italics suggest, the word *relationships* is critical. Weyewa do not usually blame misfortune on the malevolence of an individual human or spirit agent. Instead, they ask whether the relationships among all those—human and spirit—with an interest in the event have been conscientiously maintained. Kuipers illustrates the point with the case of a man who broke his arm when his horse threw him after seeing a snake. A diviner seeking the cause of the misfortune ultimately focused on the man's late father's failure to fulfill a bargain he had made with the earth spirit and on the man's subsequent failure to assume responsibility for the bargain after his father's death. No one was deemed solely responsible for the calamity; rather, there was a collective lack of attention to the essential lines of communication between father and son and between the human and the spirit worlds. As the diviner put it, "*nda'iki li'i pana'u/*there were no words of instruction"; "*nda'iki li'i pananggo/*there was no voice of command" (Kuipers 1990:42).[8]

What emerges from this subtle analysis is a picture of a society whose outlook on misfortune is difficult to pigeonhole. On the one hand, it would be an oversimplification to class the Weyewa among Lévy-Bruhl's "primitives," to whom "the very idea of accident is inconceivable" (Goldman 1993:45). On the contrary, Kuipers reports that many Weyewa are familiar with Western scientific explanations of calamity and see them as useful in certain limited circumstances. But it would be grossly inaccurate to describe Western notions of chance and causation as dominant or even widely accepted among the Weyewa. As Kuipers (1990:53–54) concludes: "For Weyewa, misfortune (*podda*) results when persons exercise their judgment as individuals and thus fail to recognize the authority of, or otherwise abide by, collective agreements and conventions." Such failures lead to imbalance in relationships among people and between people and spirits; that imbalance, if uncorrected, can lead to calamity.[9]

Conclusion: Has Legal Anthropology Missed the Point?

So is Goldman wrong? Does Kuipers's analysis, drawing on linguistic resources as rich as Goldman's, undercut the latter's claim that legal anthropology has missed the point about accident? In a narrow sense, perhaps; but in a broader sense, the answer to these questions is clearly no. In fact, the Weyewa case helps to make Goldman's ultimate point even more convincingly. The Weyewa case, while it may not support the universality of accident on the Western model, does underscore the significance of a language-based anthropology of law.

This realization leads us back to the most fundamental question: whether the whole discipline of legal anthropology stands on suspect terrain because of its practitioners' lack of linguistic skills. Only time and more work like that of Goldman and Kuipers will tell. But regardless of what it eventually proves about the soundness of legal anthropology's received wisdom, such work does demonstrate incontrovertibly that in any culture a full appreciation of the law and its power depends on a thorough understanding of everyday linguistic practice.

CHAPTER SEVEN

The Discourses of Law in Historical Perspective

I f legal discourse analysis has demonstrable utility across cultures, it is logical to ask whether it can be employed across time as well. Can we examine the discourse practices of past societies in order to understand how legal power was exercised and reproduced in other times? Can we discover historical analogs to such things as the gender relationships that are encoded in our own legal discourse? The historical study of law is a vast field, of course, and for many societies, the documentary record is enormous. For medieval England, for example, we have the case reports of the *Year Books,* Sir Edward Coke's commentaries, and much more; for ancient Rome, we have the second-century *Institutes* of Gaius, the sixth-century *Code* and *Digest* of Justinian, and numerous other surviving sources, which collectively capture centuries of Roman legal thinking. But can we gain access to the linguistic events that constituted the legal *practice* of societies of the past?

The problem is a complex one. By definition, we cannot watch and listen to historical legal practice. The Huli may be speaking an unfamiliar language, but they are there, practicing their law, permitting people such as Laurence Goldman to observe, record, and interpret. When we move into the past, written texts become our sole window on legal discourse. We can interpret only those discourse events that someone thought important enough to write down, and then only when the record happens to survive. Since we cannot be in attendance at those events, we become dependent on an intermediary whose interests, values, and biases affect what is available to us. Moreover, the accounts we receive are frozen. We cannot observe the reaction of the intended audience, nor can we collect further evidence on enigmatic issues.

With all these difficulties, is the effort worth making? One answer is that the historical record of legal discourse is similar in many significant ways to the record of legal anthropology that we discussed in chapter 6. In both instances, the record we have to work with has been received through intermediaries, often in summary form. In the historical case, those intermediaries are the people in the past who compiled and reported on their societies' legal proceedings. In the case of anthropology, they are the ethnographers themselves and the interpreters and informants on whom the ethnographers relied in selecting and translating the legal raw materials. And in both instances, the work of the intermediaries must be viewed with skepticism: the chroniclers of extinct legal systems did not work to modern historiographic standards, while (if Goldman is right) many ethnographers of law may not have fully understood the proceedings they have presumed to analyze.

But traditional legal anthropology, for all the flaws that Goldman identifies, has greatly advanced our understanding of comparative law, and of culture generally. This suggests the potential value of historical discourse analysis, as long as we remain aware of the nature and limits of the record available to us.

In this chapter, we consider two prominent attempts to extend the analysis of legal discourse into the historical past. Natalie Zemon Davis's *Fiction in the Archives: Pardon Tales and Their Tellers in Sixteenth-Century France* (1987) examines the texts of requests for pardons submitted to the king of France by convicted felons. Her interest is in both the storytelling techniques that the requests embody and the culture they reflect. The subject of Judith Evans Grubbs's *Law and Family in Late Antiquity* (1995) is the legislation pertaining to marriage and the family promulgated by the early-fourth-century Roman emperor Constantine. Evans Grubbs goes beyond the substantive legal content of the legislation to consider its implications for the evolving Mediterranean ideology of gender and family power dynamics. Davis's book comes closer to the kind of discourse analysis done by scholars of the contemporary legal world in that the pardon requests constitute actual legal practice—they *are* the accounts presented to the king in order to secure the remission of punishment. Evans Grubbs's texts, by contrast, are statements of legal principles. Nonetheless, they are statements of principles that arose in response to concrete problems. As a result, their linguistic details reveal things about dominant concepts of gender and family that are not evident from their legal substance alone.[1]

Gender and Power in the Archives

The pardon requests, or remission letters, that Davis examines were written to seek royal remission of a sentence of death or lengthy imprisonment. Most pardon seekers had committed murder, but remission was occasionally sought for other crimes, such as theft, rape, and heresy. Some supplicants sought pardon after having been convicted and sentenced; others had fled from the law and were seeking a prospective pardon.

All of the remission letters had at least two authors: the supplicant and a royal notary (a scribe who helped people construct legal documents), together with the latter's secretary and clerks. The notary listened to the supplicant's story, prepared a draft of the letter, and then wrote a final version in the required legal form. Each letter was phrased in the form of a royal pronouncement, which the king could sign if he were inclined to grant the remission. After a set-piece introduction, in which the king announced himself and identified the supplicant (often with such sympathetic appellations as "poor young plowman, responsible for wife and children"), the letter told the supplicant's story. The notary closed the letter with a formulaic conclusion, which summarized the facts and fit the request into a category for which royal mercy was appropriate (for example, *chaude colle,* or "hot bile") (Davis 1987: 16).

Some supplicants, particularly the better-off ones, also consulted lawyers about the preparation of their letters. The lawyer might make substantive suggestions about framing the letter to conform to the law. He might point out, for example, that it would go better for the supplicant if the deceased had been killed with a utilitarian craft knife rather than a weapon or if the victim had had time to receive the sacraments before dying (Davis 1987: 17). The lawyer might also participate in the drafting of the actual letter.

Despite the collaborative nature of the remission letter, Davis concludes that the supplicant was "the first author"; his or her voice was "the primary one in a collective endeavor" (Davis 1987: 18). There are two reasons to believe that this was the case. First, the letter was a request for mercy, not a claim to some legal entitlement. Thus, it made sense for the notary and his functionaries to preserve the personal tone of the supplicant in the body of the letter. Second, although the letter was nominally a direct interaction with the king, in fact it had to pass a number of judicial and administrative reviews. At one stage of review, a panel of judges read the letter and then questioned the supplicant at length, scrutinizing the answers for conformity to the letter and the facts that had been developed at trial. Attempting to memorize someone else's account of the crime would be a risky undertaking for a supplicant facing the death penalty.

Each of the potential co-authors would have brought particular storytelling skills to the collaboration. Poised between the medieval and the modern worlds, the sixteenth century was an epoch of storytelling. The petitioners themselves ranged from the high to the lowly, from the educated to the illiterate. Even the least educated were likely to have had substantial storytelling experience. They probably participated in evening gatherings, or *veillées,* which featured reading, storytelling, and verbal games. Stories were also common as a diversion at work, a means of transmitting news, and a vehicle for educating the young. Most people also had regular experience with framing their misdeeds in story form for the priest in the confessional. Educated supplicants and university-trained lawyers would also have known the storytelling traditions of French literature, and the lawyers would have been familiar with the classics of rhetoric. Even the notaries and clerks, though they were unlikely to have been people of literary accomplishment, "ought to have been able to recognize a good tale when they heard it" (Davis 1987:16).

It is thus clear that letters of remission were far more than formulaic imprecations. On the contrary, they were real stories, told in a cultural environment where stories were understood and valued. As a result, Davis argues, they are compelling evidence of the discourse practices of many elements of society. By analyzing what these stories say, how they say it, what they include, what they leave out, and how they were received, we can learn a great deal about the dynamics of the society that produced them. Of particular interest to us is what we can learn about the relations between men and women and their respective interactions with the law and its power.

The Distribution of Remissions

An initial observation is that women did not seek remission very often. Of about 4,000 letters that Davis studied, only 1 percent were written on behalf of women. Part of the explanation must be that women, then as now, were less violent than men. But Davis also notes that witchcraft and infanticide, the two capital crimes with which women were most likely to be charged, were not pardonable in the sixteenth century. The law, reflecting changing social mores, treated all other forms of crime—including, significantly, the full range of male homicides—as potentially pardonable, but it viewed these two specifically female crimes as beyond the pale.

In addition, women's letters of remission emerge from a distinctive social context. The events that gave rise to women's capital crimes were ordinary ones. Whereas men often invoked the special circumstances of rituals and festivals to justify their egregious actions, women typically told stories of escalating violence in the kitchen or barnyard. The reason for this, Davis argues, is that women killed when "wifeliness and/or woman's sexual honor [were] at stake, and it [was] easier to honor and excuse what happened in the setting of her everyday life" (1987:89). Women were most credible, in other words, when defending themselves within their own domain, and that domain was domestic life.

A wife's real or apparent refusal to make dinner sometimes led to homicide because "making meals was a major arena for obedience struggles in sixteenth-century marriage" (Davis 1987:92). In two of Davis's cases, husbands killed their wives after such refusals, claiming righteous anger in the face of so outrageous an affront to their honor. In another instance, a wife who did not move fast enough to suit her husband's whim ended up killing him. The husband came home with guests as his wife and son were preparing dinner. He cursed and beat the son for not having dinner prepared already. When the wife tried to calm him by pointing out that it was not yet dinner time, he knocked her down and attacked her with a wooden stake. On her knees and holding the bloody knife with which she had been decapitating chickens, she pleaded that he should not beat her when she had done no wrong. He ran at her once again and this time fell on the knife, impaling himself just below the heart. Unaware of her husband's mortal wound, the wife got to her feet and, ignoring her own injuries, went off to pick currants to appease him.

This remission letter, which produced a royal pardon, emphasized repeatedly that the wife had known her place and had been in it. When the husband returned home, bringing men of affairs as dinner guests, he found her in the kitchen. She never contested her duty to cook, but merely pointed out that he had misunderstood the extent of her compliance. As he beat her, she argued not that domestic violence was inherently unjust but that it was unwarranted under the circumstances. Ironically, he died because she never put aside the carving knife, an essential tool of the wifely trade. Even as he lay dying, she strove instinctively to satisfy his gustatory demands. How, the letter seems to ask, could one condemn a woman who was so thoroughly immersed in the details of domesticity? The king and his judges apparently found the question to be a compelling one.

Emotions and the Law

It is evident from the remission letters that sixteenth-century French law did not recognize the full range of human emotions as appropriate for both men and women. Anger, for example, was an acceptable emotion only for men. Many men sought remission on the grounds that they had committed their crimes in the heat of anger—*chaude colle.* Davis's archives are replete with stories of men who sought and obtained pardon after responding to some lesser provocation with an outburst of lethal violence—such as the man from Lyon who, when his wife threw a wine bottle, a loaf of bread, and a tureen at him, stuck a knife in her stomach, "in anger, upset and furious" (1987:79).

Chaude colle on the part of men was understandable because it was thought to be caused by the same combination of humors that produced courage in battle. For men, anger was a resource rather than a character defect. The legal system, which was an exclusively male domain, was usually ready to forgive anger's occasional untoward consequences.

The outlook on women's anger was very different. There were, according to Davis, few situations in which the consequences of women's anger could be forgiven. "If a woman's anger erupted into violence, it could be approved in the exceptional case of defending her children or her religion . . . but most rightful bloodshed was better left to men" (Davis 1987:81). She quotes writers of the period to the effect that a woman's physical weakness is a blessing in that it prevents her, in most cases, from acting on her anger.

Women seeking pardons often blamed their actions on their emotions, but seldom on anger alone. They tended to describe their emotional state as a complex melange of feelings. When anger was cited, it was as a contributing motive rather than a driving force. Women apologized for their anger, rather than relying on it as a self-evident justification. To illustrate the point, Davis reproduces the remission letter of Marguerite Vallee, a mother of newborn twins whose husband beat her with a board and then attacked her with an ax. In the midst of the attack, she managed to get hold of the ax and strike her husband two or three times, inflicting a fatal wound. In seeking pardon for this homicide (which was granted on grounds of self-defense and in consideration of her prior good conduct), she never described herself as angry. She characterized herself at various points in the narrative as "disturbed, bewildered, and distracted," "sick at heart and a desperate woman," and "in despair, mourning, and displeasure," but never as angry (Davis 1987:77–78). Right up to the instant when she struck back with the ax, she saw her own death as the only appropriate outcome and in fact invited her husband to kill her as he advanced with the weapon. After she killed him, neighbors had to coax her to return to her twins, several times stopping her from drowning herself en route.

The issue is not whether Marguerite Vallee actually did and thought these things in 1536. The point, rather, is that she and her legal advisers thought that this was the way to frame her pardon request—not as a tale of righteous anger but as a narrative of confusion, despair, and remorse. The obvious inference to be drawn is that, whereas the dominant legal discourse of the day saw male anger as a necessary evil, if not a virtue, it saw female anger, however justified, as something unseemly.

If anger was a defining male emotion, its female counterpart may have been jealousy. Cuckolded men often cited anger in justifying the killing of their wives or wives' lovers, but never jealousy. A husband responded with righteous anger when his wife violated her duties of honor and obedience; jealousy was a weak and thus demeaning response. A woman in parallel circumstances, however, might well admit to jealousy as an inciting factor, as in the case of the peasant wife who was moved to throw stones at her husband's lover by both *chaude colle* and *force de la jallosie* (Davis 1987:83).

The manipulation of emotions by pardon seekers is revealing. Anger, a man's justification, is an emotion of power and autonomy. To recognize the defense of anger is to say that in some circumstances an actor is possessed of such autonomy that he can disregard the consequences of his actions. Men rely on anger frequently, and without elaboration; women rarely do so, and then apologetically. Jealousy, a woman's justification, is an emotion of dependency. The angry husband strikes out to punish those who have dishonored him. The jealous wife strikes out to regain her rightful—and subservient—position from the woman who has superseded her. Women admit to jealousy, but men do not. Women also admit to a range of essentially powerless emotions—confusion, despair, desperation—that rarely appear in men's narratives.

Law and Society in Sixteenth-Century France

Through the analysis of the substantive and emotional content of remission letters, Davis gives us a window on the values that dominated the legal and social order of sixteenth-century France. Through some combination of personal choice and the influence of the men who assisted them, female pardon seekers fashioned their remission letters out of the stuff of everyday life. Whereas men often justified their crimes on the basis of exceptional circumstances, women immersed themselves in domestic detail. As Davis puts it, "[T]hey created atmosphere by building up dialogue or prosey detail alone. Like thrifty housewives, they wove their fictions from materials ready at hand" (1987: 104). And whereas men highlighted their righteous anger, women suppressed it, if indeed they felt it at all, highlighting instead such emotions as jealousy and sadness. Men, in other words, were likely to claim to have acted in moments of special empowerment; women, on the other hand, portrayed themselves as reacting when events had turned their routine powerlessness into utter desperation.

Because of what they were, the remission letters must be seen as the most vivid possible reflection of dominant social beliefs and practices. They were not works of self-analysis, defiant resistance, or ironic commentary, but last-ditch efforts to survive. They would succeed only if they evoked for their readers—the king and his officials—the appropriate images of virtue and propriety. Where women were concerned, these were images of powerlessness, of domestic subservience and emotional dependency. It makes no difference to the analysis whether these images came naturally to the authors themselves or were foisted on them by their legal advisers. In either case, by allowing the letters to go forward, the women acquiesced in the view that these were the dominant values of the time—and they were right, as the pardons were almost always granted.

This conclusion is in no sense surprising. Anyone with any knowledge of the history of women's social roles would have predicted as much. Davis's analysis is, however, remarkably rich in at least two respects. First, the extent to which the texts are suffused at every level with the dominant values of law and society is striking. The letters do not simply lay overt claim to the virtues of the ideal woman: domesticity, obedience, loyalty, and the like. Rather, they present detailed narratives about practicing these virtues. Readers did not have to accept the conclusion that a supplicant was virtuous. They could draw that inference themselves from what must have been a reassuringly familiar context of characters, roles, and relationships. Four centuries later, we get an unexpectedly revealing look at the interaction between norms and practices in medieval France.

This leads to the second point, which is that Davis's research also shows the timelessness of the process whereby dominant legal values are reinforced and reproduced. In their moments of ultimate crisis, pardon-seeking women and their advisers took care to frame their experiences in conformity to the dominant values of the time. Each of the repeated acts of conforming simultaneously reflected and reaffirmed those values. Because few, if any, pardon seekers would have seized on the remission process as an opportunity for resistance, the process of reaffirmation must have been especially powerful. Those in positions of legal authority were not presented with alternatives to their preferred interpretation of women's lives. Instead, they saw that interpretation played out over and over again in the narratives of the pardon seekers. In the terms we have used elsewhere, the dominant discourse of the law was inscribed in the linguistic practice of the remission letters. Davis's analysis of this practice reveals not only the content of the law's discourse but also an important mechanism for perpetuating its dominance.

Family Law and Family Practice in the Roman Empire

The work of classical scholar Judith Evans Grubbs provides an additional illustration of the value of analyzing legal discourse in historical contexts. In two related projects (Evans Grubbs 1995, 1996), she has endeavored to use legal texts from the middle and later years of the Roman Empire to understand the Roman family. In her book *Law and Family in Late Antiquity* (Evans Grubbs 1995), she analyzes legislation promulgated by the early-fourth-century (A.D.) emperor Constantine. This "legislation" was in fact a set of decrees, for by Constantine's time "the emperor's word was the law" (Evans Grubbs 1995:2). (Classicists debate the extent to which Constantine himself, as opposed to his advisers, was actually responsible for the content of the legislation.)

Constantine's rule came at the end of more than a century of social upheaval, during which members of the old Italian senatorial families were displaced as officeholders and courtiers by new people from the provinces, especially Spain and Africa. During the same period, Christianity evolved from persecuted sect to state religion. As a result of such developments, much of Constantine's legislation reflected an effort to restructure society, to reconcile Roman values and traditions with the new social order. And because control over marriage and the family provides the most direct means for the state to influence social structure, more than 20 percent of Constantine's legislation dealt with marriage, sexual relations, and the family (Evans Grubbs 1995:2, 28). Thus, while the legislation does not have the narrative quality of Davis's remission letters, it provides a vivid, if indirect, reflection of the lives of people of the times.

In her more recent work, Evans Grubbs (1996) examines the texts of imperial rescripts dating from the second, third, and fourth centuries A.D. Rescripts were the emperor's responses (usually drafted by specialists in the civil service) to specific legal questions posed by cities, officials, or individual citizens. The requests and responses were posted in public places and were often copied into the official legal records of the Empire. Many have been preserved as papyri and some in the form of stone inscriptions. Because of the narrative framing of the requests, the rescripts contain explicit evidence of the social contexts in which the legal disputes arose.

Much of Evans Grubbs's analysis of Constantine's legislation focuses on the changes he made in divorce law. In ancient Rome, divorce, like marriage, was accomplished by the parties stating their intentions rather than by formal legal proceedings. Throughout most of the period of the Roman Republic (Roman history up until the accession of the first emperor, Augustus, in the late first century B.C.), only the husband could declare a divorce, and then only on the grounds of serious fault on the wife's part, especially adultery. During the Empire prior to Constantine, divorce became much easier to obtain. The spouses could jointly declare a no-fault divorce, or either one could send the other a written notice of divorce called a *repudium*. No justification was necessary, although wrongdoing by one spouse might affect the disposition of the dowry that the wife had brought to the marriage.

In A.D. 331, Constantine radically restricted the availability of divorce through the following decree.

> It is pleasing that a woman not be permitted to send a *repudium* to her husband because of her own depraved desires for some carefully contrived cause, such as the fact that he is a drunkard or gambler or a womanizer, but neither should husbands be permitted to dismiss their own wives for just any reason whatever.
>
> But in the sending of a *repudium* by a woman [it is pleasing] that these crimes alone be looked into: if she has proved that her husband is a murderer or a preparer of poisons [this offense includes both poisoning and magic] or a disturber of tombs, so that not until then shall she receive back her entire dowry. . . . But if she has sent a *repudium* to her husband for any reason other than these three crimes, she should leave it [the dowry], down to a hairpin, in her husband's home and be deported to an island. . . .
>
> Also in the case of men, if they send a *repudium*, it is fitting that these three crimes be inquired into: if they want to repudiate an adulteress or a preparer of poisons or a go-between. For if he has ejected a woman free from these crimes, he should restore the entire dowry

and not marry another woman. (Evans Grubbs 1995:228–29, as translated by the author)

Several details of this text are striking. Its practical intent seems to be to limit divorce and to create a rough equality between husbands and wives. However, it opens with a luridly detailed description of a great evil that is to be avoided: the propensity of women, driven by "depraved desires," to defame their husbands with "contrived" accusations of such stereotypically male sins as drinking, gambling, and womanizing. This recitation is not balanced by any discussion of parallel propensities that afflict men.

It is also interesting to compare the three-part lists of offenses that are so heinous that they provide absolute grounds for unilateral divorce. Women must charge their husbands with committing murder, poisoning, or disturbing tombs. Men must charge their wives with committing adultery, poisoning, or acting as a sexual go-between. The only item in common is poisoning, which had overtones of magic. The other two most serious crimes that a man could commit were murder and the religious offense of disturbing tombs. The female list reflects no comparable concern with harm to others or to the religious integrity of the community. On the contrary, the other two items on the list—adultery and sexual facilitation—relate to a woman's sexual purity and her status as sexual property.

Further evidence for the characterization of women as property comes from Evans Grubbs's study of imperial rescripts (1996:38ff.). Several of her sources refer to a procedure with the extraordinary title of *de inspiciendo ventre* (literally, "on the inspection of the abdomen"). This was the procedure to be followed if a woman whose husband died claimed to be pregnant with his child. Paternity had serious consequences for the inheritance of the deceased's estate. To protect the rights of her late husband's relatives, the widow had to give them immediate notice of the claimed pregnancy and allow them to send "experts" (midwives presumably) to examine her and confirm the pregnancy. The widow was then required to give further notice to the husband's family thirty days before the birth was expected. To prevent the substitution of a spurious child (who, if undetected, would become the husband's heir), the relatives could require the widow to be confined in a locked and guarded house and could send observers to the birth—which had to take place in a room with at least three lights.

The image of women as weak, unstable, and prone to sexual misconduct had wide currency in other legal decrees and commentaries of the time. Evans Grubbs (1995:328–29) cites numerous examples of laws that limited women's participation in business and legal affairs in order to protect their *pudor,* which she translates as "modesty, especially, though not exclusively, sexual modesty," and to avoid the consequences of their frivolity (*levitas*) and fickleness (*mobilitas*). One remarkable law prescribed "exquisite tortures" for any judge who sent a bailiff to the house of a married woman "who keeps herself within her home" in order to "drag her into public" to answer for unpaid taxes. At the other extreme, women who had so little *pudor* that they worked as tavern waitresses could not be prosecuted for adultery, since "the baseness of their life has not considered [them] worthy of the law's observation" (Evans Grubbs 1995:329).

As was the case with Davis's medieval French texts, the construction of the nature and role of women that emerges from Evans Grubbs's Roman legal texts is not at all surprising. Indeed, she repeatedly emphasizes that similar constructions have been a commonplace of Mediterranean cultures down to the twentieth century. What is of interest to us is her analysis of the interaction between the legal texts—a kind of linguistic practice—and the dominant cultural ideas about women, divorce, and family life.

In analyzing this interaction, the basic question is whether Constantine was using the law to change social values or changing the law to conform to social values. By one interpretation, Constantine's divorce laws were a conscious attempt to reestablish old-fashioned republican values in the face of social mores that had become far more liberal. That is, Constantine's legislation was an effort to use authoritative legal discourse to change the day-to-day practice of family life, and ultimately the values that underlay that practice. In the alternative view, the purpose of the legislation was to bring divorce law into line with social practices that were in reality far more conservative than the lenient laws of the pre-Constantine Empire would suggest. Some authorities argue that the permissive divorce laws had been tailored to the interests of the urban elite of Italy, whose day-to-day social lives bore little resemblance to those of the ordinary people of the rest of the Empire.[2] By this account, Constantine, himself a provincial, sought to make the law more reflective of the conservative social world from which he had emerged.

The linguistic evidence bearing on the interpretation of Constantine's divorce laws is mixed. On the one hand, a number of Constantine's laws bear a strong resemblance to some of republican Rome's most ancient legal texts, suggesting that he was indeed trying to reaffirm the family values of a quasi-mythic past. On the other, inscriptions and other nonlegal texts from Constantine's era reflect the growth of a "silent majority," who adhered to traditional ideals of the family and rejected notions such as ready access to divorce and female autonomy. This evidence supports the view that the liberal pre-Constantine divorce laws were unrepresentative of cultural practice.

Regardless of which interpretation ultimately prevails, Constantine's legislation reflects a moment of discontinuity between legal discourse and social values, a clear, if somewhat unorthodox, instance of resistance. In one view,

Constantine was making a radical change in authoritative legal discourse in order to influence social practices of which he disapproved.[3] In another, he was altering legal discourse because it had become disconnected from the day-to-day social reality of most of his constituents.[4] But in either case, one set of Roman divorce laws—the old or the new—would have stood in opposition to cultural practice.

In many of the chapters of this book dealing with American law, we have attempted to show how the everyday discourse of law can both reflect and reinforce broader cultural values. Chapter 4, which deals with the patriarchy of Anglo-American law, is a prime example. Here, by contrast, legal discourse is being used to transform social values or, alternatively, is being itself transformed to conform to changes in those values. Under the former interpretation, authoritative legal discourse is being deployed to overcome social resistance; under the latter, the emperor himself is at the forefront of popular resistance to the elitist values that had previously been embodied in the dominant legal discourse. What is most significant for our purposes is the fact that both views depend on attention to the details of the law's language. Here, as in the case of the French pardon letters, such features as the topics chosen and the words used to talk about them reveal the social context in which the law was practiced.

Conclusion: The Timelessness of Legal Discourse

The work that historians do in combing through written texts from other time periods is remarkably like that of anthropologists who scrutinize the details of spoken legal discourse from the contemporary world. Both anthropologist and historian study the details of how things are said—whether spoken or written—not simply for the inherent interest that the words hold but also as a means for understanding the broader social and cultural patterns that they reveal.

The textual materials from the past discussed in this chapter, although drawn from different time periods and sources, yield important insights about the societies that produced them. Indeed, what they show about the role of law in supporting the hegemony of men's interests over women's interests echoes what we know about law's role in our own time. In earlier chapters, we saw how the legal system manages what rape victims can and must say, as well as how mediation plays on the vulnerabilities of many women. And we reviewed evidence that shows how many of women's ways of speaking or telling their stories are undervalued by the legal system in comparison to styles more commonly associated with their husbands and brothers.

The French texts analyzed by Davis tell a remarkably similar story of patriarchal privilege. It is a story revealed through the linguistic details of remission letters—the different emotions attributed to women and men and the different conventions that bound women and men as they pleaded for the king's favor in a final effort to save their lives or regain their freedom. It is through such details that Davis crafts her argument about a legal system that reinforced male privilege and female dependency.

The materials that Evans Grubbs had at her disposal for the study of Roman law and society are in many ways even more remote from the resources we have available for studying present societies. The Roman texts contain no reports of dialogue or personal narratives of the sort that Davis used. Despite these differences, the tale that they tell about Roman society is indistinguishable from the one that Davis uncovered. The Roman laws that codified rules about women, divorce, and family life specified a world of power and privilege for some citizens, while prescribing subordination for others.

Law and language research shares with the discipline of history a focus on texts. In both instances, texts are explored, examined, and mined for what they reveal about social processes. In the study of the past, texts are often all that is available as a window on social and cultural processes. Historians accordingly mine them as thoroughly as possible because what can be learned must be found in them. By contrast, for legal anthropology and for law and society, texts compete with other forms of data—surveys and other "more comprehensive" ways of exploring social relationships. Texts that require detailed analysis are often seen as "soft," "limited," or "merely anecdotal." They are passed over by those unfamiliar with what they might reveal through careful scrutiny. Law and language offers the same lesson as history about method: that texts that may seem frozen can be thawed and made to yield unsuspected insights.

In both of the instances we discuss in this chapter, historians working with texts from past societies make the same point that we have made throughout the book: that society's big picture—its macrodiscourse—is best understood by examining the little details of a society's linguistic practice—its microdiscourse. The success of Davis and Evans Grubbs is compelling evidence that the microlinguistic analysis of legal discourse need not be limited to contemporary materials collected for research purposes. Although there are obvious advantages to studying complete and precise transcripts of events such as trials, mediation sessions, and lawyer-client conferences, the work reviewed in this chapter reveals the power of the method to explicate even the fragmentary discourse bequeathed to us by the historical record. Indeed, when we look into the past, we find the antecedents of some of the most significant sociolegal issues in our own world.

CHAPTER EIGHT

Conclusion

If we were to state the arguments of the previous chapters in a single sentence, it would be this: the details of legal discourse matter. First and foremost, the details of legal discourse matter because language is the essential mechanism through which the power of the law is realized, exercised, reproduced, and occasionally challenged and subverted. Most of the time, law is talk: the talk between disputants; the talk between lawyers and clients; the courtroom talk among lawyers, parties, judges, and witnesses; the legal talk that gets reduced to writing as statutes and judicial opinions; and the commentary on all of this other talk that people like us engage in. Therefore, if one wants to find particular, concrete manifestations of the law's power, it makes sense to sift through the microdiscourse that is the law's defining element. If the objectives are to understand the nature of the law's power, to see how that power is exercised over real people, to identify points at which it might be challenged, and to assess which challenges are likely to work, then microdiscourse is the place to look.

In this book, we have argued that the details of legal discourse matter from a series of different empirical perspectives. In chapter 2, we presented evidence that the law's power to revictimize rape victims is not an abstraction but a concrete linguistic reality. The feeling of revictimization seems to emerge from a limited number of things that lawyers routinely say to and about rape victims during trial. Ironically, and tellingly, they are not the things that advocates for rape victims' rights have usually focused on.

In chapter 3, we examined the language of mediation, particularly as it is used in divorce. Our first objective was to document how mediation "works," in the sense of providing an environment in which hostile parties begin talking again in an effort to agree on a solution to a dispute. The key seems to be a set of linguistic strategies that mediators use to steer the parties away from the conversational structure of argument. We then considered whether mediation—which is usually advertised as a balanced, value-neutral, participant-controlled process—is subject to bias. That is, are there ways in which certain kinds of disputants, with the at-least-implicit connivance of the legal system, can exert power and pursue their own agendas? The answer is clearly yes; the subtle but convincing evidence lies in the linguistic details of mediation practice.

In chapter 4, we sought linguistic evidence for the widespread claim that Anglo-American law is patriarchal. We found it on at least two levels: in the legal system's preference for a speech style that is used preponderantly by males and in its parallel devaluing of account structures and forms of argument that derive primarily from the social experiences of girls and women.

In chapter 5, we took a microlinguistic look at the natural history of disputes. We developed a descriptive typology that accounts for the different kinds of linguistic events that can occur over the life of a dispute. By examining these various linguistic events in detail, we argued, it is possible to understand more fully the ways in which disputants, their representatives, and the decision makers before whom they appear can exercise and contest for power.

Finally, in chapters 6 and 7, we presented two variations on a single theme: the portability of legal discourse analysis to other places and times. Chapter 6 reported on the effort to use linguistic analysis to resolve some longstanding questions about the jurisprudence of societies far removed from our own. Chapter 7 offered a complementary discussion of how legal language can illuminate power relationships in societies from the historical past. In these very different contexts, we reemphasized a point made repeatedly throughout the book: that claims about the nature and purpose of law—its macrodiscourse—are highly suspect unless grounded in a thorough understanding of the microlinguistic realities of legal practice.

In making these varied claims for the indispensability of legal discourse analysis, we have also intended to connect the historically distinct research traditions of sociolegal scholarship and sociolinguistics. As we discussed in chapter 1, the core claim of sociolegal scholarship is that the law in practice does not live up to the ideal of fairness. Justice is contingent, and the critical contingencies are such categories as gender, race, and class. What has been missing from much sociolegal research, in our view, is a detailed explication of what injustice looks like as it happens.

Sociolinguistics, on the other hand, has a rich tradition of showing precisely how linguistic events—stories about troubles, requests for help, collaborative searches for blame, and so on—unfold. However, the sociolinguistic lens has not always been focused on events that "count" in the legal and political world. Throughout our respective teaching careers, we have often heard the complaint that sociolinguistics "sometimes seems to be learning more and more about less and less" as it has catalogued and described innumerable instances of the social conditioning of language.

A significant theoretical motive in writing this book is to highlight some important connections between the sociolegal and the sociolinguistic traditions and thereby to suggest the potential for future collaborations in law and language. In this concluding chapter, we discuss several areas of incipient collaboration that offer particularly exciting prospects: the search for the origins of legal language, the cross-cultural analysis of legal discourse, and the use of law and language to influence political and legal reform.

Where Does Legal Language Come From?

As sociolinguistics probes ever deeper into the details of disputing language, a recurrent theme is how elegantly patterned that language seems to be. Members of every society appear to have vast stores of cultural knowledge about disputing, as well as an elaborate sense of how to conduct themselves and interpret the behavior of others in a variety of legal and quasi-legal contexts. But where do they get this knowledge? Aside from its inherent intellectual interest, the question is of vital practical importance to those interested in reforming some problematic aspects of disputing behavior. Consider, for example, the evidence presented in chapter 3 that the disputing styles of many women end up getting turned against them by divorce mediators. In order to provide equal access to justice for everyone, it is essential for reformers to understand how the women as well as the mediators acquire their respective approaches to disputing.

In a society such as this one, with a complex, professionalized dispute resolution system, the question of origins has at least two parts. The first is, Where do the lay members of society learn how to conduct themselves in disputes? The second part asks how legal professionals learn the particular discourse styles and strategies that have been in evidence throughout the book. These styles and strategies are very different from their everyday counterparts, but how are they acquired? Promising beginnings have been made in answering these questions.

Learning How to Argue

When seeking the origins of any social behavior, a logical place to start is with children. A good deal of research has now been done on the disputing language of children.[1] Some of the most interesting current work is being done by Amy Sheldon and Diane Johnson (1994; see also Sheldon 1993). Their inquiries have focused on gender differences in disputing language among preschool children. They have identified two distinct styles of disputing discourse. *Single-voice discourse* is characterized by unmitigated self-assertion. It involves direct, confrontational speech acts in which the speaker pursues his or her own goals without regard to the dispute's effect on the other party. In *double-voice discourse,* by contrast, "self-assertion is accomplished with linguistic mitigation" (Sheldon and Johnson 1994:42). That is, while the speaker is oriented primarily toward the self, double-voice discourse also evidences sensitivity to and a feeling of responsibility for the well-being of the other disputant. Sheldon and Johnson stop short of characterizing these two styles as, respectively, masculine and feminine. They argue instead that double-voice discourse is typical of interactions in the "solidarity-based" groups in which young girls usually play. Single-voice discourse, on the other hand, is a defining characteristic of the "dominance-based" groups in which boys typically play. Although the gender correlation is apparent, it is the norms of the two kinds of groups that select one or the other discourse style rather than the gender of the group's members per se.

Although Sheldon and Johnson are restrained in drawing implications from their studies, the possibilities are provocative. They note, for example, the obvious connection between dominance-based disputing discourse and patriarchy. Elsewhere, Sheldon (1993) has elaborated on the connection between the affiliative, relationship-focused conflict style of little girls and Carol Gilligan's (1982) theory that women's moral reasoning derives from an ethic of care, whereas men's moral reasoning grows out of an ethic of rights. We have argued throughout this book that Anglo-American law expresses a preference for linguistic practices that are more typical of men than women. Sheldon and Johnson may have discovered some of the earliest manifestations of these preferences in the lives of individual men and women.

Sheldon and Johnson also comment on the ways in which women and girls may be disadvantaged in various dispute settings. Clearly girls' (and women's) double-voicing is well-suited to the social norms that govern self-assertion in all-female, solidarity-based groups. However, in mixed-sex conversations, double-voice discourse may not serve girls as well, because dominance-based norms are often operating there (Sheldon and Johnson 1994:61).

These findings have potentially profound implications. They can help us understand, for example, the source of many of the problems that women experience in divorce mediation. If in their earliest social disputes girls learn to temper their pursuit of self-interest with concern for the needs of the opponent, while boys learn precisely the opposite, then it should come as no surprise that women should at once like mediation and fare badly in it. We might expect women to prefer mediation because it is designed to be nonconfrontational, relational, and affiliative. At the same time, we would expect women to be disadvantaged because men are likely to ignore these aspects of the process and devote all their attention to the single-minded pursuit of a favorable outcome.

How Do Lawyers Learn Legal Discourse?

As we have repeatedly seen, the discourse of legal professionals is distinctive on multiple levels. The most superficial level is legal jargon. Lawyers and judges regularly use words and phrases such as *directed verdict, j.n.o.v.,* and *mens rea,* which are not part of the everyday vocabulary of lay people, as well as common words and phrases that have specialized legal meanings such as *consideration, pleading,* and *complaint.* The source of legal jargon in the practice of the law is obvious: law students are required to learn it in law school.

Other aspects of the law's professional discourse are far more subtle, however. We saw in chapter 3, for example, that divorce lawyers transform their clients' stories in regular and predictable ways. They do so by imposing a particular discourse structure on those stories. Similarly, we argued in chapter 4 that the legal system prefers certain kinds of story structures and logical frameworks. The source of these preferences is far from obvious. Law school does teach a process that law professors often refer to as "thinking like a lawyer." This means knowing how to infer rules of law from the comparative analysis of judges' written decisions in particular cases. Especially in the first year, law students read large numbers of cases and study the relationship between facts and outcomes. Their objective is twofold: to become familiar with the paradigm cases that have yielded rules of wide applicability and to learn how to predict the reactions of courts to novel situations. Almost every law school exam question presents the students with an original (and often bizarre) fact pattern and demands that they predict the likely legal response. The theory of this kind of testing is that this is just what lawyers do when clients appear in their offices and tell them about their problems.

This approach to legal education selects rather ruthlessly for a particular style of analysis. Students who get high grades usually read quickly through complex fact patterns, zeroing in on "relevant" facts—that is, facts that judges and law professors will see as having a bearing on legal rights and remedies—and immediately discarding everything else. Students who go to their professors to ask about low exam grades are often told that they "got bogged down in irrelevancies" or "never got to the point."

The demand that students learn how to think like a lawyer has both positive and negative consequences. On the positive side, it seems clear that judges often *do* think in precisely this way. Thus, the predictive skill that traditional legal education seeks to impart is a real and significant aspect of professional competence. On the negative side, it seems equally clear from the evidence presented throughout this book that the consumers of the law *rarely* analyze their problems in the same way. Accordingly, by its exclusive focus on the professional mode of analysis, legal education may be sending the message that the thought processes of the people the profession purports to serve are irrelevant and inadequate.

Until recently, legal education has paid virtually no attention to this problem. The analysis of legal education's contribution to the lawyer-client communication gap is just beginning to progress beyond the kinds of general observations made in the preceding paragraphs. Some of the most significant work to date has been done by Elizabeth Mertz (1996, n.d.), a law professor trained as both an anthropologist and a lawyer. Mertz has asked what it is about legal education that so transforms the discourse practices of law students that they seem to lose touch with their own society. She and her colleagues are in the process of recording, transcribing, and analyzing first-year classes in eight different law schools.

Mertz's preliminary observations include the following:

1. *The social context of disputes is treated differently than in the everyday world.* When ordinary people talk about their troubles, social context is always very important; often it is everything. Yet when law professors lead their students through discussions of cases, a common tactic is to abstract the disputants from their social context, to conceive of them as "acontextual" (Mertz n.d.: 15). When law professors propose hypotheticals (as they often do), Mertz observes, the characters are typically "average" farmers or "average" home buyers with a standard set of attributes and apparently no social connections. While some degree of abstracting is undoubtedly necessary in order to simplify the rule-deducing process for beginning students, an obvious question is whether at some point the students begin to adopt the unreal world view that such acontextual discourse embodies.

2. *The discourse practices of law professors appear to be influenced by their backgrounds.* Mertz finds that "issues of gender and race appear to come up more directly and more frequently in classes taught by women and by men of color" (Mertz n.d.: 12). While law professors generally treat context as something that is relevant only in exceptional cases (as, for example, when a "bad" judge may act on some sort of bias), such commentary is more common in classes taught by women and by men of color. Interestingly, it is not always the professors themselves who are injecting these factors: students seem more willing to raise issues of context in classes taught by professors who are not white men. Perhaps these professors have had more occasion to think about the importance of context in their own lives than have their white male colleagues, and they thus are more inclined to see it as relevant to legal outcomes. In any

event, Mertz's preliminary findings suggest that "thinking like a lawyer" may come more naturally to people with particular social experiences.

3. *The language of law professors fosters an "us/them" divide between law and society.* Mertz identifies the propensity of law professors to use a collective *we* to refer to the professor, the student being questioned, and the court that is hearing the case, as in "Where are we in the case? We're in Wisconsin." The regular use of this collective-professional *we,* Mertz argues, has several significant effects. It unites the professor and the student as professionals who are reading the legal text from a perspective that is different from that of the ordinary people who are engaged in the dispute. Likewise, it transports the student and the professor, together, into the case. When they arrive, their vantage point is that of the court rather than that of the disputants.

The effect of these various discourse practices is to perpetuate "a universalist language capable of translating almost any conceivable event or issue into a common rhetoric" (Mertz n.d.:23). Law schools inculcate both a way of talking about problems and the logic that lies behind that way of talking. Because such logic is an essential tool of current legal practice, law schools could not give up teaching it even if they wanted to do so. What Mertz reminds us, however, is that the discourse of legal education has other consequences that have not been identified or thought through with sufficient care. As law professors use language to socialize their students, they are simultaneously distancing them from the social contexts from which they emerged, the same social contexts that their future clients will inhabit.

Mertz's work has demonstrated convincingly that legal education is fundamentally a linguistic process. Law professors do not conspire to strip students of their social consciousness; on the contrary, the vast majority of American law professors are card-carrying social progressives. What seems to be happening is that law professors are insufficiently attentive to the relationship between discourse and power. As law students emulate the ways that law professors talk about people and their problems, they also begin to take for granted the patterns of thinking that such talk embodies. If legal education is interested in understanding and dealing with the consequences of its classroom discourse practices, then much more work of the sort that Mertz has undertaken will be essential.[2]

Comparative Legal Discourse

We included chapters 6 and 7 in an effort to show the comparative potential of legal discourse analysis. In chapter 6, using the work of Laurence Goldman and Joel Kuipers, we attempted to relate the methods of discourse analysis to the traditions of legal anthropology. Goldman, in a polemical way, shows how to use discourse analysis to challenge the conventional wisdom of legal anthropology, whereas Kuipers's work is an elegant demonstration of how to analyze legal discourse in another culture. The overall point of the chapter was that traditional legal anthropology, as a result of inadequate attention to the details of discourse, has sometimes missed the point in studying comparative law. Indeed, as Goldman's work illustrates, it has on occasion gotten things backwards. In chapter 7, we suggest the potential for the comparative analysis of legal discourse across time.

The next step, in our judgment, must be the development of a new, discourse-based legal anthropology. This new discipline will share legal anthropology's traditional concern with the imposition of legal systems and substantive legal concepts, but will add to it a concern for the subtleties of legal reasoning that can be appreciated only at the microlinguistic level. It will, for example, enable us to analyze the natural history of disputes in other societies at the same level of detail at which Gail Jefferson, Anita Pomerantz, and others have analyzed Western disputes. The new legal anthropology will not simply report that the Azande attribute the collapse of a granary to witchcraft or summarize facts and outcomes of Barotse tribal court cases in the manner of Western case reports. Rather, it will use the details of how the members of a particular society talk their way through disputes in an effort to illuminate their legal process and its power dynamics.

As much of the work cited in chapter 6 illustrates, the call for a new, discourse-based legal anthropology is not limited to us. A number of scholars are in the field trying to practice just this sort of approach in their own work. As an exemplar of the benefits of merging the traditional concerns of legal anthropology and the power of discourse analysis in a single ethnographic project, we have chosen Susan Hirsch's (forthcoming) recently completed study of family law among the Muslim inhabitants of coastal Kenya. In the tradition of Max Gluckman and Paul Bohannan, Hirsch spent several years living in the community, learning the language, talking with people about their domestic disputes, and observing and recording many of the disputes that find their way into the Islamic courts. She explores the conventional model of the patriarchy of Islamic law, which gives women a starkly defined position of subordination, subservience, and powerlessness. Her analysis of disputing language reveals far more complexity.[3] Gender is not simply a fixed category that the law responds to in consistent and predictable ways. The linguistic evidence reveals that the legal relationships between men and women are the subject of ongoing negotiation. It is true that women are often victimized by the dominant ideology as they work to resolve domestic problems through the legal system; Hirsch's linguistic data document how this happens. But Hirsch also finds that women have opportunities to resist and challenge patriarchal power and that they sometimes succeed.

Rather than simply reporting that Islamic law is an instrument of patriarchy, Hirsch asks what patriarchy means in terms of the law's everyday linguistic practices. Rather than simply asking what the law *is,* she examines how it *works* at a level of detail unavailable in traditional legal ethnography. The result is not only a sharper picture of the particular legal system with which she is concerned, but also an original perspective on the general question of how gender is inscribed in law. Her work is, we believe, an appropriate model for future legal anthropology, as well as a blueprint for the cross-cultural study of sociolegal issues.

Deconstructing Law Reform

Legal audiences in particular often ask whether law and language research has any practical significance. The answer is an unqualified, if not always obvious, yes. One area where the merger of traditional sociolinguistic and sociolegal concerns can make a particularly significant contribution is the evaluation of legal reform efforts. Gregory Matoesian's analysis of rape shield laws, reviewed in chapter 2, illustrates this potential. Advocates of rape shield have long argued that prohibiting defense lawyers from inquiring into a woman's prior sexual history will significantly alleviate the feeling of revictimization that dissuades many rape victims from going ahead with prosecution. Matoesian demonstrates, however, that defense lawyers do not need to exploit prior sexual history in order to humiliate and demoralize the victim. Instead, ordinary and hitherto noncontroversial cross-examination techniques can be used to the same effect. If he is right, the reform efforts have missed the point because of their proponents' failure to understand the linguistic reality of revictimization.

In parallel ways, the work on mediation that we reviewed in chapter 3 reflects the law of unintended consequences at work in the legal reform process. The widespread adoption of divorce mediation was celebrated as the most progressive kind of reform. It was (and for the most part still is) widely seen as promoting the psychological well-being of the divorcing spouses and their children; responding to the prevailing desire of women for a more supportive, nonconfrontational forum; and saving money for everyone. But it is now suspected that in material terms women may be worse off in mediation than in traditional adjudication. Linguistic evidence is reinforcing these suspicions by identifying some of the pathways through which gender bias might operate.

An interesting counterexample—a case of listening before you leap, as it were—is unfolding in Colorado. Like their counterparts everywhere, judges and bar officials in Colorado are increasingly concerned about excessively adversarial behavior on the part of trial lawyers. They worry about such particular misbehavior as filing frivolous lawsuits, withholding or even destroying documents that the other side is entitled to see, making endless unnecessary motions in an effort to exhaust the opponent's resources, and badgering witnesses during depositions and trials. The Colorado courts have already initiated some modest reforms intended to get at the underlying problem.[4]

At the same time, however, officials of the Colorado bar asked a number of social scientists, including the authors, to participate in a discourse-based ethnographic study of the state of the adversary system. They worried about whether a general sense of crisis, even one that was almost universally shared, was an adequate basis for designing major reforms of longstanding legal procedures. They clearly understood that it would be reckless to attack a behavioral problem without a precise description of the offending behavior, and they also appreciated that the behavior in question was almost entirely linguistic. The study is ongoing. We and the other researchers share the general perception that the adversary system is out of control and hope that our work can contribute to its diagnosis and treatment. More broadly, we hope that other people responsible for law reform will also come to appreciate that intelligent and effective efforts to improve legal practice require a great deal of sensitivity to the language that constitutes the practice.

Sociolinguists in the Legal World

By this point, we hope that we have amply demonstrated that microlinguistic analysis is an extraordinary tool for studying social problems. Political concepts such as power, domination, and bias come vividly to life when the linguistic processes through which they are enacted are revealed. We believe that this potential to illuminate and influence the law imposes some responsibilities on those who work in the various traditions of microlinguistic analysis.

First, sociolinguists, conversation analysts, and other scholars of language must shed any lingering reluctance to deal with questions of power. For example, when reading the works of Jefferson, Pomerantz, and other seminal conversation analysts, one often senses an unwillingness to go beyond the discovery of the rules of interaction to a consideration of what their social consequences might be. There are some exceptions to this rule. For example, in *Order in Court,* a conversation analysis of judicial proceedings, Max Atkinson and Paul Drew (1979:228) acknowledge that their work "is suggestive of ways in which certain features of court-room interaction that may have organizational advantages in facilitating the accomplishment of a court's work simultaneously provide a basis for moral assessments to be made about particular speakers." In a different vein, much of Deborah Tannen's work on gender differences in conversational style (e.g., Tannen 1993) revolves around questions of power. Nonetheless, there is in our judgment a need for a more explicit recognition of the fact that the rules of linguistic interaction, especially in legal contexts, have profound implications for the distribution of power in our society.

The second point is difficult to make in a polite way: people who do this kind of work need to write more clearly. With very few exceptions, recent work in conversation and discourse analysis—whether done by conversation analysts, linguists, or anthropologists—is virtually impenetrable to the nonspecialist. A certain amount of jargon may be defensible. There is no justification, however, for the convoluted constructions, odd in-group usages, and apparently intentional obscurity that plague the writing in the field. In our experience, people in the legal world are eager to know the kinds of things that law and language scholars can tell them. Often, however, they find the form of the presentation so opaque and off-putting that they give up before understanding the content. This is regrettable, since it is vitally important that lawyers, judges, and legal educators come to appreciate the significance of their discourse practices. Much of the important research in law and language is truly elegant, and there is no reason that it cannot be described in straightforward language.

Those of us who do law and language research must also rethink our transcription conventions. Since the early work of Jefferson, the goal of conversation analysis has been to transcribe conversation in a way that captures as much of the original sound pattern as possible. This remains an appropriate practice for scholarly discourse among specialists. Such transcripts are extremely difficult for nonspecialists to work with, however. Researchers might consider publishing parallel transcripts, one designed to meet the needs of their professional linguistic audience, the other the needs of legal readers without a linguistic background. (To illustrate the difference, compare the transcription styles in Matoesian [1993] and Matoesian [1995].) The objection that the former is somehow "purer" than the latter is unpersuasive. Since no transcript can ever capture fully the sounds of a conversation, every set of conventions necessarily involves a number of judgments and choices driven by the needs and interests of the audience.

Law and Society, Law and Language

The ultimate objective of each of these recommendations is to promote a fuller integration of law and language into law and society scholarship. The two fields have shared a similar focal point: the failure of the law to live up to its ideal of equal treatment. They have, however, approached the issue from opposite poles. Law and society has attacked the problem from the top down, combining political claims with empirical research that has often been conducted at a fairly high level of abstraction from daily practice. Law and language has worked from the bottom up, beginning with descriptions of linguistic practices and working gradually toward a capacity to test political claims. In carrying out their respective research programs, both have emphasized the effect of variation, especially in such dimensions as race, class, and gender. Law and society has argued that these kinds of variation have affected access to justice. Law and language has documented how such variation manifests itself in the linguistic practice of the legal system, inviting—although rarely making—judgments about political significance. If this book succeeds, it will remind each of these research traditions of its need for the other. It will also remind a broader audience that a meaningful appreciation of justice requires understanding both the concept of power and the mechanisms through which it is applied.

CHAPTER NINE

Language Ideology and the Law

Much of the recent work on the relationship between language and power has been done under the heading of *language ideology*. (*Ideology of language* and *linguistic ideology* are used more or less synonymously.) In everyday usage, the word *ideology* suggests a body of ideas, a philosophy, or an outlook. It often has political connotations, as in "Marxist ideology" or "conservative ideology." The word also frequently has a pejorative undertone, an implication that one who holds to an ideology is an inflexible and uncritical true believer—I have a well-reasoned political philosophy, but you are a "mere ideologue."[1] Applying everyday thinking to the term *language ideology* yields a definition along the lines of "a body of ideas about language," with a particular focus on political contexts. Although the scholarly definitions of both ideology and language ideology are endlessly debated, the most common social-science usages do not differ materially from their everyday counterparts.

The linguistic anthropologist Michael Silverstein (1985) provides a vivid historical example of language ideology at work. It involves the history of the second-person pronoun *you,* which modern English uses in both the singular and the plural. In Old English, before the Norman Conquest in 1066, the singular variants of this pronoun were *thou* (nominative, or subject) and *thee* (accusative, or object)—*thou* love me, and I love *thee.*[2] The plural forms were precursors of *ye* and *you—ye* love me, and I love *you.* The post-Conquest dominance of Norman French speakers added a new element to this pattern of usage: the French practice of always using the plural form in formal speech or in addressing someone of higher social status. Thus, a teacher would address a student in the singular *tu,* but the student would reply in the plural *vous.* By the thirteenth century, this practice had become established in English as well, to the point where "to *thou*" had become a verb meaning "to speak down to." A French language ideology had been imported into English, leading to a change in the meaning and usage of English pronouns.

By 1700, however, *thou* and *thee* had disappeared from English, and Silverstein asks why. Remarkably, it seems to have been the Quakers' fault. The seventeenth century was a time of great upheaval in England, with the beheading of Charles I, Cromwell's commonwealth, the restoration of Charles II, and finally the Glorious Revolution that brought William of Orange to the English throne. Silverstein (1985:247) identifies two significant ideological themes in this century of tumult: "constant struggles between the authority of institutions—Crown, Church, et cetera—and the authority of what we might term the 'empirical evidence of individuals,'" and the "emergence of consciousness of English as a 'language.'" On the question of authority, the Quakers took an extreme pro-individual and egalitarian position. This had a linguistic manifestation: the deliberate and pointed use of *thou* in addressing any individual, regardless of status. Taking advantage of the growing awareness of English as a language, prominent Quakers advanced linguistic purity as a justification for the practice. Historically, they argued, *thou* and *thee* were always and only singular forms, and *you* was just the opposite. In linguistic parlance, these pronouns "indexed," or pointed to, number and number only. To refer to an individual as *you* was thus without linguistic warrant and simply wrong.

The Quaker practice posed a dilemma for those on the authoritarian side, however. I might be *thouing* you because I think you are of lower status, but how could listeners be sure that I was not using the subversive, leveling Quaker *thou*? In order to avoid association with a disfavored fringe group, those in the mainstream eschewed *any* use of *thou* and *thee,* and the forms all but disappeared from the language in favor of the universal *you.*

Silverstein's point in telling the story is to illustrate the interaction between ideas about the meaning of language—language ideology—and the very structure of language, in this case the norms for using personal pronouns. Over the course of about four hundred years, speakers of English reversed these norms twice in reaction to political and social forces. In the second instance, the precipitating cause was the subversive effort of a dissenting sect, the Quakers. They played upon the evolving idea that there was such a thing as a "language" in the sense of a rule-bound system whose traditions and precedents deserved to be taken seriously. Language ideology thus found itself at the intersection of language and society, and in particular at the center of an ongoing struggle for power. At various points people's ideas about language responded to power, abetted its assertion, and spearheaded an effort to subvert it.

In this chapter we will expand our consideration of law, language, and power by analyzing some more recent examples of language ideology at work in legal contexts. We begin by examining in some detail the efforts of anthropologists, linguists, and others to define ideology generally and language ideology in particular. We will then review two contemporary case studies. The first involves an American criminal trial that was strongly influenced by ideas about the nature of language and the hierarchical relation among languages. The second explores the interaction of language ideologies and cultural ideas about gender in an Islamic court in coastal Kenya. Despite the radically different settings, the two studies make a similar point about how language, interacting with ideology, can simultaneously reflect and constitute power.

Defining Terms

Anthropologist Sally Merry (1990:6) has defined *ideology* broadly and inclusively as "a set of symbols which are subject to various kinds of interpretation and manipulation." Writing at the same time, we defined "the core element of ideology as a system of beliefs by which people interpret and impart meaning to events" (Conley and O'Barr 1990:210 n. 10). Following Merry (1986), we distinguished anthropology's emphasis on ideology as a constitutive system of meaning from the Marxist focus on ideology's role in the maintenance of power relations.

A more recent analysis of the meaning of ideology by another anthropologist, Kathryn Woolard (1998), suggests that these same themes continue to dominate the discussion of this elusive concept. Woolard (1998:5) characterizes the very word "ideology" as "itself a text, woven of a tissue of conceptual strands," four of which she discusses in detail. The first strand treats ideology simply as the realm of mental phenomena, having to do with "consciousness, subjective representations, beliefs, ideas," and comprising "the more intellectual constituent of culture." Some writers in this tradition have insisted that ideology must have an intentional, deliberate, thought-out element, whereas others see it as "behavioral, practical, prereflective, or structural." In the latter sense, ideology is a matter of "the lived relations by which people are connected" in society (Woolard 1998:6), and overlaps with such concepts as hegemony, Bourdieu's notions of *doxa* and *habitus,* and Foucault's idea of discourse (or *macrodiscourse,* as we have defined it in chapter 1).

Woolard's second strand builds on the first, adding an element of sociocultural relativity to the basic concept of shared ideas and practices. In this view, which Woolard (1998:6) characterizes as "the most widely agreed-upon," the components of ideology are inevitably "derived from, rooted in, reflective of, or responsive to the experience or interests of a particular social position." That is, even though ideologies are often presented as self-evidently true and beyond the need for explanation, they can always be deconstructed and shown to be the product of someone's wants and needs. Ideology, in other words, is "dependent on the material and practical aspects of human life" (Woolard 1998:6).

The third strand is essentially the second with an important new wrinkle: "a direct link to inhabitable positions of power—social, political, economic" (Woolard 1998:7). Specifically, "ideology is seen as ideas, discourse, or signifying practices in the service of the struggle to acquire or maintain power." In law, for example, we have demonstrated that the "official" ideology retailed by legal professionals reflects their experiences and advances their interests. By contrast, the varied legal ideologies held by lay litigants reflect their very different experiences and support their efforts to challenge professional dominance (Conley and O'Barr 1990:150).

The fourth and final strand adds the element of "distortion, illusion, error, mystification, or rationalization." Often, this can be associated with "the defense of interest and power," as with Engels' notion of "false consciousness" (Wollard 1998:7). To return to the example of law, lawyers have long been accused of using language and symbols to mystify inherently simple concepts in order to maintain their monopoly. Richard Abel (1989:18–19) has described this process as "the task of constructing the professional commodity," and insuring that consumers "purchase it rather than simply produce it themselves."

Woolard (1998:7) sees a "great divide" between the second and third strands, between those who view ideology as "neutral" and those who imbue it with "negative values." In the specific case of language ideology, the prevailing definitions seem to be neutral, but much of the research focuses on power relations. It is as if those who study language ideology begin with a neutral stance but are drawn inevitably to questions of power. That has certainly been our personal experience.

In what may be at once the most elemental and most widely cited definition of language ideologies, Alan Rumsey (1990:346) has characterized them as "shared bodies of commonsense notions about the nature of language in the world"—in other words, ideas about language held by groups of people. Judith Irvine and Susan Gal (2000:35) extend this minimalist definition to encompass the relationship between language and society: "the ideas with which participants and observers frame their understandings of linguistic varieties and map those understandings onto people, events, and activities that are significant to them." The linguistic anthropologist John Haviland (2003:764) glosses these two formulations, elegantly and helpfully, as "what ideas the people we work with (and, indeed, we ourselves) have regarding what language is or what language is good for." He further observes that "insofar as ideas about language rub off onto ideas about people, groups, events, and activities, we may find that linguistic ideologies pervade the very stuff of anthropology: social life and its comparative organization."

Tracking the differences in approach to the general concept of ideology, many have focused more explicitly on power. Irvine (1989:255; emphasis added), for example, has defined language ideology as "the cultural system of ideas about social and linguistic relationships, *together with their loading of moral and political interests.*" Haviland's (2003:764) version is "ideas about language and its place in social arrangements or its use and usability for social and political ends." And in a definition that presumes awareness and intent— and is splendidly illustrated by his account of *thou* versus *you*—Silverstein (1979:193) proposes "sets of beliefs about language articulated by users as a rationalization or justification of perceived language structure and use."

The Importance of Studying Language Ideology

Regardless of the details of one's preferred definition, most scholars agree that the current attention to ideology has had two significant effects on linguistics itself. The first is renewed respect for "the linguistic 'awareness' of speakers," or "native consciousness" (Kroskrity 2000:5, 8)—in other words, what people think about their own language. These "local models," in Paul Kroskrity's (2000:7) words, are "by definition 'real' to members of the groups in question," and "can provide resources for members to deliberately change their linguistic and discourse forms." Students of language ideology see the linguistic models of speakers not as "competing with expert or scientific systems," as many early linguists did, but rather as complementary forms of sociocultural data.

With a few exceptions, until recently linguistics had chosen to discount or ignore speakers' linguistic theories in favor of the "scientific" perspective of the analyst (see Kroskrity 2000:6–7).[3] This was true even of disciplines that emphasized the detailed analysis of language usage. Thus, conversation analysis has generally avoided consideration of speakers' ideas, even as it combs transcripts for the rules that those same speakers appear to attend to. Similarly, William Labov (1979:329), who pioneered the correlation of language variation with social factors, dismissed the possibility that ideology could "alter the socially determined pattern of linguistic variation."

Nonetheless, Labov's work, sometimes described as *correlational sociolinguistics,* also provides a vivid illustration of the salience of native consciousness. As we described in chapter 1, Labov demonstrated strong correlations between patterns of linguistic variation and social class. One can read his research as relating not only to speakers' experience of class but also to their class aspirations. In what may be his most famous study, Labov (1966) showed that employees of an upscale New York department store pronounced *r* after vowels (for example, saying "New York" rather than "New Yawk")—thought to be an upper-class tendency—more frequently than their counterparts in a discount store. In addition, the post-vocalic *r* was more common when the speakers were asked to repeat themselves and, presumably, were paying more conscious attention to their speech.

Although Labov (1979:329) expressly denied the power of language ideology, at least in the sense of "native consciousness," to alter the pattern of linguistic variation, the current view would be that he had demonstrated precisely the effect that he had denied. Recall that he characterized the pattern of variation as "socially determined." But how does social determination work? What, specifically, is the social agent of determination? The answer must be *language ideology*. In Irvine and Gal's (2000:35) phrasing, Labov's *r*-pronouncers had some ideas with which they framed their understandings of linguistic varieties, and they mapped those understandings onto events that were significant to them. Labov discovered *how* language can vary according to social context. Language ideology helps to explain *why*.

The influence of language ideology can also be seen in conversation analysis. In the 1998 edition of this book (pp. 19–20), we wrote, accurately, that "most conversation analysts have limited themselves to the study of *how* people manage conversations, prescinding from such questions as *why* they do what they do. The focus has been on the mechanics of conversation rather than on the social and political objectives the parties may be pursuing." This has changed. Responding to the concerns that have animated the study of language ideology, conversation analysts have increasingly sought to tie speakers' explicit language practices to their implicit purposes. Some scholars doing work that is methodologically indistinguishable from conversation analysis have self-consciously called their research "discourse analysis" in order to distance themselves from conversation analysts' longstanding aversion to questions of power. Much recent work has been done under the rubric of "critical discourse analysis," with "critical" meaning "focused on power relations." Several new collections (all published in Europe and hard to find in this country) have used conversation analysis to examine ideologies of language and gender (see Hellinger and Bußmann 2000; Litosseliti and Sunderland 2002; McIlvenny 2002). Conversation and discourse analysts have begun to debate "what counts as context for analyzing talk, what it means to say something is relevant to participants, the relative status of analysts' and participants' understandings of participant actions, and, most broadly, the role of objectivity and politics in intellectual inquiry" (McElhinny 2003:849).

The second effect of paying attention to language ideology has been to highlight "the non-referential functions of language" (Kroskrity 2000:7). The most basic definition of *referential* is suggested by its root, *refer,* "meaning simply to point out something for the purpose of describing or saying something about it" (Mertz 1985:8). As the linguist John Lyons (1968:404) put it a generation ago, "the relationship which holds between words and things (their referents) is the relationship of *reference:* words *refer to* (rather than 'signify,' or 'name') things." Thus, the referential function of language involves using it to denote, or refer to, things that are being talked about. This is the function of language that people are most attuned to when they are beginning to study a foreign language, studying lists of words and phrases, listening to tapes, and generally trying to learn "how to say things."

The nonreferential functions comprise everything else that language can do, including constructing, reflecting, and resisting social structure. As Kroskrity (2000:7) points out, "much of the meaning and hence communicative value that linguistic forms have for their speakers lies in the 'indexical' connections between the linguistic signs and the contextual factors of their use—their connection to speakers, settings, topics, institutions, and other aspects of their sociocultural worlds." In other words, much of the work of language is done in the nonreferential realm.

We believe that Kroskrity's claim that attention to ideology has opened up the previously neglected nonreferential aspects of language is somewhat overstated. To cite one example, our own work in the 1980s and early 1990s on rule-oriented versus relational accounts of legal problems (Conley and O'Barr 1990) seems to be precisely about the connection between linguistic signs and settings, topics, and institutions, even though we failed to characterize it in terms of language ideology. And William Labov, even as he disavowed the efficacy of language ideology, seemed to be proving its importance. We think it might be more accurate to say that the current focus on language ideology has sharpened linguists' appreciation for the nonreferential by making explicit that which was formerly implicit.

Kroskrity also identifies four substantive features of language ideologies that have proven to carry particular analytical power. First, "language ideologies represent the perception of language and discourse that is constructed in the interest of a specific social or cultural group" (Kroskrity 2000:8). This is the self-interested aspect of ideology in the general sense that we discussed earlier. Kroskrity gives the example of national language movements: although their stated purpose is usually to promote efficiency in communication, they can almost always be shown to benefit some groups at the expense of others. In fact, the same argument can be made about linguistic scholarship itself: its ostensibly disinterested (and, in theory, purely referential) texts can "be read subversively as powerful means of controlling the process of producing and receiving discourse" (Bauman and Briggs 2000:139).

Krsokrity's (2000:12) second point is that language ideologies are "grounded in social experience which is never uniform." That is, language ideologies should be presumed to be multiple, since every sociocultural group can be subdivided along such axes as gender, class, generation, and elite status. In simplest terms, when you find *a* language ideology, look for more. Third, "members may display varying degrees of awareness of language ideologies"

(Kroskrity 2000:18). Awareness is likely to correlate with the way in which an ideology is put into practice. Those who are more aware tend to be more active in contesting existing, dominant ideologies, whereas "merely practical consciousness" typifies "relatively unchallenged, highly naturalized, and definitively dominant ideologies" (Kroskrity 2000:19). The Quakers who advocated for the status-neutral *thou* were certainly aware of the ideological contest in which they were engaged, as were, more recently, the feminists of the 1970s who began the movement to displace the generic *he* (Silverstein 1985). By contrast, before these respective subversive actions, English speakers who made the *thou/you* status distinction or referred to a generic human being as *he* probably thought rarely if ever about what they were doing.

Kroskrity's (2000:21) final point is the most subtle and in some ways the most powerful: "members' language ideologies mediate between social structures and forms of talk." Language ideologies, in other words, are not mere abstractions. They are, rather, bridges between the sociocultural experiences of speakers and the ways in which they actually speak. The Quaker case is again pertinent: one can trace an unbroken link from social and political experience through language ideology to the very structure of the English pronoun system.

An example that illustrates all four of Kroskrity's points is the question of whether *United States* is singular or plural. In the eighteenth and early nineteenth centuries, the United States *were* plural, as in Article III of the Constitution: "Treason Against the United States shall consist only in levying War against them, or in adhering to their Enemies, giving them Aid and Comfort." This usage began to change during and immediately after the Civil War; for example, by its 1888 edition, *Encyclopedia Britannica* had switched to the singular. Now, speaking of the United States in the plural sounds like a conscious archaism or rhetorical flourish, as when someone says "in these United States."

First, both usages reflect ideas about language—specifically, about the significance of the category "number"—that serve the interests of particular social groups. In the Constitution, the plural may be indicative of deference to the sensibilities of those who were reluctant to sacrifice the autonomy of the uniting states. As the states' rights leader John C. Calhoun said in 1849, "the United States are not a nation" (Schwartz 1993:239). Alternatively, it may simply reflect the traditional British practice of rendering governments and other corporate bodies in the plural. Even if the latter interpretation is correct, it is interesting that there was no attempt in the Constitution to make a point by using the singular. In either case, the standard historical view (e.g., Bishop 2003) is that the post–Civil War singular serves a newly ascendant nationalist ideology.

Second, the ideologies in question were not uniform. One can find published examples of the singular usage before the Civil War, as well as the persistence of the plural in the decades thereafter. Surprisingly, the Thirteenth Amendment, which was pushed by the strongly Unionist Radical Republicans immediately after the Civil War, abolished slavery "within the United States, or any place subject to *their* jurisdiction."[4] Third, the historical record suggests varying degrees of awareness of the ideological change. It is widely believed that Lincoln was the pivotal figure in the switch to the self-consciously nationalist singular, but there is evidence of him using both forms—on the same day![5] Now, of course, the once-controversial singular has been fully "naturalized" for as long as most living people can remember.

As to Kroskrity's fourth point, it is hard to imagine a clearer example of ideas about language mediating between changing sociocultural experiences and the forms of everyday talk. The Civil War and the events that precipitated and followed it were the pivotal sociocultural experiences, of course. Mark Twain captured the point perfectly (and anticipated linguistic anthropology by more than a hundred years) when he observed that the Civil War was fought over whether "United States" was singular or plural (see Venners 1997).

The Power of Language Ideology in Legal Contexts

We turn next to two specific examples of the study of language ideology in legal contexts. In each instance, attention to language ideology helps to clarify the ways in which language functions (nonreferentially) both to reinforce existing power relations and to facilitate their subversion. The first is a report by linguist John Haviland (2003) of an Oregon murder trial in which he served as an expert witness. Several witnesses, including the defendant and the critical prosecution witness, were speakers of Mixtec, an indigenous Mexican language, but the court presumed them to be Spanish speakers because of their nationality. Haviland uncovers the complex ways in which the case was influenced, if not determined, by a set of ideas about language itself and the relationships among languages that are embedded in the American legal system. The second example is the work of anthropologist Susan Hirsch (1998) in Islamic divorce courts in coastal Kenya. Through attention to the linguistic details of trials and mediation sessions, Hirsch illuminates the interaction between linguistic and cultural ideologies about gender. She reveals the dilemma faced by divorcing wives who must play to one ideology in order to justify themselves as wives and women while simultaneously invoking its opposite in an effort to assert their rights under Islamic law.

Language Ideologies in American Courts

Haviland served as an expert witness for the defense in a homicide case against a defendant he identifies as Santiago V., a Mixtec-speaking Indian from the

Mexican state of Oaxaca. The victim, Ramiro, was stabbed to death in a migrant labor camp near Portland, Oregon. According to the prosecution's version of the case, Margarito, a friend of Ramiro, had provoked a fight at a party. Afterwards, the two had driven off into the strawberry fields, pursued by another car full of young men. After Ramiro and Margarito abandoned their car and ran off, the second group—which included Santiago—found it and burned it. They then captured Ramiro and, according to eyewitness testimony, Santiago stabbed him while he was held at gunpoint. The defense contended that there were several cars in the fields, that the lack of bloodstains proved that Santiago could not have done the stabbing, and that the eyewitness testimony had been coerced from men who were under threat of prosecution for the car burning. Santiago V. was convicted and sentenced to life imprisonment. The critical linguistic feature of the trial was that none of the witnesses to the events in question spoke English. Almost all were native speakers of Mixtec, and few had meaningful competence in Spanish. Nonetheless, the only translator provided by the court was a native speaker of Cuban Spanish (which is quite different from Mexican Spanish) who knew no Mixtec.

Haviland's account focuses on some beliefs about language that were critical to the outcome of the trial. The first (Haviland 2003:767) is the notion of "referential transparency." He characterizes this as "the 'Verbatim' theory, or the assumption that expressions in one language can be unproblematically rendered into propositions and translated 'verbatim' into another." This belief underlies the way in which the court structured the relationship among witnesses, jurors, and interpreters. The judge instructed the interpreter to function as a translation machine (p. 768): "[T]ranslate the responses of the witness verbatim, word for word. In other words, I don't want you to say, 'Well, the witness says,' forget that part. Just translate it verbatim, word for word." This is impossible, of course, since no one language can be mapped directly onto another in "verbatim" fashion. As Haviland (p. 768) puts it, the judge's instruction rested on the fallacy that "the truth-functional core of what someone says can be decoupled from the actual saying itself."

The same can be said of the judge's instructions to the jury about the translation process. Following a long-established principle of American law, the judge told the jurors that they must ignore any competency that they might have in Spanish.

Text 9.1 (Haviland 2003:768)

> The translation of the Spanish language that you must rely on in the course of this case is that translation that is made by the court interpreter that will be translating the language as it's spoken from the witness stand. . . . I don't know whether any of you, as I say, understand

5   Spanish, but we don't want to get into a situation where we have some
juror in the jury room saying, "Well, that's not what the witness really
said, you know."

Thus, the interpreter's "verbatim" translation of a witness's answers—presumably bereft of any commentary, paraphrases, or, ironically, "interpretation"—was to be the sole source of evidence for the jurors. They were to ignore everything they heard between the lawyer's question and the interpreter's English rendering of the answer, regardless of whether they understood it. This legal rule is apparently informed by a fear of jurors arriving at competing translations that are not verbatim. The rule has an internal logic only if, as Haviland argues, one accepts the verbatim fallacy.

So the *Santiago V.* case, like most U.S. cases that involve non-English-speaking witnesses, began with the promulgation of a flawed language ideology. As the trial progressed, other language ideologies came into play to complicate the situation even further. As we noted earlier, some of the key witnesses were speakers of a third language that neither the English-speaking judge and lawyers nor the English-Spanish interpreter understood at all. In Text 9.2, the testimony of the Mixtec-speaker who claimed to have seen the defendant stab the victim degenerated into dark comedy. Note that the district attorney was speaking in English and the witness in Spanish. The interpreter was going back and forth between the two languages, but the transcript—which forms the sole basis of a defendant's rights on appeal—reproduced only her English renderings.

TEXT 9.2 (Haviland 2003:769)

DISTRICT ATTORNEY (DA): Do you understand Spanish well?
WITNESS: No.
DA: What is the word you know in Spanish for stabbing?
INTERPRETER: May I ask how I can ask him without giving the
5   word?
DA: Okay. Let me rephrase the question. What word do you
use to say how the knife went into the man's body?
WITNESS: I call it knife.
DA: How do you describe a knife being stabbed into someone
10 hard?
INTERPRETER: I don't know if you want it in Spanish or English?
DA: In Spanish.
WITNESS: I don't know.
DA: You don't know the word to describe that in Spanish?
15 WITNESS: I don't understand much.
DA: What language do you usually speak?
WITNESS: In my village, only Mestica [*sic*].

DA: Is it different very much from Spanish?
WITNESS: Yes.

Note the multiple absurdities. First, the district attorney established that the witness had limited facility in Spanish. Then he asked the interpreter to ask the witness, *in Spanish,* for the Spanish word for "stabbing." When the interpreter pointed out the circularity of the request, the lawyer asked the witness to provide a word for sticking a knife into someone. The witness responded with "knife." When the witness demurred to the lawyers' follow-up questions, it finally occurred to the district attorney to ask whether "Mestica" is very different from Spanish.

But even this was not enough to discourage the prosecutor from seeking the testimony he needed. Several pages later in the transcript, he tried to cure the problem by asking the witness to write out an appropriate "Mestica" word, and then "spell it in Spanish"! The witness responded that in addition to being unable to speak Spanish, he could not write, at least in Mixtec.

What was happening here? One possible interpretation is that the district attorney was an idiot. How complicated is it to understand that there are people in Mexico who speak indigenous languages? That such languages are radically different from *all* European languages? That an interpreter who speaks Spanish does not necessarily speak every language found in every Spanish-speaking country? The clinching evidence for the DA's idiocy might be his lack of preparation for all of these problems. District attorneys are elected. Murder trials are rare, so there is plenty of time to prepare. Such trials usually command intense media attention. Smart district attorneys try to avoid looking like fools in front of the voters. How hard would it have been to locate an English-Spanish-Mixtec interpreter for this trial?

In considering alternative explanations, it should be pointed out initially that the district attorney won: Santiago V. was convicted and sentenced to life imprisonment. It appears that the "tragicomic" (Haviland 2003:769) discourse did not strike the jurors as sufficiently absurd to upset their faith in the prosecution. So perhaps the district attorney was dumb like a fox.

Haviland's linguistic explanation invokes two additional language ideologies that the district attorney may have shared with the jurors. The first is what Haviland (2003:769) calls the "standard language" notion. That is, the conduct of the trial seems to have assumed not only that verbatim translation is possible, but that translation *into English* is especially easy. In linguistic terms, English is treated as "a maximally unmarked and neutral vehicle of propositional communication"—in other words, a "standard language" into which all others should be readily translatable. The negative implication of this belief is that all other languages must be nonstandard, and thus less suitable than English for unambiguous expression of meaning, and generally inferior to it.

The second relevant ideology is what Haviland (2003:769) calls the "handi-cap" notion. Oregon law treats non-English speakers (along with those whose hearing or speech is impaired) as "disabled persons." The accommodation for this particular disability is the appointment of an interpreter. To Haviland, this approach to language rights reflects a belief that English is not only a standard language, but "is also somehow in the repertoire of skills of a 'standard per-son,' one who is socially and, perhaps, morally whole or 'normal.'" Once again, there is a powerful negative implication: those who do not speak English are not only "disabled," but "substandard."

Taken together with the verbatim fallacy, these two additional notions ex-plain a great deal about both the judge's instructions and the district attorney's conduct. The instructions seem built on the premises (a) that verbatim trans-lation is possible and (b) that something about English makes it a particularly appropriate endpoint for the process. Point (b) (the standard-language ideol-ogy) both prompts and is reinforced by (c) the handicap ideology. It works both ways: you are defined as disabled because you cannot speak the standard language, and you cannot speak it because of your disability. With these three ideologies in place, the district attorney can be seen not as manipulative but as simply struggling to deal with an abnormal, substandard person. And this per-son is doubly abnormal: not only can he not speak *the* standard language, En-glish, but he is little better at the next best thing, Spanish. Perhaps the jury sympathized with the prosecutor in his desperate efforts to deal with such a thoroughly dysfunctional person.

Haviland might have added a fourth point to his list of ideologies: the no-tion of national languages.[6] Taken as a whole, the trial embodies the idea that nations have languages that are standard, normal, and natural. In the United States, that language is English, of course. However, the ostensibly ludicrous employment of an English-Spanish interpreter to aid the Mixtec-speaking wit-nesses implies the belief that Mexico, too, has a natural language: Spanish. Stu-pidity or sheer malice could explain the court's failure to have a Mixtec inter-preter present, as well as the district attorney's befuddlement at his witness's stubborn refusal to be able to speak Spanish. But it is also possible that this tragic farce was set in motion by the operating assumption that "normal" Mex-icans would be able to speak their country's "normal" language. Once again, the jurors, sharing this ideology, might have sympathized with the prosecu-tion's dilemma.

Haviland (2003:773) concludes on a discouraging note. He admits that his readers will inevitably expect "a triumphal cry for linguistic anthropology as an antidote to bad theories of language." But he concedes that he has no prac-tical solutions, and we cannot do much better. There are barriers to reform at every level, some legitimate and some spurious.

First, the legal system has a compelling reason for reducing every trial to an

English-language transcript: facilitation of appeals. Appellate review of judicial decisions has long been viewed as a fundamental component of due process. Unless appeals are to involve a live retrial of every case—a logistical impossibility—then trials must be reduced to written transcripts in a language that every appellate judge can be presumed to understand.[7] In this country at this time, the reality is that there is only one such language, English. Even under the simplest circumstances, transcribing is an act of interpretation (Ochs 1979). The problems become infinitely more complex when multiple languages are involved. Courts can do a better job of addressing these problems, certainly better than the Oregon court in Haviland's case, but no amount of ideological adjustment will make them go away.

A related practical issue is how much linguistic competence and sophistication courts can be expected to have. The competence aspect of this issue is whether every defendant has a right to interpretation in every language spoken by every witness. In a murder or other major felony case, we think, the answer is clearly yes; it violates any reasonable standard of fairness to send someone away for life on the basis of a colloquy between a lawyer and a witness who barely understood each other. It seems equally obvious that a traffic case should not grind to a halt while an interpreter in a rare (in that venue) language is found, trained, and qualified. Where to draw the line is an excruciatingly difficult question that is beyond the scope of this discussion.

The sophistication prong of the issue brings us back to Haviland's lament about the "bad theories of language" that are so much in evidence in the *Santiago V.* case. That is, is there any hope that judges and lawyers will become knowledgeable consumers of the theory of language ideology? On the evidence of the transcript excerpts that Haviland quotes, the answer would be a resounding no. Haviland's reported experience suggests that legal practitioners are just too dim to get it.

But can this be true? Every day, lawyers everywhere make use of extremely complicated scientific theory and data, from genetics to toxicology to economics. As the following chapter demonstrates, forensic linguists are becoming increasingly prominent as experts. Why, then, is language ideology such an impenetrable mystery? One answer might be that Haviland participated in a truly unrepresentative case, with the lawyers and the judge exhibiting extraordinary levels of incompetence. We have no reason to think so, but, as is almost always the case with qualitative research (including our own), it is impossible to determine how well a particular set of data represents any larger population.

Another factor might be the way that linguists and anthropologists write about language ideology. That is, maybe lawyers and judges would be interested in language ideology, and capable of dealing with it, were the writing on the subject not so unnecessarily dense. Haviland's own article is the exception that proves the rule, straightforwardly written and probably comprehensible to most educated nonspecialists (lawyers, for example). Regrettably, this is not the case with much of the work in the field. The development of specialized terminology is inevitable as a discipline matures. But obscure diction and convoluted syntax are not. Language ideology both deserves and is capable of straightforward exposition. Instead, we find the very mystification for which social scientists rightly criticize the law. In fact, too much of the writing about language ideology embodies its own language ideology: the apparent belief that obscurity is a mark of theoretical sophistication.

A final question about the relationship between linguistics and American law is also prompted by Haviland's complaint about "bad theories of language." What about linguists' theories of law? Are linguists' ideologies of law as flawed as lawyer's ideologies of language? Two points that Haviland makes are especially provocative.

First, Haviland (2003:770) describes his expert efforts on behalf of Santiago V. as "trying to get an innocent man (and he was innocent) out of prison." In a footnote appended to the parenthetical, he explains that "post-conviction research by defense investigators, as well as by the author and Lourdes de Leon aided by others from the accused man's village in Oaxaca, soon revealed the identity of [*sic*] actual knife-wielder." Few things are as problematic to critical theorists as the law's historical claim to determine "truth," what "really happened." A trial is seen as a competition of narratives (Bennett and Feldman 1981), with the outcome contingent as much on power dynamics as the "facts." Yet here a critical theorist states a conclusion about "what really happened" without any reflection on the problematic nature of truth, or any apparent awareness of the extraordinary irony of his absolute claim. Even allowing for the limitations of space, it is striking that words such as "innocent" and "actual" are unexamined. Linguistics claims a position of privilege that it would not (and should not) grant to the law.

Haviland (2003:773; emphasis added) concludes his discussion of the *Santiago V.* case with an ambivalent "postscript" on the final outcome. The conviction was ultimately reversed and the innocent defendant freed after five years in prison. However, to Haviland's evident regret, the release "was based not in the least on the theory-laden analysis and critical deconstruction of the linguistic flaws in the investigation and trial." Instead, "it was based on a *technicality*. His lawyers persuaded the court of appeals that he had been incompetently defended, since his lawyer had refused to allow him to testify in his own defense." The word "technicality" carries heavy ideological baggage. To nonspecialist observers of the legal system it has such implications as "insubstantial," "unrelated to the merits of the case," and, often, "inconsistent with the interests of justice," as in "the high-priced lawyer got the crook off on a technicality." Yet here it is applied to a right—the assistance of counsel—that is explicitly enumerated in the Constitution (the Sixth Amendment) and that most lawyers would regard as a cornerstone of justice. By what warrant, and for what purpose, does Haviland treat it so dismissively? Is it not an exercise in ideology to value the assistance of counsel below "theory-laden analysis and critical deconstruction"?

Haviland's remark about Santiago V.'s lawyers having "persuaded the court of appeals" is also interesting. Recall that Haviland's own judgment about guilt and innocence was pronounced with unproblematic authority: the man *was innocent.* No such certainty attends the appellate court's judgment about the competence of the defendant's trial lawyer. We are not told that the lawyer *was incompetent,* but rather that a higher court was *persuaded* that he or she was. Once again, why is it that the law's construction of reality needs "critical deconstruction" by linguistics, while the linguist's version of the same process is to be taken for granted?

None of this is intended to detract from the excellence of Haviland's analysis. He demonstrates, persuasively, how language ideology came into play in the trial of Santiago V., and how its manipulation led to a denial of justice. His work is a model for a new level of linguistic analysis of the production and maintenance of legal power. Our point, rather, is one made frequently by students of language ideology, including Haviland himself: linguistics, like any other institutionalized activity, has its own language ideologies.[8] It is anomalous that Haviland, otherwise so acutely attuned to ideological relativism, chooses to ignore this point in dissecting his own interaction with the law. Perhaps this anomaly can help to explain why the law proved so unreceptive to his approach: physician heal thyself and all that.

Language Ideologies in Kenyan Divorce Courts

Anthropologist Susan Hirsch (1998) studied language ideology in the Kadhi's Courts of coastal Kenya. A *kadhi* is an Islamic judge who is empowered by the state to apply Islamic law in certain cases (including divorce) that involve Muslim parties. Hirsch's particular focus is on ideas about language and gender that are implicated in what she calls (Hirsch 1998:17) "the discursive construction of gender." The title of her book, *Pronouncing & Persevering,* captures an ideological dichotomy that has long been powerful in Kenyan Swahili[9] society, the contrast between "a Muslim husband pronouncing divorce and his persevering wife silently accepting the decree" (Hirsch 1998:2). In this stereotype, the husband's authority to pronounce both reflects and reaffirms his autonomy and agency, whereas women, "devoid of agency" (Hirsch 1998:1) in language and in fact, "are expected to endure marital hardships without complaint and to accept divorce in the same spirit" (Hirsch 1998:3). Hirsch sets for herself the task of questioning this beguilingly simple paradigm through the analysis of the language of divorce cases.

Lacking the power to pronounce, wives who find themselves in intolerable marriages must go before the kadhi and make a case. By Hirsch's account, women confront a seemingly irreconcilable dilemma. Swahili women should personify the cultural ideal of *heshima,* which involves respect, honor, and modesty. An important part of *heshima* is shielding private matters from public scrutiny; instead of making public complaints about marital troubles, one perseveres quietly. A parallel cultural ideal is that of *haki,* which includes the concepts of justice and rights. It is especially powerful because *haki* is guaranteed by Islam and Islamic law. The obvious quandary is that in order to seek *haki* in the marital context, a woman inevitably jeopardizes *heshima.* To achieve her rights as a wife, a woman puts at risk the very qualities that make her deserving of such rights. But women regularly bring and win divorce cases (they lost fewer than 2% of the cases Hirsch studied), meaning that they somehow walk this exceedingly fine line.

The solution seems to lie in the ability to negotiate a minefield of culturally significant and often conflicting language ideologies. Specifically, women invoke ideologies that index, or point to, themselves as proper wives, while at the same time stepping outside the traditional bounds of propriety to assert their rights. As Hirsch (1998:219) puts it, "Swahili women who complain in court embody a contradiction. Through their participation in cases and mediations, they generally stand in gross violation of appropriate speech, and yet, in so many dialogues, they are also routinely depicted as compliant wives."

One important language ideology involves the belief that "words expose"; that is, "exposing household problems is damaging to family members" (Hirsch 1998:229). As one divorcing husband described the principle (Hirsch 1998:230), "It's shameful like that. People stay, they—they conceal together about anything they have, they don't have. Indeed, this is how people get along." For a wife to bring a divorce case, or even to protest her treatment, is inevitably to violate this belief, leading many husbands to complain about their wives' complaining. As one of them testified (Hirsch 1998:230–31), "She took the opportunity to—to bring my brother-in-law to the house and to mention these matters . . . I don't want her speaking to him about anything at all." For the wife, however, there is no alternative. To win her case, she must persuade the kadhi that she has persevered in the face of her husband's unjust behavior, so that behavior must be exposed. In other words, in order to justify her breach of the linguistic norm, the wife must breach it even more.

A related belief is that "words harm": "bad words 'cause' bad events" (Hirsch 1998:232). Talk about conflict produces more conflict, bringing down evil on speakers and hearers. As a kadhi said in urging a husband and wife to stop arguing and reconcile (p. 233), "But don't—don't you, don't be ready all the time to cause trouble, meaning, it's bad to argue." In a similar vein, a husband reported that after an argument with his wife (p. 232), "I went out to avoid this evil." Here again, a wife seeking a divorce must necessarily go against a belief that Hirsch describes (p. 232) as "widespread in Swahili culture." To compound the problem, the violation is at two levels. The first occurs simply by virtue of talking about trouble in the marriage. In addition, to show that she has been a persevering wife, the woman must describe the trouble in graphic detail, repeating many of the argumentative and abusive "bad words" that her husband has directed at her. The repetition of profanity is especially problematic. So strong is the cultural antipathy to bad words that kadhis will often interrupt wives' narratives with such admonitions as "leave aside these careless words" or "don't say those things here" (p. 234).

All of this takes place against a more general ideological background pertaining to language and gender. Specifically, women are expected to be story-tellers: "Swahili women perform experiences of conflict as animated stories, using many conventions of narrative common to storytelling outside court" (Hirsch 1998:140). By contrast, "[m]en tell stories less frequently, and their stories include fewer features of storytelling performances" (p. 140). Consequently, women must tell stories to "index" themselves as women, and those stories must contain the private details of their perseverance. In order to conform to one ideological norm, and to create an entitlement to relief, wives must violate other strongly held beliefs. Their husbands are quick to criticize these transgressions, both in and out of court. Yet wives persist and succeed.

Hirsch's analysis suggests no simple explanation of how they do it. One hypothesis might be that women are effectively subverting the dominant ideologies through their resistance, but Hirsch finds no evidence that this is happening. Instead, it seems that women accommodate themselves to the existing belief system. Hirsch reports that the cases that come to court involve truly compelling stories of patient and long-suffering perseverance. She believes that the barriers posed by language and gender ideologies exert a screening effect on the filing of cases. Given the adverse reactions that their unavoidable violations of these norms will provoke, women wait until they have an unimpeachable record of their own compliance with the obligations of *heshima* and their husbands' contempt for the ideals of *haki*. Thus, women almost always win when they seek a divorce, but their winning percentage is illusory, since they only try in the direst of circumstances. If the denominator were bad marriages rather than divorce cases filed, women would appear far less powerful.

Another sign of the power of prevailing ideologies is a decline in the prestige of the Kadhi's Courts. Hirsch reports that men constantly criticize the kadhis for giving relief to women who breach the norms of *heshima*. "Accordingly, kadhis face the hostility of men who lose in court and of other men who criticize their lack of solidarity" (Hirsch 1998:129). Men condemn the Kadhi's Courts as "women's courts," unfaithful to the true tenets of Islamic law. One such man expressed his dissatisfaction with a decision by stabbing the kadhi. Although this judge heroically returned to the bench, and others soldier on in less dramatic fashion, there is a real danger that these courts will not survive.[10]

Hirsch, like the Kenyan women whose cases she studied, finds ironies and contradictions at every turn. Initially, wives who are badly treated seem trapped by a set of interlocking ideologies of language and gender. But, as Hirsch discovered, some of them prevail in court by the tactic of openly and notoriously violating those same ideologies. The necessity of using that tactic, however, dooms all but those with the most egregious cases to persevere in silence. Finally, we learn that the men who lose when women win may defeat the insurgency by simply pronouncing the dangerous system out of business.

Conclusion

Recent studies of language ideology represent, in our view, not an entirely new theoretical perspective but a useful reframing and refocusing of work that has been going on for a generation or more. In the first edition of this book we criticized conversation analysis and other methods of linguistic microanalysis for deliberate inattention to connections between language and social, cultural, and political contexts. We particularly emphasized the need to consider the role of language in creating and reflecting power relations. The current focus on language ideology has been a strong corrective to this inattention. By making context a starting point rather than an afterthought, language ideology scholars remind us that we cannot usefully study how people practice language without paying attention to how they think about it.

For people like us who have done comparable research framed in terms of discourse, the concept of language ideology may provide greater analytical precision. We have written extensively, for example, on the rule-oriented and relational "orientations" that lay people have toward the law (Conley and O'Barr 1990). We would have done better to characterize these orientations as language ideologies, for that is exactly what they are: shared ideas about language. Specifically, they are ideas about the linguistic practices that are appropriate in legal contexts. Because different social groups have differential access to these divergent ideologies, and because only one is compatible with the dominant ideology of the law, the power implications are clear.

The two research projects we have reviewed in detail in this chapter—Haviland's analysis of a multilingual American trial and Hirsch's study of Kenyan divorce courts—demonstrate further the power and potential of the concept of language ideology. Haviland uncovers a subtle but strong, even determinative connection between shared ideas about language (and individual languages) and the workings of the American criminal justice system. For those of us who are as much interested in the law as in its language, the next step is to figure out what to do with his revelation. Hirsch, working in a very different setting, reminds us that the power relations embedded in language ideology are neither simple nor linear. Her sometimes contradictory findings are compelling evidence of the power of attending to power in studying language.

CHAPTER TEN

Forensic Linguistics

In their new book, *Language on Trial,* the lawyer-linguists Lawrence Solan and Peter Tiersma (2004) tell a remarkable story of the role of a self-proclaimed "author attribution expert" named Donald Foster in the still-unsolved JonBenet Ramsey murder case. JonBenet, a six-year-old beauty queen, was killed in her Boulder, Colorado, home on Christmas night in 1996. At the center of the case is an unsigned ransom note that was found at the scene. In June 1997, Foster wrote a dramatic and apparently unsolicited letter[1] to JonBenet's mother Patricia, a prime suspect, saying, "I know that you are innocent—*know* it, absolutely and unequivocally." He concluded that the ransom note had been written by a young adult with an addiction to crime literature and Hollywood thrillers, and pointed the finger at John Andrew Ramsey, JonBenet's half brother. Foster believed that this young man was communicating over the Internet using the name "Jameson." When it turned out that "Jameson" was really a woman, Foster changed his theory to allege that John Andrew Ramsey and the woman had worked together. Finally, when the Boulder police consulted with Foster, he changed his story once again, claiming that the child's mother was actually the author of the ransom note. Foster's key piece of evidence, it seems, was the way that Patricia and the unknown author wrote the letter *a.*

Knowing only this much, most people might conclude that Foster was a crackpot. But who is he in fact, and why did many people, including the police, pay attention to what he had to say? Donald Foster is indeed a serious person, a well-known Shakespearean scholar who is an English professor at Vassar College. In 1989, he had published his Ph.D. dissertation as a book called *Elegy by W.S.: A Study in Attribution,* in which he claimed, on the basis of stylistic similarities, that Shakespeare was the author of a poem entitled "A Funeral

Elegy" (Foster 1989). His claim did not go unchallenged, however. Another Shakespearean scholar found fault with Foster's analysis on several grounds (including the facts that Shakespeare's style had changed by the date the text was published, that Shakespeare did not have a known connection to the subject of the poem, and that Shakespeare's name was appropriated by many others in this period before the advent of copyright). After this and other challenges, Foster withdrew his claim about Shakespeare and the literary community now considers the real author to be someone else.

Foster had also achieved some popular acclaim shortly before interjecting himself into the JonBenet case. A 1996 best seller called *Primary Colors* (Anonymous 1996) depicted a presidential campaign conducted by a thinly disguised Bill and Hillary Clinton and a raft of characters who closely resembled prominent Clinton insiders. The author was listed only as "Anonymous," a gimmick that greatly enhanced the book's cachet. It was endlessly discussed in the media as the Washington elite alternated between looking for themselves in the text and trying to guess who wrote it.

On the basis of his notoriety in the Shakespeare controversy, *New York* magazine hired Foster to analyze the text of *Primary Colors* and attempt to determine its author from a list of 35 "suspects." Applying his best techniques (e.g., looking for unusual words, spellings, syntax, and so on), Foster concluded that Joe Klein, a *Newsweek* columnist, was the author (see Foster 2000). After the *Washington Post* acquired a copy of the manuscript annotated in Klein's handwriting, Klein capitulated. Foster had been right this time.

What does this unusual series of episodes say about the role of language scholars in the courtroom? If the Ramsey case ever goes to trial, Foster is unlikely to have any part in it. After Foster's multiple flip-flops, a police source quoted by Solan and Tiersma concluded that "the defense would eat him alive." In the end, the sober Shakespearean scholar had devolved into the writer of the overwrought letter to JonBenet's mother and a caricature of the self-promoting "expert." It was not a good time to be arguing that students of language have important contributions to make to the litigation process.

In this chapter we review some of the areas in which linguists and other language experts have been routinely welcomed as expert witnesses, as well as some areas in which the role of linguistics has remained controversial. We compare the legitimate contributions of language experts with the more dubious efforts that are exemplified by the Foster fiasco. We argue that, although such experts have made important contributions to litigation, their work has not been without at least three sets of troubling consequences.

The first issue concerns who gets the benefit of linguistic expertise. In some cases, it seems to be a simple question of who can pay. In other situations, language scholars have donated their services in pursuit of fairness and equity. Even in those cases, however, there is evidence of another form of rationing, this time along political lines. A second and related question deals with subsequent access to the work that experts do. In an adversary system, the work of experts is usually viewed as proprietary, effectively owned by the party for whom it is done. Is it appropriate for language researchers to devote significant time to work that may never see the light of day? Third, there is reason to be concerned about the effect of allowing the needs of the legal system to determine which issues get addressed. While all kinds of research are, of course, influenced by practical considerations (see, for example, the ongoing debate about whether medical research funding is directed disproportionately to "men's" or "women's" diseases), we argue that the problem is particularly acute here, as a vast amount of research time and energy is devoted to pursuing an agenda set by the law. As we have done in other chapters, we explore the implications of these issues for the power relations that are embodied in the legal system. We turn first, however, to a brief digression on the law that applies to expert testimony.

The Law of Expert Witnesses

In court, most witnesses are limited to testifying on the basis of firsthand knowledge—things that they actually saw, experienced, or (rarely) heard. "Experts" are people with special qualifications who are allowed to express opinions about topics that ordinary jurors cannot be expected to understand. A doctor, for example, would be allowed to testify that a person suffered a concussion as a result of an automobile accident. A psychiatrist might be allowed to express an opinion that a criminal defendant was incompetent to stand trial, or an engineer might be allowed to opine (the legal verb for "give an opinion") about the cause of a building collapse. Had the police and prosecutor in Boulder tried to use Donald Foster in a case against any of the suspects he identified, the questions for the court would have been (1) whether he was qualified, based on his specialized linguistic knowledge, to offer an opinion about the authorship of the ransom notes; and (2) whether that opinion would be sufficiently reliable.

In answering these questions, all federal courts must follow Federal Rule of Evidence 702 (as must most state judges, as a practical matter, because most states now have evidence rules based on the federal model). According to Rule 702, "[i]f scientific, technical, or other specialized knowledge" will be helpful to the judge or jury, then "a witness qualified as an expert by knowledge, skill, experience, training, or education, may testify thereto in the form of an opinion or otherwise, if (1) the testimony is based on sufficient facts or data, (2) the testimony is the product of reliable principles and methods, and (3) the witness has applied the principles and methods reliably to the facts of the case."

Rule 702 raises several distinct questions. We consider them specifically with reference to Donald Foster and the JonBenet case. First, is the witness qualified? Note that the rule is very flexible about forms of qualification: an M.D. degree with specialized board certification might be necessary in one case, whereas years of experience as an auto mechanic would suffice in another. Foster, with his Ph.D., his Shakespeare book (a serious endeavor, even if he was ultimately proved wrong), his years of teaching and research experience, and his successful unraveling of the *Primary Colors* mystery, would be found to be a qualified practitioner of author-identity scholarship by any judge in the country.

That finding would lead us to a second, more difficult question: would such expertise be helpful to the jury? Initially, most judges would conclude that author identification is a highly technical field in which few jurors would have any competence; this would weigh in favor of admitting Foster's testimony. But even so, would knowing about this field and Foster's findings really help the jurors to decide the case, or would it simply mislead them? This gets us to the issue that pervades the second half of the rule and that proves decisive in most determinations of the admissibility of expert testimony: will the expert's opinion be *reliable*?

The rule instructs the judge to apply a three-part test of reliability. First, is the opinion based on "sufficient" facts or data? In other words, did the expert look at all the available evidence, and was there enough there to support a conclusion? This would be hard to determine in Foster's case. How could a court tell whether Foster had looked at all the available evidence, short of commissioning another author-identity expert to study the entire case? And are there any standards in the field for determining how much evidence is enough?

The second part of the test would be even more difficult: was Foster applying "reliable principles and methods"? In a 1993 case called *Daubert v. Merrell Dow Pharmaceuticals, Inc.* (which is still good law), the United States Supreme Court held that "scientific" experts should base their opinions on the scientific method.[2] The Court instructed judges to examine experts' methods for indicators of reliability usually associated with positivist or "hard" science (experimental physics, for example), including testability of theories, calculation of error rates, peer-reviewed publications, and general acceptance in the scientific community. Then, in a 1999 case called *Kumho Tire Co. v. Carmichael,* the Court held that in dealing with experts who did not fit the scientific model (in that case, a "tire wear expert"), the trial judge should still insist on a showing of reliability, but could be more flexible in deciding what factors to consider.[3]

How would Foster fare under these standards? For starters, is his work "scientific"? If so, his general methods of investigation had surely been peer-reviewed (if nothing else, his dissertation must have satisfied a faculty committee), and the long and serious debate over his Shakespeare conclusion suggests that his methods were viewed as generally accepted. But are those methods testable? It would seem possible to devise a test for authorship analysts, but has anyone done so? Have rates of error ever been calculated? And if Foster is not a scientist, what alternative measures of reliability might a judge employ?

Finally, Rule 702 requires that the reliable principles and methods be reliably applied to the facts of the case. That is, an expert with a track record of reliability cannot depart from his or her established methods and say whatever comes to mind. If we assume that Foster had developed and employed reliable methods in his earlier work on Shakespeare and Klein, were his inferences about the JonBenet case based on the same methods conscientiously applied? Or was he using his credentials as a license to speculate?

We have both worked as expert witnesses, and one of us teaches scientific evidence and has examined many experts in court. We doubt that many trial judges would admit the sort of opinions that have been attributed to Foster in the Ramsey case. The point we seek to make is more general, however. It is that those who seek to appear in court as linguistic experts must satisfy not their fellow linguists but judges seeking assurances of "reliability." We remind our readers to keep this standard in mind as they consider the examples that follow.

Defining Forensic Linguistics

The word *forensic,* derived from the Latin *forum,* means (according to the Oxford English Dictionary) "of, used in, or pertaining to a court of law." Thus, in its most straightforward sense, *forensic linguistics* means "linguistic expertise applied to legal cases." It should be noted, however, that many people now use the term as synonymous with "law and language." For example, in his preface to John Gibbons' (2003) *Forensic Linguistics: An Introduction to Language in the Justice System,* the distinguished linguist Peter Trudgill locates it within the context of applied linguistics (itself defined as the application of the findings of linguistic research to the solution of real-world problems). For Trudgill (2003:vi), forensic linguistics is "the application of linguistic research—in sociolinguistic areas such as discourse analysis, dialectology, linguistic variation and stylistics, and other core linguistic areas—to different societal issues connected with the law."

Gibbons (2003:12) himself distinguishes between a narrow and a broad definition of forensic linguistics. In the narrow sense, it refers to linguistic evidence used in and by the law. In the broad sense, it refers to the entire range of law and language issues, including (1) the language of the law, including both the written language used in legal documents and the language spoken in legal fora; (2) legal translation and interpretation; (3) efforts to alleviate linguistic disadvantages resulting from the language of the law; (4) linguistic evidence provided by experts in court; and (5) linguistic expertise applied to problems of legal drafting and interpretation.[4]

In this chapter we will focus on the fourth element of Gibbons' definition, largely because the preceding chapters are devoted to the other components. And as we have done elsewhere in this book, we emphasize the relationship between forensic linguistics and power.

Tracking the Footprints of Linguistics in the Law

In the United States and other common law countries where lawyers must make their cases in an adversarial process, they seek expert testimony on an enormous range of topics. Thus, it is not surprising that in some situations they would turn to linguists and other scholars of language for assistance. Two scholars, Elizabeth Loftus and Roger Shuy, began their work in the 1970s when such expert testimony was novel and rare. As a result, their articles and books became foundational texts in the emergent field we now call forensic linguistics. Although Loftus holds a Ph.D. in cognitive psychology rather than linguistics, her work deals directly with language. Shuy was trained as a linguist and taught linguistics for many years at Georgetown University. Examining their work is instructive because it illuminates both the contributions that language experts have made to the law and the problems that their work has raised.

Elizabeth Loftus and Eyewitness Testimony: Access to Expertise

The psychologist Elizabeth Loftus began studying eyewitness testimony in the 1970s. Although her focus as a psychologist is on cognition and memory, the fact that what is remembered is typically reported *through language* makes her work of interest to law and language scholars. In her early and perhaps best-known research, Loftus (1979:77–78) studied eyewitness testimony by asking questions of experimental subjects who had watched a videotape she had produced showing a car crash. In a particularly provocative set of questions, Loftus asked subjects how fast two cars were going when they collided with each other. She varied the words used to describe the action of the cars in the videotape: *How fast were the cars going when they / hit / smashed into / each other?* Subjects reported variations in speed from 25 miles per hour to more than 55, depending on the verb used to describe the action. Not surprisingly, the subjects who were asked the "smashed" version of the question reported much higher rates of speed.

In a follow-up study a week later, Loftus asked the same subjects, *Did you see any broken glass?* There had been no broken glass in the videotaped accident. Nonetheless, those subjects who had been given the "smashed" question the week before reported seeing broken glass almost three times as frequently as those who had been asked the "hit" question—presumably, Loftus (1979: 78) inferred, "because broken glass usually results from accidents occurring at high speed." Loftus interprets these results as evidence of the power of new information to influence an eyewitness's memory of a complex event. (Linguists would also be reminded of the extraordinary power of language to shape understanding.)

Findings such as these convinced Loftus that the formation of memory is an ongoing process subject to external influences, not a discrete event that creates an immutable record. The obvious significance of her findings for law led to opportunities to work as an expert witness, assisting lawyers in and out of court in assessing the validity of eyewitness testimony.[5] As she became more involved in legal issues, she came to question the law's historical practice of elevating eyewitness testimony above other forms of evidence, and to worry about the harm that it might cause. As Loftus (1979:xi) acknowledges in the very first sentence of her now classic *Eyewitness Testimony,* "A major reason for writing this book has been a longstanding concern with cases in which an innocent person has been falsely identified, convicted, and even jailed."

Loftus has appeared as an expert witness in numerous reported cases, almost always to testify on behalf of criminal defendants about the unreliability of eyewitnesses. Judges have varied in their willingness to admit such evidence. According to one recent decision by a federal appellate court (*United States v. Smithers*), "[c]ourts' treatment of expert testimony regarding eyewitness identification has experienced a dramatic transformation in the past twenty years and is still in a state of flux."[6] When such evidence began to be offered in the 1970s—largely in the person of Elizabeth Loftus—courts were skeptical, finding, among other things, that the scientific theory was not generally accepted, or that jurors, aided by cross-examination, could figure the question out for themselves. During the 1980s, courts increasingly found such testimony admissible, influenced by the mounting body of research that suggested a "dichotomy between eyewitness errors and jurors' reliance on eyewitness testimony." Indeed, the *Smithers* court cited Loftus for the proposition that "half of all wrongful convictions result from false identifications" (2000:311). Currently, under the evidence rules reviewed at the start of this chapter, trial judges are required to give close scrutiny to the reliability of eyewitness expert testimony and its capacity to help or mislead the jury. The 1980s trend toward admissibility seems to be continuing, although not without exceptions.[7] Psychology and linguistics have appeared too "unscientific" to some judges.[8]

Loftus's work raises squarely the question of access to language expertise.

When experts charge, then help is available only for defendants who have the money, or whose states provide subsidies for experts. And even if all the available experts were to work pro bono all the time, only a tiny fraction of the criminal defendants around the country who were facing eyewitness accusers could possibly expect to get help.[9] It is logical to assume that experts appearing without charge would limit themselves to cases in which they thought the defendant was deserving of their help.

A remarkable example of the latter point—and the difficulties that political screening of cases can create—is provided by Loftus's involvement in the case of John Demjanjuk, a Cleveland autoworker alleged to have been "Ivan the Terrible," a notoriously cruel guard at the Treblinka death camp during the Holocaust. He was convicted of crimes against humanity by an Israeli court in 1988. According to an account Loftus gave in a 1987 *Newsweek* op-ed piece (Loftus 1987), she was called by one of Demjanjuk's lawyers before the trial. He said that he believed in his client's innocence and asked for her help in challenging the eyewitness testimony of the elderly Treblinka survivors on whose identification of Demjanjuk the prosecution's case rested.

Loftus wrote that her initial reaction was sympathetic. Her entire research career had led her to question criminal convictions based solely on eyewitness identifications—particularly those based on observations made long before the trial. This was just such a case. Loftus then referred to her desire to promote the legal ideal of insuring a fair trial for all defendants, even unpopular ones. Loftus also cited her obligations to what she called "my science," implying that a scientist has a duty to pursue significant research opportunities regardless of personal and political consequences.

In the end, however, she rejected the engagement because of personal and social conflicts. Her own Jewish heritage played a part in the decision. Most troubling to her, however, was the hurt expressed by some close friends, also Jewish, when she raised the possibility of helping Demjanjuk. They persuaded Loftus that giving the expert testimony sought would heap a final and terrible indignity on those Holocaust survivors who claimed to recognize Demjanjuk more than forty years later.

This was obviously an excruciating personal judgment that we are glad we did not have to make. Nonetheless, the analytical and emotional process that Loftus chose to detail in the press raises some important questions about forensic science. Few research scientists would share her sense of obligation to contribute to the legal system, and we suspect that just about all would have rejected the case out of hand on political grounds. So Loftus came closer than most would have to offering her expertise even to the most unsympathetic of defendants. But in the end she could not do so, underlining the problem of selective access.

Loftus's work also helps to frame the issue of the proper relationship between basic and applied research. Her career in the laboratory and the courtroom would appear to represent an ideal progression from theory to practice, from basic research to real-world application. She has made significant and fundamental contributions to the science of memory. She is absolutely correct when she writes (Loftus and Ketcham 1994:5), "My work has helped to create a new paradigm of memory, shifting our view from the video-recorder model . . . to a reconstructionist model." Lawyers discovered her work and asked her to apply it. She has done so, guided by an admirable ethic of concern for the unjustly accused.

But as her work has developed, one might wonder about the relationship between science and law. In 1994, she reported having "testified in hundreds of court cases where a person's fate depended on whether the jury believed the eyewitness's sworn testimony" (Loftus and Ketcham 1994:3). Even spread out over fifteen or twenty years, "hundreds" of court appearances represent a phenomenal commitment of time. As she described it, again in 1994, "my world has been turned upside down. As grant applications pile up in the corners of my hopelessly cluttered office, I spend my days talking on the phone to strangers accused of the most loathsome crimes imaginable" (Loftus and Ketcham 1994:5). Her published output also came to focus heavily on the legal application of her research. In 1991, for example, she wrote *Witness for the Defense: The Accused, the Eyewitness, and the Expert Who Puts Memory on Trial* (Loftus and Ketcham 1991), while her 1994 book, *The Myth of Repressed Memory* (Loftus and Ketcham 1994), deals entirely with her experiences in sexual abuse cases. (Both books were coauthored by Katherine Ketcham, a writer of popular self-help and recovery books).

We admire Loftus's commitment to the rights of the accused. What concerns us is the prospect of a major field of research—in this case, the study of memory and its interaction with language—having its development driven primarily by the needs of a class of litigants, which needs happen to coincide with the political beliefs of the field's principal figure. We do not mean to suggest in any way that Loftus's *answers* are driven by the interests of her clients; her integrity and competence are unimpeachable. We do mean to wonder about a field in which the *questions* seem to be dictated by those interests.

Recall Loftus's reference to her obligation to "my science" in her *Newsweek* piece about the Demjanjuk case. She agonized over whether, *as a scientist,* she was duty-bound to try to answer a question posed *by the law.* Helping the legal system might be part of one's duty as a citizen, but is it one's duty as a scientist (or a basic researcher in any field) to pursue an agenda set by a legal advocate? Is that in fact "science"? Does a researcher's responsibility not include the framing of the questions to be studied?

Roger Shuy's Linguistic Battles: Questions of Ownership and Agenda-Setting

Roger Shuy's distinguished career is similarly revealing of the strengths and weaknesses of the field of forensic linguistics. Shuy is a widely published and highly regarded linguist who has worked often as an expert in legal contexts (according to his Web site, he has consulted on over 500 cases and testified in 52). As he wrote in 1993, "I have worked on behalf of a number of nationally known public figures, entertainers, politicians, industrial giants. I have also worked on behalf of the little guys" (Shuy 1993:xvii). Two of his books (Shuy 1993, 2002) can be characterized as chronicles of his courtroom experiences in, respectively, criminal (*Language Crimes: The Use and Abuse of Language Evidence in the Courtroom*) and civil (*Linguistic Battles in Trademark Disputes*) cases.

Language Crimes is a compelling book that details some of the ways in which linguistic evidence can promote criminal justice. In separate chapters dealing with bribing, agreeing, threatening, admitting, truth-telling, and promising, Shuy (1993:8) outlines basic linguistic understandings of how these speech acts work and shows some of the ways the law can misinterpret them. He begins his analysis by discussing some common misconceptions about language: meaning is found primarily in individual words; a single listening to a tape is enough to determine its content; reading a transcript is as good as hearing a tape recording; all parties to a conversation understand the same things by their words; people say what they mean and intend. For a linguist, these assumptions are problematic. They become the basis for Shuy's demonstration of what applied linguistics can deliver to the law.

For example, in discussing the problem of bribery, Shuy (1993:43–65) points out that there are a variety of ways that offers can be made, ranging from the overt (or performative) offer to the indirect and embedded varieties. The most direct sort of offer would be something like *I hereby offer you a bribe for such and such*. One could make the same offer indirectly, as in *If you will do me a little favor, I'll make it up to you real good*. Least direct of all is the embedded offer, which "lacks both the explicitness of the performative offer and the inferred comprehension of the indirect offer" (Shuy 1993:55). It might consist of nothing more than the mention of two activities occurring simultaneously, such as an otherwise legal campaign contribution to a politician and some action to be taken by the politician. How overt and direct does an offer of a bribe have to be in order to count legally? How should the above examples be interpreted? Should the law consider them bribes or not? The answers to these questions are, of course, legally consequential: they could mean the difference between a jail term and going free.

In another chapter, Shuy (1993:118–35) asks how direct an admission must be in order to be legally binding. Or alternatively, how indirect may it be and still be considered by the law to be an admission? These examples illustrate the quandary: *I admit that I overslept / I slept till 7AM / I missed my bus / I was here as soon as anyone else / My alarm clock didn't go off.* These statements vary from the direct, performative admission (*I admit that . . .*) to the indirect admission (*I slept till 7 AM; I missed my bus*) to the excuse that contains an implied admission (the last two).

Linguistic distinctions like these proved consequential in a case in which Shuy testified in 1986, *The State of Alaska v. Larry Gentry.* Gentry was charged in a homicide, and a critical question was whether he had admitted that he knew in advance that his car was to be used in a murder. In an earlier hearing concerning a search warrant, Gentry's statements had included the following (Shuy 1993:124–25; italics in original): "I *wasn't too sure* on it even being a shooting . . . I *wasn't sure,* but I *kind of knew* and I *kind of didn't know*" / "I was *pretty sure* of it, yes" / "*I'd done figured it out*" / "No, *I did not know* he was going to use that car" / "I was still *trying to ignore it.*" Analyzing these and other inconsistencies, Shuy argued that Gentry had never made anything that the law should characterize as an admission. Finding that the issues were beyond common understanding, that Shuy had used established linguistic techniques, and that his testimony would help the jury, the judge allowed him to testify. Nonetheless, "the jury deliberated briefly and found Gentry guilty as charged" (Shuy 1993:135).

Despite the adverse outcome, it is hard to dispute that Shuy's presence assured Gentry of a fairer trial than he otherwise would have gotten. Indeed, in all of his criminal cases Shuy is undoubtedly using his expertise to advance the interests of justice when he appears in court to demand that language issues be addressed in a linguistically sophisticated way. Nonetheless, the issue of access remains. Who gets the kind of help Shuy can provide? Is politics a determinant, as in Loftus's case? Economics? Shuy (1993:xxi) writes that he is politically neutral: although he has testified only on behalf of defendants, he has consulted with prosecutors and stands willing to help them. But in the course of speculating about why prosecutors almost never call on him, he mentions (Shuy 1993:xxi) that "[t]here may be budget constraints," suggesting that money plays a role in the allocation of his expertise.

The more recent *Linguistic Battles in Trademark Disputes* (Shuy 2002) recounts the civil side of Shuy's career as an expert witness. The role of linguistic experts in trademark cases is longstanding and well established. A trademark is a distinctive word (*Coca-Cola*), phrase (Nike's *Just do it!*), symbol (the Nike swoosh), etc., that identifies a company's product or service. The decisive issue in most cases is whether the defendant's mark is so similar to the plaintiff's that it is likely to confuse consumers about the source of the relevant products (suppose, for example, that a competitor of Nike adopted the slogan

Go ahead and do it!). In some cases, the defendant claims that the plaintiff's mark is invalid because it has become the generic name for a class of products; cellophane, aspirin, trampoline, and escalator are all former trademarks that fell victim to "genericide."

Linguists regularly contribute to the resolution of these issues. One of the cases Shuy (2002:125–43) writes about, *AutoNation, Inc. v. Acme Commercial Corp. d/b/a CarMax,* is illustrative of the types of analyses they do. The legal issues were (1) whether "AutoNation USA" was confusingly similar to Car-Max's "AutoMation" trademark (the name of its computerized inventory system); and (2) whether AutoNation's slogan, "The Better Way to Buy a Car," was confusingly similar to CarMax's "The New Way to Buy Used Cars." The jury ultimately found in favor of AutoNation.

Shuy was initially contacted by AutoNation's lawyer, with whom he had worked in the past. Because the case was far from his home, Shuy suggested that the lawyer contact his friend and colleague (and ours), Duke University linguist Ron Butters. A few weeks later, Shuy got a call from CarMax's lawyer. He had used Butters in the past, and had intended to hire him here. But when he learned that Butters was already working for the other side, he offered the engagement to Shuy, who accepted. Beyond being mildly amusing, this story speaks volumes about the role of linguists in trademark cases. Everyone understands that, in every significant case, there will be a "battle of experts"; there are a limited number of "regulars"; everyone knows everyone else; and experts compete without hard feelings. Indeed, the professional behavior of the experts seems indistinguishable from that of the lawyers (including being well-compensated). Implicit in this is the understanding that a good linguist, just like a good lawyer, should be able to construct a plausible argument for either side.

Shuy and Butters prepared reports for their respective clients and testified in depositions (sworn testimony given before a trial, usually in a lawyer's office, to permit the opponent to learn what the witness will say). The technical linguistic issues they debated included the following:

1. *Phonetic similarities and differences:* The two experts agreed on the number of sound units, or *phonemes,* in the AutoNation USA and AutoMation marks. Butters emphasized, however, that the "o" in AutoNation was long, whereas in a CarMax television commercial the "o" in AutoMation was pronounced "uh" (what phonologists call the "schwa" sound). He argued that this difference helped to prevent confusion. Shuy emphasized the similarity of the "n" and "m" sounds in the respective marks, and pointed out that they are easily misperceived or confused by listeners. He also stressed the visual similarity of the two marks.
2. *Morpheme differences:* Butters contended that the "Auto-" morphemes (a morpheme is a unit of sound that conveys meaning) in

the two marks were different: in AutoMation, auto means "self," whereas in AutoNation it means "automobile." Shuy pointed out that both were derived from the Greek *automata,* meaning "self-directed" or "propelled," and hence were a source of potential confusion.

3. *Pragmatic meaning differences:* Butters testified that AutoNation and AutoMation were used to refer to different things. The former referred to a used car store in its entirety, and the latter to a computerized inventory system that was "a relatively minor aspect of the Carmax operation" (Shuy 2002:134). Shuy viewed this as Butters' strongest evidence of the absence of confusing similarity.

In their reports and depositions, the two experts went back and forth on these and other technical points. When the trial finally came, the two were sequestered in different hotels by their lawyers for eight days and told little about what was going on. In the end, neither testified. Shuy, who in hindsight regretted having taken the case, found out about the result only much later (a recurrent irritant in both his civil and criminal cases). What can we learn about forensic linguistics, and linguistics generally, from Shuy's accounts of cases like this? Five significant points emerge.

First, the linguistic analyses are of very high quality. The issues in such cases are close, and there is indeed much to be said on both sides. Shuy and Butters applied well-accepted linguistic theories and methods to the facts at hand and produced persuasive reports. If we were teaching linguistics, Shuy's cases would be an excellent source of illustrative materials on a range of topics. It is not surprising that courts routinely find that such analyses meet the standard of scientific reliability.

Second, at least in the instance of Shuy and Butters, the experts seem to succeed in walking the fine line between science and advocacy. As Shuy acknowledges in his writings, he understands that he is participating in an adversary process and that the lawyers may ignore an answer that does not advance their case. He stresses, though, that he is absolutely impartial in performing his work. As he puts it, "I do *not* call myself a forensic linguist . . . I consider myself a linguist who, in this instance, happens to be carrying out his analysis on data that grows out of a court case . . . the linguist analyzes the language evidence from a position of neutrality" (Shuy 1993:200).

Third, the participation of Shuy and other linguists in such cases raises some questions about equal access to justice, although they are not as troubling as in the criminal context. These are purely commercial disputes, with both sides paying their experts as part of the cost of maintaining their trademarks. It would be a rare trademark case in which linguists refused to appear on some sort of political grounds.[10] It would be an equally rare trademark case, however, in which language experts volunteered their services. Consequently, there are likely to be cases in which only one side can afford linguistic assistance. Losing a trademark is obviously not as serious a matter as going to jail, but the problem is still worth noting.

A fourth point concerns the ability of the expert witness to publish. In our experience, the lawyer and client effectively *own* the expert's work (see Conley and Peterson 1996). One cannot disclose the results of an investigation without permission. Some lawyers would argue that an expert is bound by a more far-reaching duty of loyalty, amounting to an implied agreement not even to comment on the case in a way that might be detrimental to the client's interest. Shuy's writings suggest that, at least for him, permission to disclose and comment is regularly forthcoming. But it is a matter of concern that many linguists appear to spend much, or most, of their time on work that is not automatically part of the scholarly public domain.

The fifth point involves the implications of the experts' work for linguistics itself. Shuy is correct, as we have noted, that he and others are applying established linguistic techniques to interesting problems. Once again, however, linguistics is answering questions posed by the law. This is very different from using the law as an arena for investigating questions raised by linguistics itself on theoretical grounds. A comment by Shuy is revealing. After describing his work in a case involving the trademark "doctrine of foreign equivalents" (it is possible to infringe an English-language trademark by using a foreign translation or a similar foreign word), Shuy (2002:149) writes, "I was never informed about the conclusion of this case . . . Like other linguists, I am still anxiously awaiting the outcome of a salient case." In his expert role, Shuy would be understandably anxious to learn the outcome of the case. But why should he and other linguists, *as linguists,* care about who won? How would a court's decision affect the progress of linguistics? Is the legal tail wagging the scientific dog?

A simple but interesting experiment is to examine the contents of recent issues of *Forensic Linguistics: The International Journal of Speech, Language and the Law,* the journal of the International Association of Forensic Linguistics. The journal publishes a mix of papers that pursue linguistic questions in legal contexts and those that attempt to answer questions of primary interest to the law. In, for example, volume 10, number 1 (2003), one of the articles falls into the former category: Anna Wierzbicka's "'Reasonable Man' and 'Reasonable Doubt': The English Language, Anglo Culture and Anglo-American Law" (Wierzbicka 2003). Using semantic theory, she explores the meaning of the word "reasonable" in historical and cultural perspective, arguing that the original meaning—so central to the evolution of the common law—is no longer understood by most English speakers. Here, linguistics both poses the questions and provides the answers. The linguist is an outside critic, not an invited guest. From the law's perspective, both question and answer are probably unwelcome.

The rest of the papers in the issue, however, can be fairly categorized as linguistics acting at the invitation of the law. The titles include "Identifying the Source of Critical Details in Confessions' (Hill 2003; testing a method of validating confessions made to the police); "Not So Fresh in the Mind: A Forensic Linguistic Analysis of Suspected Memorized Narrative Essays" (Kennedy 2003; applying new software to uncover impermissible memorized passages in the Hong Kong Certificate of Education writing exam); "Better Tools for the Trade and How to Use Them" (Woolls 2003; assessing programs for detecting plagiarism and determining authorship); and "Earwitness Identification over the Telephone and in Field Settings" (Yarmey 2003; testing the ability of witnesses to describe and identify a voice in various settings, including lineups). All of these are interesting topics, and the research may ultimately improve the administration of justice. But should we be concerned about the diversion of so much linguistic time and talent from fundamental critique of the law to pursuing the law's agenda?

A final comment about *Forensic Linguistics* concerns a review of the work on powerless language that we did in the 1970s. An issue from 2002 included an essay by Joanna Kerr Thompson (2002) entitled "'Powerful/Powerless' Language in Court: A Critical Re-evaluation of the Duke Language and Law Programme." Thompson makes many excellent points. She argues, for example, that too many researchers who have used and built upon our work have failed to appreciate its methodological limitations (which we readily acknowledge), and that we should have been more engaged in the critical reappraisal of the work (a fair comment). Her concern, however, seems to be less with improving the theoretical model than with "proffering advice on so sensitive a topic [witness credibility]," in particular to "ensure an adequate 'duty of care' to those potentially on the receiving end of linguistic counsel" (Thompson 2002:153–54). Elsewhere she writes that "the 'duty of care' owed by linguists to their 'clients' must be more closely defined" (Thompson 2002:153).

At this point we are puzzled. We have no clients; we have not given linguistic counsel, whatever that is; and we do not proffer advice. We asked questions that interested us as linguistic anthropologists. We published our findings in several academic journals, and presented them before all kinds of legal and social science audiences. Whether we were right or wrong is a valid and important question, but its importance in no way depends on or derives from the use that experts may choose to make of our work.

Forensic Linguistics and Power

Much of the work that forensic linguists do is clearly on behalf of the powerless. The appearances of people like Loftus and Shuy in criminal cases have helped to redress the power imbalance that typically obtains between the state and the accused (the occasional celebrity felon notwithstanding). In Australia, the linguist Diana Eades (1995) has long worked to minimize the language barriers that Aborigines must overcome in dealing with the legal system. In this and many other countries, Susan Berk-Seligson and others have labored to improve court interpretation, to the benefit of immigrant and other litigants who do not speak the national language.[11]

A great deal of other work in the field can be characterized as at least power-neutral. The *Forensic Linguistics* articles on confessions and earwitness testimony discussed above, for example, should be of value to both prosecutors and defense lawyers, and should ultimately promote conviction of the guilty and acquittal of the innocent. So also with Shuy's trademark cases, where two relatively powerful litigants seek to protect their investments. Neither side is inherently favored by forensic linguistics, and competent testimony should help the courts get it right.

In fact, it is hard to identify any instance in which forensic linguistics seems to be advancing the interests of the powerful in any overt and direct way. The potential problem, we believe, lies in the law's agenda-setting role. If forensic linguistics spends most of its time answering questions of interest to the law, then its contribution to promoting justice will necessarily be incremental. Consider, for example, the issue of gender bias in the courtroom, which was a major implication of our research on powerless language style. In her critique of our work, Thompson (2002) worried about "linguistic counselors," who presumably would help women and other powerless speakers to become better-received witnesses. The legal system has a problem, and forensic experts bring social science to bear to ameliorate it.

Contrast this approach with that of Gregory Matoesian, whose work we reviewed at length in chapter 2. Matoesian dealt with the most powerless of all situations confronted by women in court: testifying as rape victims. Matoesian, however, did not begin with the law's assumptions. Instead, he used theory and methods developed elsewhere to examine rape victim testimony as a linguistic event. Far from discovering possibilities for incremental improvement, he delivered the radical message that the rape trial, with all the gender-based cultural baggage it carries, is structured in such a way as to make justice almost impossible. This is not a message that could have emerged if the law had set the agenda. This is bleak news, but is it the job of science to be hopeful and helpful?

Mateosian challenged the law's premises in a fundamental way. Much of the ad hoc work in forensic linguistics does not. As we have repeatedly argued throughout this book, the law reflects and reproduces society's power relations. Research such as Mateosian's unsettles those relations in a way that responding to the law's agenda cannot. Moreover, encouraging linguistics to become, in effect, an agent of the law may be a positive distraction from pursuing deeper questions. In this subtle and indirect way, then, contemporary forensic linguistics, even as it strives to promote just outcomes in individual cases, may be working to strengthen the structures that create injustice in the first place.

Going Forward: A Linguistically Driven Forensic Linguistics

We conclude this chapter with the book with which we began: Solan and Tiersma's (2004) *Language on Trial.* After examining the vast and growing body of literature that now appears under the heading of forensic linguistics, we believe that Solan and Tiersma's work offers the best model for the future of the field. Rather than being linguists working for the law, they are linguists looking at the law, in ways that are determined by linguistics. They answer many questions that are of interest to the law, but, more importantly, they also ask many questions that would not have occurred to the law.

Solan and Tiersma deal with a range of situations in which the law appears to be practicing linguistics, as, for example, when courts interpret speech acts. In deciding on the legality of police conduct, judges must regularly decide, for instance, whether a suspect *asked for* a lawyer. Once the suspect does so, the police must stop the questioning until a lawyer is on the scene. In everyday interactions, we often ask for things in very indirect ways. A restaurant patron might say to the server, "I'd like the salmon special," or even, "I'm in the mood for the salmon." Although ostensibly mere expressions of desire, these utterances function as requests in the pragmatic context of the restaurant service encounter. But what about when a suspect under interrogation by the police says such things as "when I talk to my lawyer I'll [answer questions]," "I will get a lawyer," "maybe I need a lawyer," or "I'd like to have one [a lawyer] but you know it would be hard to get hold of one right now" (Solan and Tiersma 2004:57–58)? Courts have refused to recognize these nonliteral requests, permitting police officers to ignore the suspect's obvious intent and continue the questioning.

The law's handling of expressions of *consent* is exactly the opposite, according to Solan and Tiersma. Whereas suspects must make explicit and literal requests for counsel, police officers have been permitted to obtain consent to search a suspect's property in the most roundabout way. For example, the U.S. Supreme Court has found consent to search the trunk of a car where the officer asked, "Does the trunk open?" and the suspect responded in the affirmative. The problem is broader than merely the words used, as the pragmatic context of the encounter must be taken into account. Indeed, Solan and Tiersma (2004:59) conclude that when someone in a position of power or authority asks or requests us to do something, we will normally interpret it as a command.

Many of the issues they cover are also discussed in Shuy's (1993) *Language*

Crimes. Many of the same linguistic points are also made in both books. What is different is the intellectual approach. It may seem to be a fine distinction, but it is, we believe, a significant one. Shuy's book is a set of stories about linguistic analyses that he performed when lawyers presented him with particular cases. Solan and Tiersma began with a set of linguistic concerns and sought out legal contexts in which to explore them. Their answers involve both concrete suggestions for law reform and more basic critiques of the law's working assumptions. But their work is, in every case, linguistics applied to law, not linguistics responding to law. Any biases that may be present in their selection of issues have not been imposed by the law and thus do not reflect the power hierarchies that are embedded in it. Also, their findings are accessible to all, never the property of any particular client.

Testimony by forensic linguists in individual case is both necessary and desirable. When courts confront linguistic issues (whether they are aware of them or not), competent experts must appear to offer guidance. But case-by-case work should not be the driving force in the field of forensic linguistics (or the predominant activity of forensic linguists), nor should case reports comprise the bulk of its literature. "Theory" should not be merely the sum of what can be inferred from individual cases. Solan and Tiersma's work is, we believe, the model for a far more effective forensic linguistics, one in which linguistics challenges the primacy of the law rather than simply serving needs that the law defines.

NOTES

Chapter One

1. Danet studied a Massachusetts trial in which a doctor who had performed an abortion was prosecuted for manslaughter. She analyzed the different ways in which prosecution and defense categorized the entity that had been aborted: "baby" and "little baby boy" by the prosecution, "fetus" and "products of procreation" by the defense.

2. We mean two things by *linguistic analysis*. First, we mean it in the narrow, technical sense of analysis that draws explicitly on linguistic theory and methods. We also use it in a broader sense to refer to any kind of analysis, whether or not formally linguistic, that focuses on language in an intensive way.

3. Language is also the medium of argument, persuasion, threat, and other extralegal means to settle disputes. The exceptions, of course, are physical fighting and warfare, which can be seen as nonlinguistic efforts to resolve disputes.

4. The term *utterance* is also difficult to define. We have in mind something akin to what conversation analysts mean when they describe a complete turn at talk. Harvey Sacks, Emmanuel Schegloff, and Gail Jefferson (1974) noted that speakers in conversational exchanges normally get to speak until they reach a *turn relevance place*. A person usually speaks until a turn is syntactically complete—the turn relevance place is reached—at which point that speaker or another must negotiate who gets the next turn. An utterance, as we use the term, is very much like the *turn* Sacks, Schegloff, and Jefferson have described. For readers not familiar with this literature, it might be useful to think of *utterance* as referring to a simple sentence or something that works like a simple sentence.

5. R. A. Hudson, in his influential textbook *Sociolinguistics* (1980:4), characterizes the difference between sociolinguistics and the various forms of structural linguistics as a matter of emphasis: "I shall refer throughout to 'sociolinguists' and 'linguists' as though they were separate individuals, but these terms can simply be used to reflect the relative amount of attention given to the social side of language, without taking the

distinction too seriously." He also points out that, while most linguists recognize that one *should* pay attention to the social contexts of language, sociolinguists dedicate themselves to determining *how* to do so.

As Hudson's comments suggest, many language-oriented scholars who are not usually thought of as sociolinguists have also attempted to incorporate the social context of language into their theorizing. John Searle's (1969) speech act theory and H. Paul Grice's (1975) work on conversation are examples. Many of the issues we discuss in this book could be profitably examined from such perspectives, but that is beyond the scope of the sociolinguistic analysis that we are undertaking.

6. Perfectly formed utterances are those that follow the rules of formal (written) English grammar. It was typical for linguistics texts to devote their primary attention to explaining the structure of sentences such as "John hit the ball" or "Lions love meat and gravy" rather than the messier and more complex sentences that actually occur in everyday contexts. For illustrations, see Bloomfield 1933:17–77 and Chomsky 1964:61–84.

7. Nonideal utterances are those real-world utterances that are problematic from the perspective of a strict grammarian. For example, one commonly hears sentences such as "My mother, no I mean my aunt, lived, no well that isn't quite right, she didn't really live there, she thought about living there. Anyway . . ."

8. See generally Fasold 1990:39–64. We discuss some examples of linguistically oriented legal anthropology in chapters 6 and 8.

9. Representative work appears in Tannen 1993; some of it is discussed in more detail in chapter 8 of this book.

10. Some of the most important papers on conversation analysis in institutional contexts have been collected by Paul Drew and John Heritage (1992) in *Talk at Work*. A comment in the paper by Emmanuel Schegloff (1992:106) illustrates our point: "The issue I mean to address is *not* 'Is there such a thing as gender/class/power/status/organization/etc.?' or 'Does it effect anything in the world?'"

11. This question is suggested by Marc Galanter's classic article "Why the 'Haves' Come Out Ahead" (1974), which proposes a number of structural answers.

Chapter Two

1. The common law rule was that the slave was property, to be disposed of as the master saw fit; the only prohibition was against homicide, and then only in limited circumstances (Hall et al. 1996:192–96).

2. In North Carolina, for example, the marital defense to rape was not fully abolished until 1993. See N.C. General Statutes §14-27.8; see also Koss 1994:223–24; Bohmer 1991:327–29.

3. To illustrate again with North Carolina law, the crime of first-degree rape (N.C. General Statutes §14-27.2) against an adult victim requires the use of a deadly weapon, serious personal injury, or multiple perpetrators. Most acquaintance rapes will therefore fall into the less serious second-degree category (§14-27.3).

4. We consider later in the chapter whether these tactics and their effects are unique to rape trials or are simply generic cross-examination strategies that may be especially problematic in the rape context.

5. Van Pearlberg, Jimmy D. Berry, Julie L. Miller, and Linda A. Goldman (1995: 53A-4 to 53A-7) offer an example of a "how to" manual for defense lawyers on exploiting the victim's lifestyle and prior sexual history. Such advice is conventional wisdom among criminal lawyers.

6. North Carolina, for example, has created an Office of Coordinator of Services for Victims of Sexual Assault, the purpose of which is "to establish a network of coordinated public and private services for victims of sexual assault." See N.C. General Statutes §§143B-394.1 to 143B-394.3.

7. North Carolina (N.C. General Statutes §15-166) allows the trial judge to exclude "bystanders" (persons other than those directly involved in the trial) from the courtroom during rape trials. Efforts to restrict what the press may disclose have proved to be of dubious constitutionality. In *The Florida Star v. B.J.F.*, 491 U.S. 524 (1989), the Supreme Court struck down a Florida law that imposed penalties on a newspaper that published the identity of a sexual assault victim.

8. Federal Rule of Evidence 412 provides a model that has been widely adopted by the states. See Pearlberg et al. 1995:53A-10 to 53A-12 for examples.

9. Before proceeding with the analysis, one further comment is in order. Most of the social science writing about rape that we have discussed, including Matoesian's, seems to assume that rape defendants are guilty and that the proper task of legal reform is to eliminate barriers to convicting them. Readers may note, for example, that Matoesian's analyses of trial transcripts rarely mention one particular class of possible explanations: that the woman is not telling the truth and that the defendant is not guilty. We do some of this as well, as when, for reasons of clarity, we refer to the complaining witness in a rape case as the "victim." We, too, are convinced that rape is a problem of epidemic proportions, that acquaintance rape is not taken seriously enough, and that the prosecution of rape puts extraordinary and unfair burdens on the victim. However, we want to respect the fundamental legal values of the presumption of innocence and the right to due process. In our judgment, undermining these values in any context, even one as compelling as rape, is a risky undertaking. Readers will reach their own conclusions about these matters, of course, but they should give the issue their thoughtful attention.

10. These postulates are perhaps most appropriately limited to American and/or British English and the societies in which they are spoken, since most conversation analysis studies have been based there. We note, however, that anthropologists have often objected to the implicit assumption within conversation analysis that generalizations about how conversation works in the United States or Britain might apply elsewhere. For example, Robert Hayden (1987) noted different practices with respect to interruption in Indian *panchayats* (councils), and Elinor Keenan (1976) questioned the applicability of Grice's conversational maxims in Malagasy language and society.

11. All of the data presented here are drawn from transcripts of the cross-examination of female rape victims by male defense lawyers. This is not the result of any selection on our part. In all of Matoesian's published transcripts and in all of the rape cases we have studied, the male defendant has been represented by a male lawyer. There are still few female criminal defense lawyers, and even fewer who represent men charged with rape. Why this is so is an interesting and complex question that is beyond the scope

of this book. By contrast, female prosecutors are common, and many of them specialize in rape cases. Moira Lasch, the prosecutor in the William Kennedy Smith trial, which we discuss at the end of this chapter, is such a specialist.

12. Matoesian (1993:148) identifies a dozen distinct question forms.

13. In lines 1–2, the lawyer starts to ask an open-ended WH question but then switches to a yes-no question about the witness's age before the witness has a chance to answer the WH question.

14. The colloquy in lines 30–34 can also be seen as a single tag question. The witness's first "Mmhmm" in line 32 interrupts the question, and the lawyer then completes it by adding the tag "Correct?" in line 33.

15. After all the witnesses for both sides have testified, the lawyers are allowed to make closing arguments to the jury. The law gives the lawyers wide latitude to summarize and comment on any aspect of the evidence.

16. Witnesses are sometimes "rescued" during cross-examination by the friendly lawyer (the district attorney, in this context) or the judge. The lawyer might object to the line of questioning and ask the judge to rule that the witness be given a chance to explain her answers. Alternatively, or in addition, the lawyer can go back over the same ground on redirect examination and give the witness a chance to explain or elaborate on the answers she gave on cross-examination. These possibilities do not fundamentally alter the power imbalance we have described, however, because the witness is entirely dependent on the intervention of others.

17. This is an instance where the district attorney might have attempted a rescue by insisting to the judge that the witness be allowed to complete her answer. The fact that no rescue ensues affirms the dependency and ultimate powerlessness of the witness.

18. By focusing our analysis on the rape *trial,* we do not mean to diminish the significance of the pretrial process, during which the police and the prosecutor examine the victim to determine whether to go forward with the case. This process undoubtedly contributes to the feeling of revictimization. Indeed, in evaluating the woman as a prospective witness, the prosecutor—whether male or female—may employ some of the same discourse strategies that defense lawyers use on cross-examination.

19. The discovery that revictimization is an artifact of the adversary system would have some interesting implications for efforts to reform the prosecution of rape. If the adversary system itself dooms the complaining witness to a process of domination, thereby denying her a fair hearing for her story, then the only remedy would seem to be to divert rape cases into another kind of system. But such radical change would be beyond the power of a legislature because the right of a criminal defendant to confront his accuser publicly, and with the assistance of counsel, is guaranteed by the Sixth Amendment to the Constitution. It might be possible to evade these constitutional imperatives by handling at least acquaintance rape through a noncriminal process. Some colleges have tried to do so through their student conduct codes, in apparent recognition of the problems of dealing with rape through traditional adversary procedures. This, however, has brought criticism from all quarters: from defense lawyers screaming for due process and from victims' rights advocates decrying the trivialization of a violent crime. See, for example, Ruth Sheehan, "Campus Courts on Trial," *Raleigh News & Observer,* Sept. 29, 1996, p. 1.

20. Our colleague Marion Crain has raised the possibility of analogizing rape to robbery. Both involve the appropriation of something (sex or money), and in both cases, it is necessary to determine whether the thing appropriated was freely given or taken by force or threat. It would seem, at least a priori, that both classes of cases would present frequent instances of ambiguity about the nature of the appropriation. But we know that the question of domination comes up all the time in rape cases, almost never in robbery cases. Why? Crain asks. The answer, she suggests, lies in the cultural presumptions that we bring to bear. In economic matters, we presume self-interest; thus, we find it hard to believe that a person who claims to have been forced to turn over his or her money really meant to give it away. With rape, though, we may begin from a premise of consent because we assume that women who do certain things, wear certain clothes, or have certain kinds of friends are making themselves sexually available.

21. This comment assumes that the defense lawyer is male, which is almost invariably the case. See note 11 above.

22. Louis Bilionis has observed to us that Smith's final answer is a kind of announced silence. It is a silence that stands in ironic contrast to the silences of the female victims that we discussed earlier in the chapter, however, because Smith's silence is a powerful rather than a helpless one.

Chapter Three

1. Friedman's *A Guide to Divorce Mediation* (1993) is one of numerous recent popular books written by mediators that both advocate and explain mediation. The proliferation of such books is itself evidence of mediation's growing acceptance.

2. In interviews with a large number of divorce lawyers in Maine, sociologist Craig McEwen and political scientists Lynn Mather and Richard Maiman (1994) found them to be generally supportive of mediation. One reason that lawyers like divorce mediation is that it allows for face-to-face settlement negotiations between the parties in an atmosphere of civility. Settling cases without bringing the parties together is difficult, the lawyers report. Lawyer-to-lawyer negotiations are inefficient, with the lawyers shuttling proposals to and from their clients. Miscommunications are also common. But face-to-face discussions, even with the lawyers present, frequently degenerate into shouting matches. Mediation represents the best of both worlds. The parties are brought together, but the norms of mediation, as enforced by the mediator, ensure that they will behave themselves.

The divorce lawyers also reported to McEwen, Mather, and Maiman (1994:166) that mediation helps them resolve a difficult professional conflict. Lawyers see themselves as obligated to serve simultaneously as "client advocate" and as "reality tester." The advocate is the loyal champion of the client's cause, pushing the client's position regardless of the odds. The reality tester assesses the case from a cool professional perspective, calculates the probabilities, and tells the client the truth, even if he or she does not want to hear it. Lawyers find it easy to be advocates. But advocates who let their clients become falsely optimistic are failing to provide competent legal service and may be inviting malpractice suits. The problem is that, when the reality tester delivers bad news, the client may lose faith in the advocate and look for a new one.

The great benefit of mediation is that someone else serves as the reality tester. A lawyer can walk into the mediation room as an advocate and then sit back while the opposing party and the mediator expose the weaknesses in the client's case. When the client perceives the problem and suggests that some concessions might be necessary, the lawyer can agree reluctantly without any hint of disloyalty to the cause.

3. This variability is well documented in the ethnographic work of Susan Silbey and Sally Merry (1986). They report that mediation, as they have seen it practiced, is not a consistent process. Rather, mediators typically adopt one of two styles: bargaining or therapy. Bargainers focus on concrete agreements. They ignore the emotional demands of the parties and concentrate instead on demands that can be traded off against each other. Bargainers emphasize their professional expertise in law and the legal process. They warn the parties of the dangers of failing to agree and ending up in the costly and capricious legal system. They exert considerable control over the process. They often caucus with the parties individually and sometimes strike out on their own to draft agreements they think the parties will accept.

The therapeutic style, by contrast, "is a form of communication in which the parties are encouraged to engage in a full expression of their feelings and attitudes" (Silbey and Merry 1986:20). Therapeutic mediators stress their expertise in managing personal relationships. They, too, urge avoidance of the legal system, but their rationale is that the court will be inattentive to the parties' emotional needs. Whereas bargainers tend to dismiss feelings in pursuit of concrete objectives, therapists treat emotional concerns as paramount. Conflicts are characterized as misunderstandings or failures of communication. As a result, therapists are sometimes at an impasse when they find that the parties understand each other perfectly well but simply do not agree.

Each style has a distinctive language. Bargaining "converts the experiences and claims of the disputants into the language of negotiation and exchange." In asserting a quasi-legal kind of authority, "[t]he mediator wraps him or herself in the same mystical cloth as the jurist, the rabbi, or the priest." The language of therapy, conversely, "attempts to recast disputants' individual experiences into terms of mutually valued relationships." Therapy "seeks to cultivate a language of mutual recognition of the importance of [the parties'] relationship, shared rather than individual interests, and collective values rather than competitive demands" (Silbey and Merry 1986:26–27).

4. Many social scientists have criticized conversation analysis for avoiding questions of purpose and effect. A part of the response has always been that the publication of extremely detailed textual data allows interested readers to ask those questions themselves.

5. Garcia (1991:831 n. 18) reports that 60 percent (191 out of 321) of the accusations or complaints made in the mediation sessions she studied contained such downgrading characteristics.

6. These terms, as well as the phrase "fifty percent a parent," are marvelously evocative of Fineman's (1991) characterization of therapeutic discourse, which we discuss in chapter 4.

7. Garcia (1995:39–41) does speculate about the possible social consequences of her linguistic findings. She suggests that the mediator activism she documents may decrease

both the probability of reaching an agreement and the degree of compliance with any agreement that is reached.

8. For further discussion of this question, see Conley and O'Barr 1990:181–85.

9. Much of this work was inspired by Robin Lakoff's *Language and Woman's Place* (1975). Examples include the contributions in Tannen 1993, Philips et al. 1987, and Thorne et al. 1983. Deborah Tannen's (1986, 1990) best-sellers have been enormously successful in popularizing the analysis of language and gender.

Chapter Four

1. See chapter 3 for a detailed review of this argument with respect to divorce.

2. A case study in this approach is the campaign of Catharine MacKinnon and Andrea Dworkin for the enactment and enforcement of a restrictive anti-pornography ordinance in Indianapolis. The city ultimately adopted an ordinance they had drafted, but the courts found it unconstitutional (MacKinnon 1989:206).

3. We discuss these developments in linguistics in chapter 1.

4. This work is reported in O'Barr 1982 and Conley et al. 1978.

5. These findings were presented initially in Conley et al. 1978 and in a revised form in O'Barr 1982.

6. Subsequent studies of powerless language have confirmed the existence and significance of the phenomenon. They have also refined the definition of powerless language and developed a more precise understanding of its effects in a variety of contexts. For a review of more recent research trends, see Morrill and Facciola 1992.

7. We pointedly used the past tense in the discussion in the text. One might reasonably question the continuing validity of our findings in light of the educational and career gains that women have made over the past twenty-five years. Perhaps powerless language has become less prevalent, or at least has lost the strong gender correlation it seemed to have had in the 1970s. More recent research on powerless language continues to demonstrate its impact on listener perceptions, although the strength of the association between powerless speech and gender is unclear (Hosman 1989; Wright and Hosman 1983; Morrill and Facciola 1992).

8. A standard formulation is this: "In determining the weight to be given to the testimony of each witness as to whether he or she is to be believed, you should apply the same test of truthfulness that you would in your everyday affairs" (O'Barr 1982:95).

9. It is not clear that the law could do anything even if it wanted to. In the 1970s, we conducted an experimental test of whether jurors' assessments of credibility are affected by instruction from the judge to disregard powerless language and found that they are not (O'Barr 1982:94–96).

10. *Eisenstadt v. Baird,* 405 U.S. 438 (1972).

11. To take a single example, consider the increasingly strict limits on a lawyer's right to exercise peremptory challenges to dismiss prospective jurors during the jury selection process. Historically, lawyers were allowed to dismiss a certain number of jurors peremptorily, meaning for any reason or no reason at all. In 1986, in *Batson v. Kentucky,* 476 U.S. 79, the Supreme Court held that prosecutors could not dismiss prospective

jurors for reasons of race. (Prosecutors had often dismissed jurors of the same minority group as the defendant; defense lawyers employed an opposite strategy.) In a series of post-*Batson* cases, courts have extended the racial prohibition to criminal defense lawyers and to both sides in civil trials, and gender and religion have been added to the list of forbidden bases for dismissal.

12. See, for example, the papers collected in Briggs 1996, all of which are based on narrative studies done in the 1980s.

13. As we explained in our earlier report (Conley and O'Barr 1990: 181–85), there is a further complication. When we describe a litigant as rule- or relationally oriented, we are referring to his or her central tendency. Most litigants, through the accounts they give, display at least some elements of both orientations. "Rules versus relationships" is thus more accurately described as a continuum than as a dichotomy.

14. As law teachers, we are often struck by how this process of linguistic co-optation affects female law students. Many of them (as well as significant numbers of men) come to their first-year classes with a Gilliganesque approach to analyzing trouble situations, only to abandon it in pursuit of the ability to "think like a lawyer." We are left wondering what is happening to their thought processes outside the classroom. We deal more fully with the topic of legal education in chapter 8.

Chapter Five

1. Although interest in the developmental stages of disputes has a long history in anthropology, we are indebted to June Starr, who made a strong case for the importance of attempting to find ways to study it in a seminar she presented at Duke University in the 1970s.

2. Although many people have found the model useful, others have criticized it from the outset. For example, in the very issue of *Law and Society Review* in which it first appeared, sociologist Robert Kidder (1980–81) questioned its applicability beyond the Western individual-rights-based idea of a dispute.

3. The term *naming* may obscure an important distinction. Numerous anthropological and linguistic studies have pointed out the power associated with naming things. In a memorable paper, Brenda Danet (1980b) analyzed a trial in which a doctor who performed an abortion was charged with homicide. She found that the prosecution named the aborted entity a "baby" or even a "little baby boy," whereas the defense chose names such as "fetus" and "products of conception."

The Felstiner-Abel-Sarat model seems to lump under the heading of *naming* two conceptually distinct phases: articulating the problem and giving it a name. Pomerantz's data are about the process of articulating the problem. Giving it a name—that is, saying that this occurrence is a specific example of a particular thing, as, for example, calling it "sexual harassment" or "rape" or "robbery"—is very different from describing what happened.

4. It is, of course, possible that the initial mentioning of the problem may fix responsibility and thus obviate the interactive work. An example might be "Sam's kid hit my car with his baseball." However, the empirical data presented by Pomerantz and Gail Jefferson (1980, 1985, 1988) suggest that the announcement is more likely to take the

form of "My car got hit with a baseball," followed by an interactional sequence that leads to the responsible party. An intriguing possibility is that some people tend to make the link earlier than others. If there are such differences, it would be interesting to investigate whether they correlate with gender or other social variables.

5. The extent to which people attribute responsibility to human versus nonhuman (i.e., supernatural, accidental, etc.) causes varies across cultures, according to anthropological sources. We take up this problem more fully in chapter 6.

6. This realization reminds us that stories do not exist apart from their various tellings. It is in one sense meaningless to ask what the "real" story is, or what the "facts" are, because stories, trouble-tellings, and accounts of problems are deeply conditioned by the linguistic and interactional environments in which they are told. Receptive, encouraging listeners help us elaborate stories. By their responses, they help us produce these accounts, becoming co-authors of what we tell. If they demur, if they resist, if they turn a deaf ear, the stories may never emerge or may lose much of their potential complexity. All this flies in the face of how the law treats disputes. By conceiving of cases as being made up of core "facts" that stay the same from retelling to retelling, the law seems to presume the existence of an authoritative version of the story that can be discovered and preserved.

7. The Felstiner-Abel-Sarat model merges the processes of articulating the problem to the blamed party and requesting a remedy. The conversation analysis evidence just reviewed would suggest that in real situations articulating and requesting may occur as separate interactions, with the details largely dependent on the response of the blamed party.

8. Conversation analysts take care to point out that the word *preferred* is not intended to imply anything about the speakers' actual feelings or intentions (Atkinson and Drew 1979:59). It refers only to the linguistic structure of the exchange, in particular the way in which the speakers "attend" to the alternative second parts.

9. As evidence, they cite the fact that accusers often structure their accusations so as to preclude a simple flat denial. They also point to the legal principle that sometimes allows silence in the face of an accusation (i.e., nondenial, the unanticipated response) to be interpreted as an admission.

10. By focusing on legal channels for disputing, we do not mean to deny the possibility that disputants will resort to extra- or illegal methods. In the real world, of course, people sometimes resolve problems by threatened or actual violence (shooting a trespassing animal, for example) or by various other "self-help" remedies (such as seizing a disputed piece of property when the other side is not looking). What these methods all have in common is that they involve, or at least contemplate, physical action beyond talk. Those who are unwilling to do more than talk about their dispute must give up or resort to the legal system.

11. Material in this section is drawn from our own research on small claims courts, as reported in Conley and O'Barr 1990.

12. Variation in judicial styles among small claims judges is described in detail in chapter 5 of Conley and O'Barr 1990.

13. There is no effective appellate mechanism to prevent such things from happening. In some jurisdictions, a defendant can remove a case from small claims to formal court

at the time it is filed, but there is no appeal if it is allowed to stay in small claims court. In other places, a defendant who is dissatisfied with the judgment of the small claims court can demand a retrial in a formal court. When this happens, however, the higher court usually starts all over from the beginning, rather than reviewing the proceedings in the small claims court.

14. For a discussion of the relationship between lawyers' talk and jurisprudential theories, see Conley and O'Barr 1988.

15. An interview with a litigant after the case is an artificial context for talking about the dispute in the sense that it is a far different environment than a conversation that the litigant might have with a family member or friend. But since it is virtually impossible for researchers to position themselves as overhearers of such discussions in the real world, post-trial interviews are the best available sources of information on the further transformation that disputes may undergo after the legal case is concluded.

16. We have borrowed the natural history theme from Michael Silverstein and Greg Urban (1996), who have adapted it to the study of discourse.

Chapter Six

1. For a short overview of the field of legal anthropology, see Conley and O'Barr 1993.

2. One of Nader's chapters does provide an extended transcript of an interview with a judge (1990:97–104). Her case descriptions, however, are reminiscent of Gluckman's and Bohannan's.

3. It also suggests that in the moots "discriminatory and coercive intentions," if present, would probably be manifest in subtler forms than confrontational questioning (Goldman 1986:374).

4. Goldman translates *piaga* literally as "go" in the sense of "happen" or "occur." Goldman's idiomatic translations indicate that it acquires further meaning from its subject. Thus, his literal translation of line (5) is "water goes (habitual)," which he then renders as "people used to drown." Similarly, line (9) is literally "trees misadventures go (habitual)," while line (13) is "holes go (habitual)."

5. Habit is sometimes expressed through other grammatical constructions in English, as in *Hardwood burns slowly* and *The men burn brush on Wednesdays.*

6. However, English does have ways of distinguishing events that happen with and without agents. Compare *The house burned* with *I burned the house.*

7. A shorter report appears in an important collection of essays edited by anthropologists Jane Hill and Judith Irvine (1992). This volume, entitled *Responsibility and Evidence in Oral Discourse,* contains a series of papers on the general topic of "the relationship between the devices that manage responsibility, the local cultural understanding of responsibility and evidence, and the nature of social identity revealed by their management" (Hill and Irvine 1992:20). The papers are remarkably diverse, covering such issues as evidentiary standards in American courts (Philips 1992), verbal abuse in a Senegalese village (Irvine 1992), and the production of meaning in rituals of divination (Du Bois 1992). Since accepting or rejecting the concept of accident is a means of managing responsibility, these papers shed significant, if sometimes indirect, light on the issue that Goldman has raised.

8. The word *li'i* is central to Kuipers's analysis. He translates it as "word" or "voice" and then explains that it connotes two rather different things: a promise that creates a prolonged moral duty and an immediate performance. It thus evokes simultaneously the permanence of tradition and the ephemeral individuality of particular oral performances (Kuipers 1990:2).

9. A related piece of work is Peter Just's (1990) study of liability and equity in Indonesian Dou Donggo law. Just finds that the Dou Donggo impose "stricter than strict" liability on people for wrongs that "might have" been committed regardless of whether or not the particular accused has actually caused any damage. On the other hand, they have a very precise system for determining moral culpability for a wrong. He concludes that Western and Dou Donggo notions of liability are at once comparable and distinguishable.

Chapter Seven

1. Another interesting source of legal discourse in the ancient world is J. A. Crook's *Legal Advocacy in the Roman World* (1995), which presents and analyzes the papyrus records of numerous court proceedings from the Roman province of Egypt. Crook's book, however, focuses more on the form and content of advocacy than on the social context of the cases.

2. Some scholars also suggest that in the second and third centuries, family ties became stronger across all segments of society as a response to a widespread decline in civic order (Evans Grubbs 1995:336).

3. One might draw an analogy to what the Supreme Court did in 1954 in *Brown v. Board of Education,* when, in an effort to transform cultural practice and values, it created a legal discourse of racial equality.

4. An appropriate analogy here might be to the series of cases in the 1960s and 1970s, culminating in *Roe v. Wade,* in which the Supreme Court created an authoritative discourse of privacy in order to strike down prohibitions on birth control and abortion that it believed to be out of touch with cultural reality.

Chapter Eight

1. One of the earliest examples of such work is a comparative study of children's insults in three different cultural settings by Laura Lein and Donald Brenneis (1978). Examining the language of insults used by black working-class American, white middle-class American, and Hindi-speaking Indian children, Lein and Brenneis concluded that some aspects of disputing behavior seem universal, whereas others are culture-specific. They have been subsequently criticized for studying artificial arguments among children who were playing roles rather than naturally occurring arguments, although they did so for understandable logistical reasons.

2. Although Mertz has focused thus far on classroom discourse, this is only the tip of the iceberg. From the very first days of law school, law students mimic their class discussions in their study groups and lunchroom arguments. The classroom provides an authoritative model that they seem eager to practice at every opportunity.

3. Consistent with the practice in contemporary anthropology, Hirsch has also

discussed her findings with the people she studied and has fed their comments back into her analysis.

4. For example, following the lead of the federal courts, the Colorado system recently adopted a new discovery rule in civil cases (Federal and Colorado Rule of Civil Procedure 26), which requires each side to provide certain basic information and hand over all relevant documents to the other at the outset of the case. Under the former practice, each side was required to request particular categories of information and documents from the other. This often led to time-consuming and expensive game-playing as the parties argued over the scope and meaning of particular requests. It is too early to tell whether either the federal or the Colorado reform is having much effect on a day-to-day basis.

Chapter Nine

1. Michael Silverstein (1998:123–24) dates this pejorative term to the Napoleonic re-action against an Enlightenment effort to establish *idéologie* as the science of "human nature." "Mere ideologue" became a dismissive epithet used against those who dealt in speculative abstractions.

2. The oldest versions of the second-person singular pronouns were *thu* and *the*.

3. As this point suggests, linguistics has its own language ideologies. For a discussion of the issue see Errington (2003) and England (2003).

4. We thank University of North Carolina colleague John Orth, a legal historian, for reminding us of this language.

5. On the former point, for example, the website of the Lincoln Bicentennial Commission states that "[b]efore Lincoln's presidency . . . [t]hose referring to this country used the plural: 'the United States are'. After Lincoln's presidency . . . the United States became a singular noun: 'the United States is'" (Bishop 2003). On the latter point, Carl Sandburg (1939:38–39) reports in his famous biography of Lincoln that the president-elect, stopping in Indianapolis en route from Illinois to Washington for his inauguration, used the phrase "*these* United States" in addressing a crowd, then told the governor and legislature what would happen if "the United States should merely hold and retake *its* forts and other property."

6. For a case study of a national-language ideology (Indonesia), see Errington (2000).

7. Susan Berk-Seligson (1990:217) has long argued for preserving a recording of all non-English testimony in order to allow for the possibility of challenging and improving on the original trial transcript. This is a self-evidently excellent idea. It does not address Haviland's concern, however, since, as a practical matter, the legal system will still insist on a single "official" transcript as the basis for appeals.

8. Haviland (2003:765) discusses "the evolving 'linguistic ideologies' of anthropology itself," citing Duranti's (2001) critical analysis. For other examples see Whitely (2003) and (Errington 2003).

9. Although Hirsch (1998:293 n. 19) acknowledges that "[s]cholars disagree on the utility of 'Swahili' as an ethnic category," she uses Swahili as an adjective "to refer to those coastal Muslims of African, Arab, Asian, or mixed ancestry who would agree that 'Mswahili' is one term that *could* be used to identify them in at least *some* contexts." Their language is Kiswahili.

10. As of mid-2004, Hirsch (personal communication) reports, the situation has grown even more complicated. Kenya is debating a new constitution, and the role of religion is a major issue. Islamic courts have come under attack by some secularists and Christians. This has caused the Swahili community to rally to protect the courts as a symbol of its position in Kenya. Lurking in the background is the additional factor of terrorism and its perceived association with Islam.

Chapter Ten

1. We base the inference that the letter was unsolicited on its contents. It is available on the website www.acandyrose.com/donaldfoster.htm.

2. *Daubert v. Merrell Dow Pharmaceuticals, Inc.,* 509 U.S. 579 (1993).

3. *Kumho Tire Co. v. Carmichael,* 526 U.S. 137 (1999).

4. Gibbons' broader definition draws on a definition promulgated by AILA (Association Internationale de Linguistique Appliquée).

5. For an illustrative transcript of Loftus giving expert testimony in 1978, see Loftus (1979:217).

6. *United States v. Smithers,* 212 F. 3d 306, 311 (6th Cir. 2000).

7. For an example of a case in which Loftus was not permitted to testify, see *People v. Sanders,* 11 Cal. 4th. 475, 905 P. 2d 420 (1995).

8. Lawrence Rosen (1977) has argued that problems with the admission of social science testimony in court are related, in part, to the fact that different social scientists are likely to give variable testimony about the same issue. He contends that this is understandable because of the different theoretical frames and schools of thought in which they work. Such inconsistency, however, has led many judges to find social science unreliable when compared to the so-called hard sciences, where agreement at least appears to be more common among different specialists.

9. To illustrate the point, a recent LEXIS search of all reported cases in our state of North Carolina turned up none dealing with a Loftus-type expert, and only a single citation to one of Loftus's articles. Practicing North Carolina criminal lawyers tell us that such testimony is rare but not unheard of.

10. One can imagine academic language experts avoiding companies that had particularly notorious records as polluters, abusers of labor, etc.

11. See, for example, the collection of papers in volume 6, number 1 (June 1999) of *Forensic Linguistics.*

REFERENCES

Abel, Richard L.
1989   *American lawyers.* New York: Oxford University Press.

Allison, Julie A., and Lawrence S. Wrightsman
1993   *Rape: The misunderstood crime.* Newbury Park, Calif.: Sage.

Anonymous
1996   *Primary colors: A novel of politics.* New York: Random House.

Atkinson, J. Maxwell, and Paul Drew
1979   *Order in court: The organization of verbal interaction in judicial settings.*
        Atlantic Highlands, N.J.: Humanities Press.

Austin, J. L.
1962   *How to do things with words.* New York: Oxford University Press.

Bartlett, Katherine T.
1994   Feminist perspectives on the ideological impact of legal education upon the
        profession. *North Carolina Law Review* 72:1259–70.

Bauman, Richard, and Charles L. Briggs
2000   Language philosophy as language ideology: John Locke and Johann
        Gottfried Herder. In *Regimes of language: Ideologies, polities, and identities,*
        edited by Paul V. Kroskrity. Santa Fe, NM: School of American Research
        Press.

Bennett, W. Lance, and Martha S. Feldman
1981   *Reconstructing reality in the courtroom: Justice and judgment in American
        culture.* New Brunswick, N.J.: Rutgers University Press.

Berk-Seligson, Susan
1990   *The bilingual courtroom.* Chicago: University of Chicago Press.

Bishop, Michael F.
2003   Divided we fall: Would we still be a "United" States without Lincoln's legacy? www.lincolnbicentennial.gov/press-febr17.html.

Black, Donald J.
1971   The social organization of arrest. *Stanford Law Review* 23:1087–1111.

Bloomfield, Leonard
1933   *Language.* New York: Holt, Rinehart & Winston.

Bohannan, Paul
1964   Anthropology and the law. In *Horizons in anthropoligy,* edited by Sol Tax. Chicago: Aldine.
1969   Ethnography and comparison in legal anthropology. In *Law in culture and society,* edited by Laura Nader. Chicago: Aldine.
1989   *Justice and judgment among the Tiv.* 3rd ed. Prospect Heights, Ill.: Waveland Press (orig. 1957).

Bohmer, Carol
1991   Acquaintance rape and the law. In *Acquaintance rape: The hidden crime,* edited by Andrea Parrot and Laurie Bechhofer. New York: Wiley.

Bohmer, Carol, and Marilyn L. Ray
1994   Effects of different dispute resolution methods on women and children after divorce. *Family Law Quarterly* 28:223–45.

Brenneis, Donald
1988   Language and disputing. *Annual Review of Anthropology* 17:221–37.

Briere, John, and N. Malamuth
1983   Self-reported likelihood of sexually aggressive behavior: Attitudinal versus sexual explanations. *Journal of Research in Personality* 17:315–23.

Briggs, Charles, ed.
1996   *Disorderly discourse: Narrative, conflict, and inequality.* London: Oxford University Press.

Bryan, Penelope
1992   Killing us softly: Divorce mediation and the politics of power. *Buffalo Law Review* 40:441–523.

Caputi, Jane, and Diana E. H. Russell
1992   Femicide: Sexist terrorism against women. In *Femicide: The politics of women-killing,* edited by Jill Radford and Diana E. H. Russell. New York: Twayne.

Chomsky, Noam
1964   *Current issues in linguistic theory.* The Hague: Mouton.

Clarke, Stevens H., Laura F. Donnelly, and Sara A. Grove
1989   *Court-ordered arbitration in North Carolina: An evaluation of its effects.* Chapel Hill: Institute of Government, University of North Carolina.

Comaroff, John L., and Simon Roberts
1981   *Rules and processes: The cultural logic of dispute in an African context.*
        Chicago: University of Chicago Press.

Conley, John M., and David W. Peterson
1996   When ethical systems collide: The social scientist and the adversary process.
        In *Recent developments in forensic linguistics,* edited by Hannes Kniffka.
        Frankfurt: Peter Lang.

Conley, John M., and William M. O'Barr
1988   Fundamentals of jurisprudence: An ethnography of judicial decision making
        in informal courts. *North Carolina Law Review* 66:467–507.
1990   *Rules versus relationships.* Chicago: University of Chicago Press.
1993   Legal anthropology comes home: A brief history of the ethnographic study
        of law. *Loyola of Los Angeles Law Review* 27:41–64.

Conley, John M., William M. O'Barr, and E. Allen Lind
1978   The power of language: Presentational style in the courtroom. *Duke Law
        Journal* 78;1375–99.

Corsaro, William A., and Thomas Rizzo
1990   Disputes in the peer culture of American and Italian nursery-school chil-
        dren. In *Conflict talk,* edited by Allen D. Grimshaw. Cambridge: Cambridge
        University Press.

Cotterrell, Roger
1994   *Law and society.* Aldershot, England: Dartmouth Publishing.

Crook, J. A.
1995   *Legal advocacy in the Roman world.* Ithaca, N.Y.: Cornell University Press.

Danet, Brenda
1980a   Language in the legal process. *Law & Society Review* 14:445–564.
1980b   "Baby" or "fetus"? Language and the construction of reality in a
        manslaughter trial. *Semiotica* 32:187–219.

Davis, Natalie Zemon
1987   *Fiction in the archives: Pardon tales and their tellers in sixteenth-century
        France.* Palo Alto, Calif.: Stanford University Press.

Dixon, R. M. W.
1979   Ergativity. *Language* 55:39–138.

Dole, Gertrude
1966   Anarchy without chaos: Alternatives to political authority among the
        Kuikuru. In *Political anthropology,* edited by M. J. Swartz, V. W. Turner, and
        A. Tuden. Chicago: Aldine.

Drew, Paul, and John Heritage
1992   *Talk at work: Interaction in institutional settings.* Cambridge: Cambridge
        University Press.

Du Bois, John W.
1992   Meaning without intention: Lessons from divination. In *Responsibility and evidence in oral discourse,* edited by Jane H. Hill and Judith T. Irvine. Cambridge: Cambridge University Press.

Duranti, Alessandro
2001   An historical perspective on contemporary linguistic anthropology. *Teaching Anthropology: SACC Notes* 7(2):20–24.

Eades, Diana, ed.
1995   *Language in evidence: Issues confronting Aboriginal and multicultural Australia.* Sydney: University of New South Wales Press.

Eder, Donna
1990   Serious and playful disputes: Variation in conflict talk among female adolescents. In *Conflict talk,* edited by Allen D. Grimshaw. Cambridge: Cambridge University Press.

Eisenstein, Zillah R.
1988   *The female body and the law.* Berkeley: University of California Press.

England, Nora C.
2003   Mayan language revival and revitalization politics: Linguists and linguistic ideologies. *American Anthropologist* 105(4):733–43.

Epstein, A. L., ed.
1967   *The craft of social anthropology.* London: Social Science Paperbacks, in association with Tavistock.

Errington, Joseph
2000   Indonesian('s) authority. In *Regimes of language: Ideologies, polities, and identities,* edited by Paul V. Kroskrity. Santa Fe, NM: School of American Research Press.
2003   Getting language rights: The rhetorics of language endangerment and loss. *American Anthropologist* 105(4):723–32.

Estrich, Susan
1987   *Real rape.* Cambridge: Harvard University Press.

Evans Grubbs, Judith
1995   *Law and family in late antiquity: The Emperor Constantine's marriage legislation.* New York: Oxford University Press.
1996   Pietas and potestas: The family in Roman imperial law. Unpublished manuscript.

Evans-Pritchard, E. E.
1937   *Witchcraft, oracles, and magic among the Azande.* Oxford, England: Clarendon Press.

Fasold, Ralph
1990   *The sociolinguistics of language.* Oxford, England: Basil Blackwell.

Felstiner, William, Richard Abel, and Austin Sarat
1980–81   The emergence and transformation of disputes: Naming, blaming, claiming. . . . *Law & Society Review* 15:631–54.

Fineman, Martha Albertson
1991   *The illusion of equality: The rhetoric and reality of divorce reform.* Chicago: University of Chicago Press.

Foster, Donald W.
1989   *Elegy by W.S.: A study in attribution.* Newark: University of Delaware Press.
2000   *Author unknown: On the trail of anonymous.* New York: Henry Holt.

Foucault, Michel
1970   *The order of things: Anarchaeology of the human sciences.* London: Tavistock.
1972   *The archaeology of knowledge and the discourse of language.* London: Tavistock.
1977   *Discipline and punish: The birth of the prison.* London: Allen Lane; New York: Pantheon.
1978   *The history of sexuality.* Vol. 1, *An introduction.* New York: Random House.
1980   Two lectures. In *Power/knowledge: Selected interviews and other writings, 1972–1977,* edited by Colin Gordon. Brighton, England: Harvester Press.
1985a   *The history of sexuality.* Vol. 2, *The use of pleasure.* New York: Viking.
1985b   *The history of sexuality.* Vol. 3, *The care of the self.* New York: Pantheon.

Frake, Charles O.
1969   Struck by speech. In *Law in culture and society,* edited by Laura Nader. Chicago: Aldine.

Friedman, Gary J.
1993   *A guide to divorce mediation.* New York: Workman.

Galanter, Marc
1974   Why the "haves" come out ahead. *Law & Society Review* 9:95–160.

Garcia, Angela
1991   Dispute resolution without disputing: How the interactional organization of mediation hearings minimizes argument. *American Sociological Review* 56:818–35.
1995   The problematics of representation in community mediation hearings: Implications for mediation practice. *Journal of Sociology & Social Welfare* 22:23–46.

Gibbons, John
2003   *Forensic linguistics: An introduction to language in the justice system.* Oxford, England: Blackwell Publishing.

Gibbs, James L., Jr.
1962   Poro values and courtroom procedures in a Kpelle chiefdom. *Southwestern Journal of Anthropology* 18:341–50.

1967   The Kpelle moot. In *Law and warfare,* edited by Paul Bohannan. Garden City, N.Y.: Natural History Press.

Gilligan, Carol
1982   *In a different voice: Psychological theory and women's development.* Cambridge: Harvard University Press.

Gluckman, Max
1955   *The judicial process among the Barotse of Northern Rhodesia (Zambia).* Manchester, England: Manchester University Press.
1965   *The ideas of Barotse jurisprudence.* New Haven, Conn.: Yale University Press.
1969   Concepts in the comparative study of tribal law. In *Law in culture and society,* edited by Laura Nader. Chicago: Aldine.
1973   *Custom and conflict in Africa.* New York: Barnes and Noble.

Goffman, Erving
1959   *The presentation of self in everyday life.* Garden City, N.Y.: Doubleday.
1963   *Behavior in public places: Notes on the social organization of gatherings.* New York: Free Press.
1967   *Interaction ritual: Essays on face to face behavior.* Garden City, N.Y.: Anchor Books.

Goldberg-Ambrose, C.
1992   Unfinished business in rape law reform. *Journal of Social Issues* 48:173–86.

Goldman, Laurence R.
1986   A case of "questions" and the questions of "case." *Text* 6:345–92.

Goldman, Laurence
1993   *The culture of coincidence: Accident and absolute liability in Huli.* New York: Clarendon Press.

Greatbatch, David, and Robert Dingwall
1989   Selective facilitation: Some preliminary observations on a strategy used by divorce mediators. *Law & Society Review* 23:613–41.

Grice, H. Paul
1975   Logic and conversation: In *Syntax and semantics, Vol. 3: Speech acts,* edited by P. Cole and J. Morgan. London: Academic Press.

Grillo, Trina
1991   The mediation alternative: Process dangers for women. *Yale Law Journal* 100:1545–1610.

Grimshaw, Allen D., ed.
1990   *Conflict talk: Sociolinguistic investigations of arguments in conversations.* Cambridge: Cambridge University Press.

Hall, Kermit, William M. Wiecek, and Paul Finkelman, eds.
1996   *American legal history: Cases and materials.* New York: Oxford University Press.

Haviland, John B.
2003   Ideologies of language: Some reflections on language and U.S. law. *American Anthropologist* 105(4):764–74.

Hayden, Robert M.
1987   Turn-taking, overlap, and the task at hand: Ordering speaking turns in legal settings. *American Ethnologist* 14:251–70.

Hellinger, Marlis, and Hadumod Bußmann, eds.
2002   *Gender across languages: The linguistic representation of women and men.* Amsterdam: John Benjamins.

Henderson, Lynne
1991   Law's patriarchy. *Law & Society Review* 25:411–44.

Heritage, John, and David Greatbatch
1986   Generating applause: A study of rhetoric and response at party political conferences. *American Journal of Sociology* 92:110–57.

Hill, Jane H., and Judith T. Irvine, eds.
1992   *Responsibility and evidence in oral discourse.* Cambridge: Cambridge University Press.

Hill, Martin D.
2003   Identifying the source of critical details in confessions. *Forensic Linguistics* 10:23–61.

Hirsch, Susan
1998   *Pronouncing & persevering: Gender and the discourses of disputing in an African Islamic court.* Chicago: University of Chicago Press.

Hosman, Lawrence A.
1989   The evaluative consequences of hedges, hesitations, and intensifiers: Powerful and powerless speech styles. *Human Communications Research* 15:383–406.

Hosman, Lawrence A., and Susan A. Silfanen
1994   The attributional and evaluative consequences of powerful and powerless speech styles: An examination of the "control over others" and "control of self" explanations. *Language & Communication* 14:287–98.

Hudson, R. A.
1980   *Sociolinguistics.* Cambridge: Cambridge University Press.

Hughes, Scott H.
1995   Elizabeth's story: Exploring power imbalances in divorce mediation. *Georgetown Journal of Legal Ethics* 8:553–96.

Hunt, Alan, and Gary Wickham
1994   *Foucault and law: Towards a sociology of law and governance.* London: Pluto Press.

Hymes, Dell
1968   The ethnography of speaking. In *Readings in the sociology of language,*
         edited by Joshua Fishman. The Hague: Mouton.

Irvine, Judith T.
1989   When talk isn't cheap: Language and political economy. *American Ethnolo-
         gist* 16:248–67.
1992   Insult and responsibility: Verbal abuse in a Wolof village. In *Responsibility
         and evidence in oral discourse,* edited by Jane H. Hill and Judith T. Irvine.
         Cambridge: Cambridge University Press.

Irvine, Judith T., and Susan Gal
2000   Language ideology and linguistic differentiation. In *Regimes of language:
         Ideologies, polities, and identities,* edited by Paul V. Kroskrity. Santa Fe, NM:
         School of American Research Press.

Jefferson, Gail
1980   On "trouble-premonitory" response to inquiry. *Sociological Inquiry* 50:153–
         85.
1985   On the interactional unpackaging of a "gloss." *Language in Society* 14:435–
         66.
1988   On the sequential organization of troubles-talk in ordinary conversation.
         Social Problems 35:418–41.

Just, Peter
1990   Dead goats and broken betrothals: Liability and equity in Dou Donggo law.
         American Anthropologist 17:75–90.

Keenan, Elinor Ochs
1976   The universality of conversational postulates. *Language in Society* 5:67–80.

Kelly, Joan
1989   Mediated and adversarial divorce: Respondents' perception of their
         processes and outcomes. *Mediation Quarterly* Summer 1989:71–87.

Kennedy, Graham
2003   Not so fresh in the mind: A forensic linguistic analysis of suspected memo-
         rized narrative essays. *Forensic Linguistics* 10:75–101.

Kidder, Robert L.
1980–81 The end of the road? problems in the analysis of disputes. *Law & Society
         Review* 15:717–25.

Koss, Mary P.
1988   Hidden rape: Sexual aggression and victimization in a national sample of
         students in higher education. In *Rape and sexual assault,* edited by A. W.
         Burgess. New York: Garland.

Koss, Mary P., ed.
1994   *No safe haven: Male violence against women at home, at work and in the
         community.* Washington, D.C.: American Psychological Association.

Kroskrity, Paul V.
2000   Regimenting languages: Language ideological perspectives. In *Regimes of language: Ideologies, polities, and identities,* edited by Paul V. Kroskrity. Santa Fe, NM: School of American Research Press.

Kuipers, Joel
1990   *Power in performance: The creation of textual authority in Weyewa ritual speech.* Philadelphia: University of Pennsylvania Press.

Labov, William
1966   *The social stratification of English in New York City.* Washington, DC: Center for Applied Linguistics.
1972a   *Language in the inner city.* Philadelphia: University of Pennsylvania Press.
1972b   *Sociolinguistic patterns.* Philadelphia: University of Pennsylvania Press.
1979   Locating the frontier between social and psychological factors in linguistic variation. In *Individual differences in language ability and language behavior,* edited by Charles J. Filmore, Daniel Kempler, and William S.-Y. Wang. New York: Academic Press.

Lakoff, Robin
1975   *Language and woman's place.* New York: Harper & Row.

Lasswell, Harold
1936   *Politics: Who gets what, when, how.* New York: McGraw-Hill.

Lein, Laura, and Donald Brenneis
1978   Children's disputes in three speech communities. *Language in Society* 7:299–323.

Levi, Judith N.
1994   *Language and law: A bibliographic guide to social sciences research in the U.S.A.* Chicago: American Bar Association.

Levi, Judith N., and Anne G. Walker, eds.
1990   *Language in the judicial process.* New York: Plenum Press.

Lévy-Bruhl, Lucien
1923   *Primitive mentality* (*La mentalité primitive*), translated by Lilian A. Clare. New York: Macmillan Company.

Lind, E. Allen, and Tom Tyler
1988   *The social psychology of procedural justice.* New York: Plenum.

Litosseliti, Lia, and Jane Sunderland, eds.
2002   *Gender identity and discourse analysis.* Amsterdam: John Benjamins.

Llewellyn, Karl N., and E. Adamson Hoebel
1961   *The Cheyenne way.* Norman: University of Oklahoma Press (orig. 1941).

Loftus, Elizabeth F.
1979   *Eyewitness testimony.* Cambridge: Harvard University Press.
1987   My turn. *Newsweek,* 29 June, 10.

Loftus, Elizabeth F., and Katherine Ketcham
1991   *Witness for the defense: The accused, the eyewitness, and the expert who puts memory on trial.* New York: St. Martin's Press.
1994   *The myth of repressed memory.* New York: St. Martin's Press.

Lyons, John
1968   *Introduction to theoretical linguistics.* Cambridge: Cambridge University Press.

MacKinnon, Catherine A.
1989   *Toward a feminist theory of the state.* Cambridge: Harvard University Press.

Malinowski, B.
1985   *Crime and custom in savage society.* Totowa, N.J.: Rowman & Allanheld (orig. 1926).

Matoesian, Gregory M.
1993   *Reproducing rape: Domination through talk in the courtroom.* Chicago: University of Chicago Press.
1995   Language, law, and society: Policy implications of the Kennedy Smith rape trial. *Law & Society Review* 29:669–701.

Mauet, Thomas A.
1992   *Fundamentals of trial techniques.* Boston: Little, Brown.

Maynard, Douglas W.
1984   *Inside plea bargaining: The language of negotiation.* New York: Plenum Press.

McCann, Michael W.
1994   *Rights at work: Pay equity reform and the politics of legal mobilization.* Chicago: University of Chicago Press.

McElhinny, Bonnie
2003   Three approaches to the study of language and gender. *American Anthropologist* 105(4):848–55.

McEwen, Craig, Lynn Mather, and Richard J. Maimon
1994   Laywers, mediation, and the manguagement of divorce practice. *Law & Society Review* 28:149–86.

McIlvenny, Paul, ed.
2002   *Talking gender and sexuality.* Amsterdam: John Benjamins.

Mellinkoff, David
1963   *The language of the law.* Boston: Little, Brown.

Merry, Sally Engle
1986   Everyday understanding of the law in working-class America. *American Ethnologist* 13:253–70.
1990   *Getting justice and getting even: Legal consciousness among working-class Americans.* Chicago: University of Chicago Press.

Mertz, Elizabeth
1985   Beyond symbolic anthropology: Introducing semantic mediation. In *Semiotic mediation: Sociocultural and psychological perspectives,* edited by Elizabeth Mertz and Richard J. Parmentier. Orlando, FL: Academic Press.
1994   Legal language. In *Annual Review of Anthropology.* Vol. 23. Palo Alto, Calif.: Annual Reviews, Inc.
1996   Recontextualization as socialization: Text and pragmatics in the law school classroom. In *Natural histories of discourse,* edited by Michael Silverstein and Greg Urban. Chicago: University of Chicago Press.
n.d.   Linguistic constructions of differences and history in the U.S. law school classroom. American Bar Foundation Working Paper No. 9419.

Miller, Richard E., and Austin Sarat
1980–81 Grievances, claims, and disputes: Assesing the adversary culture. *Law & Society Review* 15:525–66.

Morrill, Calvin, and Peter C. Facciola
1992   The power of language in adjudication and mediation: Institutional contexts as predictors of social evaluation. *Law & Social Inquiry* 17:191–212.

Nader, Laura
1990   *Harmony ideology and the construction of the law: Justice and control in a Zapotec mountain village.* Palo Alto, Calif.: Stanford University Press.

O'Barr, William M.
1982   *Linguistic evidence: Language, power and strategy in the courtroom.* New York: Academic Press.

O'Barr, William M., and Bowman K. Atkins
1980   "Women's language" or "powerless language"? In *Women in language and society,* edited by Sally McConnell-Ginet, Ruth Borker, and Nelly Furman. New York: Praeger.

Ochs, Eleanor
1979   Transcription as theory. In *Developmental pragmatics,* edited by Eleanor Ochs and Bambi B. Schieffelin. New York: Academic Press.

O'Donnell, Katherine
1990   Difference and dominance: How labor and management talk conflict. In *Conflict talk,* edited by Allen D. Grimshaw. Cambridge: Cambridge University Press.

Papke, David R., ed.
1991   *Narrative and the legal divorce.* Liverpool: Deborah Charles.

Pearlberg, Van, Jimmy D. Berry, Julie L. Miller, and Linda Goldman
1995   Defense of a rape case. In *Criminal defense techniques,* edited by Amanda J. Pisani and Elizabeth L. Englehart. New York: Matthew Bender.

Philips, Susan U.
1990   The judge as third party in American trial-court conflict talk. In *Conflict talk,* edited by Allen D. Grimshaw. Cambridge: Cambridge University Press.

1992   Evidentiary standards for American trials: Just the facts. In *Responsibility and evidence in oral discourse,* edited by Jane H. Hill and Judith T. Irvine. Cambridge: Cambridge University Press.

Philips, Susan U., Susan Steele, and Christine Tanz, eds.
1987   *Language, gender, and sex in comparative perspective.* Cambridge: Cambridge University Press.

Pomerantz, Anita
1978   Attributions of responsibility: Blamings. *Sociology* 12:115–21.

Rosen, Lawrence
1977   The anthropologist as expert witness. *American Anthropologist* 79:555–72.

Rumsey, Alan
1990   Wording, meaning and linguistic ideology. *American Anthropologist* 92(2):346–61.

Russell, Diana E. H.
1984   *Sexual exploitation: Rape, child sexual abuse, and workplace harassment.* Beverly Hills, Calif.: Sage.

Sacks, H., E. Schegloff, and G. Jefferson
1974   A simplest systematics for the organization of turn-taking for conversation. *Language* 50:696–735.

Sandburg, Carl
1939   *Abraham Lincoln: The war years.* New York: Harcourt, Brace and Co.

Sankoff, Gillian
1980   *The social life of language.* Philadelphia: University of Pennsylvania Press.

Sarat, Austin, and William Felstiner
1995   *Divorce lawyers and their clients.* London: Oxford University Press.

Schegloff, Emmanuel
1992   On talk and its institutional occasions. In *Talk at work: Interaction in institutional settings,* edited by Paul Drew and John Heritage. Cambridge: Cambridge University Press.

Schwartz, Bernard
1993   *Main currents in American legal thought.* Durham, NC: Carolina Academic Press.

Searle, John
1969   *Speech acts.* Cambridge: Cambridge University Press.

Shearing, C., and R. Ericson
1991   Culture as figurative action. *British Journal of Sociology* 42:481–506.

Sheldon, Amy
1993   Pickle fights: Gendered talk in preschool disputes. In *Gender and conversational interaction,* edited by Deborah Tannen. New York: Oxford University Press.

Sheldon, Amy, and Diane Johnson
1994   Preschool negotiators: Linguistic differences in how girls and boys regulate the expression of dissent in same-sex groups. *Research on Negotiations in Organizations* 4:37–67.

Shuy, Roger W.
1993   *Language crimes: The use and abuse of language evidence in the courtroom.* Cambridge, MA: Blackwell Publishing.
2002   *Linguistic battles in trademark disputes.* New York: Palgrave MacMillan.

Silbey, Susan S., and Sally E. Merry
1986   Mediator settlement strategies. *Law & Policy* 8:7–31.

Silverstein, Michael, and Greg Urban, eds.
1979   Language structure and linguistic ideology. In *The elements: A parasession on linguistic units and levels,* edited by Paul R. Clyne, William F. Hanks, and Carol L. Hofbauer. Chicago: Chicago Linguistic Society.
1985   Language and the culture of gender: At the intersection of structure, usage, and ideology. In *Semiotic mediation: Sociocultural and psychological perspectives,* edited by Elizabeth Mertz and Richard J. Parmentier. Orlando, FL: Academic Press.
1996   *Natural histories of discourse.* Chicago: University of Chicago Press.
1998   The uses and utility of ideology: A commentary. In *Language ideologies: Practice and theory,* edited by Bambi B. Schieffelin, Kathryn A. Woolard, and Paul V. Kroskrity. New York: Oxford University Press.

Solan, Lawrence M., and Peter M. Tiersma
2004   *Language on trial.* Chicago: University of Chicago Press.

Spohn, Cassia, and Julie Horney
1992   *Rape law reform: A grass-roots revolution and its impact.* New York: Plenum Press.

Tannen, Deborah
1986   *That's not what I meant: How conversational style makes or breaks your relations with others.* New York: Morrow.
1990   *You just don't understand: Women and men in conversation.* New York: Morrow.

Tannen, Deborah, ed.
1993   *Gender and conversational interaction.* New York: Oxford University Press.

Thompson, Joanna Kerr
2002   "Powerful/powerless" language in court: A critical re-evaluation of the Duke language and law programme. *Forensic Linguistics* 9:154–67.

Thorne, Barrie, Cheris Kramarae, and Nancy Henley, eds.
1983   *Language, gender, and society.* Rowley, Mass.: Newbury House.

Trudgill, Peter
2003   Series editor's preface. In *Forensic linguistics: An introduction to language in the justice system,* by John Gibbons. Oxford, England: Blackwell Publishing.

Turton, David
1975   The relationship between oratory and the exercise of influence among the Mursi. In *Political language and oratory in traditional society,* edited by Maurice Bloch. New York: Academic Press.

Venners, Bill
1997   The United States: Singular or plural? www.autumnleafcafe.com/lit/ESingularPlural.html.

Warshaw, Robin
1988   *I never called it rape: The Ms. report on recognizing, fighting, and surviving date and acquaintance rape.* New York: Harper & Row.

Weinberg, Steven
1977   *The first three minutes: A modern view of the origin of the universe.* New York: Basic Books.

West, Robin
1988   Jurisprudence and gender. *University of Chicago Law Review* 55:1–72.

Whiteley, Peter
2003   Do "language rights" serve indigenous interests? Some Hopi and other queries. *American Anthropologist* 105:712–22.

Wierzbicka, Anna
2003   "Reasonable man" and "reasonable doubt": The English language, Anglo culture and Anglo-American law. *Forensic Linguistics* 10:1–22.

Woolard, Kathryn A.
1998   Introduction: Language ideology as a field of inquiry. In *Language ideologies: practice and theory,* edited by Bambi B. Schieffelin, Kathryn A. Woolard, and Paul V. Kroskrity. New York: Oxford University Press.

Wools, David
2003   Better tools for the trade and how to use them. *Forensic Linguistics* 10:102–12.

Wright, John W. II, and Lawrence A. Hosman
1983   Language style and sex bias in the courtroom: The effects of male and female use of hedges and intensifiers on impression information. *Southern Speech Communication Journal* 48:137–52.

Yarmey, A. Daniel
2003   Earwitness identification over the telephone and in field settings. *Forensic Linguistics* 10:62–74.

INDEX